Falstaff:
Four Plays

Henry IV 1 and 2
The Merry Wives of Windsor
Henry V

William
Shakespeare

edited by Sasha Newborn

BANDANNA BOOKS • 2012 • SANTA BARBARA

SHAKESPEARE FOR DIRECTORS, PRODUCERS, ACTORS, WANNABEES

shakespeareplaybook.com

DIRECTOR'S PLAYBOOK SERIES. the elements of production:
storyboarding, auditions, staging diagrams, budget, publicity, costuming,
set design, playbill, stage managing, glossary, customized actor scripts

Hamlet   The Merchant of Venice Twelfth Night   Taming of the Shrew
A Midsummer Night's Dream   Romeo and Juliet As You Like It   Richard III
Henry V   Much Ado About Nothing   Macbeth   Othello

plus
SEVEN PLAYS with Transgender Characters, plus Hamlet

TWO-HOUR READS

Don't Panic: The Procrastinator's Guide to Writing an Effective Term Paper.
The First Detective: 3 Stories. Edgar Allan Poe   Gandhi on the *Bhagavad Gita*
The Everlasting Gospel, William Blake   Italian for Opera Lovers. (dictionary)
Dante & His Circle. Love sonnets   Vita Nuova, Dante's tribute to Beatrice
Ghazals of Ghalib   The Gospel According to Tolstoy
Hadji Murad, a Chechen story, Leo Tolstoy

TWO-DAY READS

Mitos y Leyendas/Myths and Legends of Mexico. Bilingual
The Beechers Through the 19th Century
 Uncle Tom's Cabin, Harriet Beecher Stowe
Frankenstein, Mary Shelley
Aurora Leigh, Elizabeth Barrett Browning

TEACHING SUPPLEMENTS

Q & A, glossaries, critical comments
Areopagitica, John Milton   Apology of Socrates, & The Crito, Plato
Leaves of Grass, Walt Whitman   Sappho, The Poem
Uncle Tom's Cabin, Harriet Beecher Stowe

CONTENTS

HENRY IV, PART TWO

Henry V

The figure of Falstaff has caught the popular imagination ever since he emerged as one of Shakespeare's premier rascals. Not just a comic figure, Falstaff somehow represents the best in the worst of us, or the worst in the best of us. He exhibits just enough of reality to make us uneasy, yet fascinated to see what he'll try to get away with next.

Falstaff's story is always a subplot in these plays, yet his trajectory intersects that of Prince Hal, who becomes King Henry the Fifth. While Hal emerges as Harry, then Henry. Falstaff goes from one scheme to another with little sign of remorse or even regret. He is unseen in the background in the final play, Henry V, though characters who knew him best speak about his moans and complaints from a back room several times in the dialogue, knowing that in his death, his presence would be missed.

One story has it that Queen Elizabeth, after seeing the Henry IV plays, urged Shakespeare to write another play to continue the Falstaff story. The result, a play with no relation to English history, was *The Merry Wives of Windsor*, with Falstaff as the fooler fooled, his ploys upended by his intended victims, as he had to escape the wrath of an irate husband more than once.

The character of Sir Toby Belch, in *Twelfth Night*, a play we believe to have been written after the *Henry* plays but before *Merry Wives*, shares many outward characteristics of Falstaff (obesity, obscenity), but is not as scandalous. An earlier non-Shakespeare play includes a similar dissolute character buddying up to a King, named John Oldcastle—but since there had been a real John Oldcastle, the name was changed. "Oldcastle died a martyr, and this is not the man" is stated clearly in the Epilogue to Henry IV, Part Two.

The role of Falstaff has understandably attracted a number of character actors—he dominates the stage when he's present. Orson Welles produced a film, *Chimes at Midnight*, a story cobbled together from the plays, and cast himself to play the character of Falstaff.

The text has been modernized (americanized, if you will) for modern actors and readers. A glossary in the back illuminates words, names, events that are no longer current.

Speaking of Shakespeare, let me put in a pitch for the most recent Bandanna Books project, Shakespeare Director's Play books for director-producers, which you can find on the Web at *www.shakespeareplaybook.com*. A dozen individual plays are set in this format, including comedies, tragedies, and a few of the history plays (*Henry V* is one of them). Check the copyright page for a list of the plays.

The Playbooks expand the scenes and parts of scenes for notes and sketches, with stage diagrams to position sets, and separate sections for entrances and exits, budget (don't start a play without it), sample publicity campaign, set designer and costumer pages, auditioning, designing a playbill, working with volunteers, coordinating and scheduling.

Shakespeare is always rewarding, alive with characters and action and emotion. Even the "extras" come alive. Actors love Shakespeare, and so do audiences.

Sasha Newborn
September 2012

Henry IV, Part One

Henry IV, Part Two

The Merry Wives of Windsor

Henry V

Act One

1

[London. The Palace]

[Enter the King, Lord John of Lancaster, Earl of Westmoreland, Sir Walter Blunt, others]

King. So shaken as we are, so wan with care,
    Find we a time for frighted peace to pant
    And breathe short-winded accents of new broils
    To be commenced in stronds afar remote.
    No more the thirsty entrance of this soil
    Shall daub her lips with her own children's blood.
    No more shall trenching war channel her fields,
    Nor Bruise her flowerets with the armed hoofs
    Of hostile paces. Those opposed eyes
    Which, like the meteors of a troubled heaven,
    All of one nature, of one substance bred,
    Did lately meet in the intestine shock
    And furious close of civil butchery,
    Shall now in mutual well-beseeming ranks
    March all one way and be no more opposed
    Against acquaintance, kindred, and allies.
    The edge of war, like an ill-sheathed knife,
    No more shall cut his master. Therefore, friends,
    As far as to the sepulcher of Christ—
    Whose soldier now, under whose blessed cross
    We are impressed and engaged to fight—
    Forthwith a power of English shall we levy,
    Whose arms were molded in their mother's womb
    To chase these pagans in those holy fields
    Over whose acres walked those blessed feet
    Which fourteen hundred years ago were nailed
    For our advantage on the bitter cross.
    But this our purpose now is twelvemonth old,
    And bootless 'tis to tell you we will go.
    Therefore we meet not now. Then let me hear

Of you, my gentle cousin Westmoreland,
What yesternight our Council did decree
In forwarding this dear expedience.

Westmoreland. My liege, this haste was hot in question
And many limits of the charge set down
But yesternight; when all athwart there came
A post from Wales, laden with heavy news;
Whose worst was that the noble Mortimer,
Leading the men of Herefordshire to fight
Against the irregular and wild Glendower,
Was by the rude hands of that Welshman taken,
A thousand of his people butchered;
Upon whose dead corpse there was such misuse,
Such beastly shameless transformation,
By those Welshwomen done as may not be
Without much shame retold or spoken of.

King. It seems then that the tidings of this broil
Break off our business for the Holy Land.

Westmoreland. This, matched with other, did, my gracious lord;
For more uneven and unwelcome news
Came from the North, and thus it did import.
On Holy-rood Day the gallant Hotspur there,
Young Harry Percy, and brave Archibald,
That ever-valiant and approved Scot,
At Holmedon met,
Where they did spend a sad and bloody hour;
As by discharge of their artillery
And shape of likelihood the news was told;
For he that brought them, in the very heat
And pride of their contention did take horse,
Uncertain of the issue any way.

King. Here is a dear, a true-industrious friend,
Sir Walter Blunt, new lighted from his horse,
Stained with the variation of each soil
Between that Holmedon and this seat of ours,
And he has brought us smooth and welcome news.
The Earl of Douglas is discomfited;
Ten thousand bold Scots, two-and-twenty knights,
Balked in their own blood did Sir Walter see
On Holmedon's plains. Of prisoners, Hotspur took
Mordake Earl of Fife and eldest son
To beaten Douglas, and the Earl of Athol,

Of Murray, Angus, and Menteith.
And is not this an honorable spoil?
A gallant prize? Ha, cousin, is it not?

Westmoreland. In faith,
It is a conquest for a Prince to boast of.

King. Yea, there you make me sad, and make me sin
In envy that my Lord Northumberland
Should be the father to so blessed a son—
A son who is the theme of honor's tongue,
Amongst a grove the very straightest plant;
Who is sweet Fortune's minion and her pride;
While I, by looking on the praise of him,
See riot and dishonor stain the brow
Of my young Harry. O, that it could be proved
That some night-tripping fairy had exchanged
In cradle clothes our children where they lay,
And called mine Percy, his Plantagenet!
Then would I have his Harry, and he mine.
But let him from my thoughts. What think you, coz,
Of this young Percy's pride? The prisoners
Which he in this adventure has surprised
To his own use he keeps, and sends me word
I shall have none but Mordake Earl of Fife.

Westmoreland. This is his uncle's teaching, this Worcester,
Malevolent to you in all aspects,
Which makes him prune himself and bristle up
The crest of youth against your dignity.

King. But I have sent for him to answer this;
And for this cause awhile we must neglect
Our holy purpose to Jerusalem.
Cousin, on Wednesday next our council we
Will hold at Windsor. So inform the lords;
But come yourself with speed to us again;
For more is to be said and to be done
Than out of anger can be uttered.

Westmoreland. I will my liege.

                    [*Exit All*]

[London. An apartment of the Prince]

[Enter the Prince of Wales and Falstaff]

Falstaff. Now, Hal, what time of day is it, lad?

Prince. You are so fat-witted, with drinking of old sack and unbuttoning yourself after supper and sleeping upon benches after noon, that you have forgotten to demand that truly which you would truly know. What a devil have you to do with the time of the day? Unless hours were cups of sack and minutes capons and clocks the tongues of bawds and dials the signs of leaping-houses and the blessed sun himself a fair hot wench in flame-colored taffeta, I see no reason why you should be so superfluous to demand the time of the day.

Falstaff. Indeed, you come near me now, Hal; for we that take purses go by the moon and the seven stars, and not by Phoebus, he "that wandering knight so fair." And, I beg you, sweet wag, when you are King, as, God save your grace—majesty I should say, for grace you will have none—

Prince. What, none?

Falstaff. No, by my troth, not so much as will serve to be prologue to an egg and butter.

Prince. Well, how then? Come, roundly, roundly.

Falstaff. Well, then, sweet wag, when you are King, let not us that are squires of the night's body be called thieves of the day's beauty. let us be Diana's foresters, gentlemen of the shade, minions of the moon; and let men say we be men of good government, being governed, as the sea is, by our noble and chaste mistress the moon, under whose countenance we steal.

Prince. You say well, and it holds well too; for the fortune of us that are the moon's men does ebb and flow like the sea, being governed, as the sea is, by the moon. As, for proof now,. a purse of gold most resolutely snatched on Monday night and most dissolutely spent on Tuesday morning; got with swearing "Lay be" and spent with crying "Bring in"; now in as low an ebb as the foot of the ladder and by and by in as high a flow as the ridge of the gallows.

Falstaff. By the Lord, you say true, lad. And is not my hostess of the tavern a most sweet wench?

Prince. As the honey of Hybla, my old lad of the castle. And is not a buff jerkin a most sweet robe of durance?

Falstaff. How now, how now, mad wag! What, in your quips and your quiddities? What a plague have I to do with a buff jerkin?

Prince. Why, what a pox have I to do with my hostess of the tavern?

Falstaff. Well, you have called her to a reckoning many a time and oft.

Prince. Did I ever call for you to pay your part?

Falstaff. No; I'll give you your due, you have paid all there.

Prince. Yea, and elsewhere, so far as my coin would stretch; and where it would not, I have used my credit.

Falstaff. Yea, and so used it that, were it not here apparent that you are heir apparent—but, I beg you, sweet wag, shall there be gallows standing in England when you are King? And resolution thus fobbed as it is with the rusty curb of old father antic the law? Do not you, when you are King, hang a thief.

Prince. No; you shall.

Falstaff. Shall I? O rare! By the Lord, I'll be a brave judge.

Prince. You judge false already. I mean, you shall have the hanging of the thieves and so become a rare hangman.

Falstaff. Well, Hal, well; and in some sort it jumps with my humor as well as waiting in the court, I can tell you.

Prince. For obtaining of suits?

Falstaff. Yea, for obtaining of suits, whereof the hangman has no lean wardrobe. 'Sblood, I am as melancholy as a gib cat or a lugged bear.

Prince. Or an old lion, or a lover's lute.

Falstaff. Yea, or the drone of a Lincolnshire bagpipe.

Prince. What say you to a hare, or the melancholy of Moor-ditch?

Falstaff. You have the most unsavory similes and are indeed the most comparative, rascaliest, sweet young Prince. But, Hal, I beg you, trouble me no more with vanity. I would to God you and I knew where a commodity of good names were to be bought. An old lord of the council rated me the other day in the street about you, sir, but I marked him not; and yet he talked very wisely, but I regarded him not; and yet he talked wisely, and in the street too.

Prince. You did well; for wisdom cries out in the streets, and no man regards it.

Falstaff. O, you have damnable iteration and are indeed able to corrupt a saint. You have done much harm upon me, Hal; God forgive you for it! Before I knew you, Hal, I knew nothing; and now am I, if a man should speak truly, little better than one of the wicked. I must give over this life, and I will give it over. by the Lord, and I do not, I am a villain. I'll be damned for never a King's son in Christendom.

Prince. Where shall we take a purse tomorrow, Jack?

Falstaff. 'Zounds, where you will, lad; I'll make one; if I do not, call me villain and baffle me.

Prince. I see a good amendment of life in you; from praying to purse-taking.

Falstaff. Why, Hal, 'tis my vocation, Hal; 'tis no sin for a man to labor in his vocation.

[*Enter Poins*]

Poins! Now shall we know if Gadshill have set a match. O, if men were to be saved by merit, what hole in hell were hot enough for him? This is the most omnipotent villain that ever cried "Stand" to a true man.

Prince. Good morrow, Ned.

Poins. Good morrow, sweet Hal. What says Monsieur Remorse? What says Sir John Sack and Sugar? Jack! how agrees the devil and you about your soul, that you sold him on Good-Friday last for a cup of Madeira and a cold capon's leg?

Prince. Sir John stands to his word, the devil shall have his bargain; for he was never yet a breaker of proverbs. he will give the devil his due.

Poins. Then are you damned for keeping your word with the devil.

Prince. Else he had been damned for cozening the devil.

Poins. But, my lads, my lads, tomorrow morning, by four o'clock, early at Gad's Hill! there are pilgrims going to Canterbury with rich offerings, and traders riding to London with fat purses. I have vizards for you all; you have horses for yourselves. Gadshill lies tonight in Rochester. I have bespoke supper tomorrow night in Eastcheap. we may do it as secure as sleep. If you will go, I will stuff your purses full of crowns; if you will not, tarry at home and be hanged.

Falstaff. Hear you, Yedward; if I tarry at home and go not, I'll hang you for going.

Poins. You will, chops?

Falstaff. Hal, will you make one?

Prince. Who, I rob? I a thief? not I, by my faith.

Falstaff. There's neither honesty, manhood, nor good fellowship in
    you, nor you came not of the blood royal, if you dare not stand
    for ten shillings.

Prince. Well then, once in my days I'll be a madcap.

Falstaff. Why, that's well said.

Prince. Well, come what will, I'll tarry at home.

Falstaff. By the Lord, I'll be a traitor then, when you are King.

Prince. I care not.

Poins. Sir John, I ask you, leave the Prince and me alone. I will lay
    him down such reasons for this adventure that he shall go.

Falstaff. Well, God give you the spirit of persuasion and him the
    ears of profiting, that what you speak may move and what he
    hears may be believed, that the true Prince may, for recreation
    sake, prove a false thief; for the poor abuses of the time want
    countenance. Farewell. you shall find me in Eastcheap.

Prince. Farewell, you latter spring! farewell, All-hallows summer!

[Exit Falstaff]

Poins. Now, my good sweet honey lord, ride with us tomorrow.
    I have a jest to execute that I cannot manage alone. Falstaff,
    Bardolph, Peto and Gadshill shall rob those men that we have
    already waylaid. yourself and I will not be there; and when they
    have the booty, if you and I do not rob them, cut this head off
    from my shoulders.

Prince. How shall we part with them in setting forth?

Poins. Why, we will set forth before or after them, and appoint them
    a place of meeting, wherein it is at our pleasure to fail, and then
    will they adventure upon the exploit themselves; which they
    shall have no sooner achieved, but we'll set upon them.

Prince. Yea, but 'tis like that they will know us by our horses, by
    our habits and by every other appointment, to be ourselves.

Poins. Tut! our horses they shall not see. I'll tie them in the wood;
    our vizards we will change after we leave them. and, sirrah,
    I have cases of buckram for the nonce, to immask our noted
    outward garments.

Prince. Yea, but I doubt they will be too hard for us.

Poins. Well, for two of them, I know them to be as true-bred cowards as ever turned back; and for the third, if he fight longer than he sees reason, I'll forswear arms. The virtue of this jest will be, the incomprehensible lies that this same fat rogue will tell us when we meet at supper. how thirty, at least, he fought with; what wards, what blows, what extremities he endured; and in the reproof of this lies the jest.

Prince. Well, I'll go with you. provide us all things necessary and meet me tomorrow night in Eastcheap; there I'll sup. Farewell.

Poins. Farewell, my lord.

[*Exit Poins*]

Prince. I know you all, and will awhile uphold
The unyoked humor of your idleness.
Yet herein will I imitate the sun,
Who does permit the base contagious clouds
To smother up his beauty from the world,
That, when he please again to be himself,
Being wanted, he may be more wondered at,
By breaking through the foul and ugly mists
Of vapors that did seem to strangle him.
If all the year were playing holidays,
To sport would be as tedious as to work;
But when they seldom come, they wished for come,
And nothing pleases but rare accidents.
So, when this loose behavior I throw off
And pay the debt I never promised,
By how much better than my word I am,
By so much shall I falsify men's hopes;
And like bright metal on a sullen ground,
My reformation, glittering over my fault,
Shall show more goodly and attract more eyes
Than that which has no foil to set it off.
I'll so offend, to make offense a skill;
Redeeming time when men think least I will.

[*Exit Prince*]

[*London. The Palace*]

[*Enter the King, Northumberland, Worcester, Hotspur,
Sir Walter Blunt*]

King. My blood has been too cold and temperate,
Unapt to stir at these indignities,
And you have found me, for accordingly
You tread upon my patience; but be sure
I will from henceforth rather be myself,
Mighty and to be feared, than my condition,
Which has been smooth as oil, soft as young down,
And therefore lost that title of respect
Which the proud soul never pays but to the proud.

Worcester. Our house, my sovereign liege, little deserves
The scourge of greatness to be used on it—
And that same greatness too which our own hands
Have helped to make so portly.

Northumberland. My lord—

King. Worcester, get you gone; for I do see
Danger and disobedience in your eye.
O, sir, your presence is too bold and peremptory,
And majesty might never yet endure
The moody frontier of a servant brow.
You have good leave to leave us. When we need
Your use and counsel, we shall send for you.

[*Exit Worcester*]

You were about to speak.

Northumberland. Yea, my good lord.
Those prisoners in your Highness' name demanded
Which Harry Percy here at Holmedon took,
Were, as he says, not with such strength denied
As is delivered to your Majesty.
Either envy, therefore, or misprision
Is guilty of this fault, and not my son.

Hotspur. My liege, I did deny no prisoners.
But I remember, when the fight was done,
When I was dry with rage and extreme toll,
Breathless and faint, leaning upon my sword,

Came there a certain lord, neat and trimly dressed,
Fresh as a bridegroom; and his chin new reaped
Showed like a stubble land at harvest home.
He was perfumed like a milliner,
And between his finger and his thumb he held
A pouncet box, which ever and anon
He gave his nose, and took it away again;
Who therewith angry, when it next came there,
Took it in snuff; and still he smiled and talked;
And as the soldiers bore dead bodies by,
He called them untaught knaves, unmannerly,
To bring a slovenly unhandsome corpse
Between the wind and his nobility.
With many holiday and lady terms
He questioned me, among the rest demanded
My prisoners in your Majesty's behalf.
I then, all smarting with my wounds being cold,
To be so pestered with a popinjay,
Out of my grief and my impatience
Answered neglectingly, I know not what—
He should, or he should not; for he made me mad
To see him shine so brisk, and smell so sweet,
And talk so like a waiting gentlewoman
Of guns and drums and wounds— God save the mark!—
And telling me the sovereignest thing on earth
Was parmaceti for an inward bruise;
And that it was great pity, so it was,
This villainous saltpeter should be digged
Out of the bowels of the harmless earth,
Which many a good tall fellow had destroyed
So cowardly; and but for these vile guns,
He would himself have been a soldier.
This bald unjointed chat of his, my lord,
I answered indirectly, as I said,
And I beseech you, let not his report
Come current for an accusation
Between my love and your high majesty.

Blunt. The circumstance considered, good my lord,
Whatever Lord Harry Percy then had said
To such a person, and in such a place,
At such a time, with all the rest retold,
May reasonably die, and never rise

To do him wrong, or any way impeach
What then he said, so he unsay it now.

King. Why, yet he does deny his prisoners,
But with proviso and exception,
That we at our own charge shall ransom straight
His brother-in-law, the foolish Mortimer;
Who, on my soul, has willfully betrayed
The lives of those that he did lead to fight
Against that great magician, damned Glendower,
Whose daughter, as we hear, the Earl of March
Has lately married. Shall our coffers, then,
Be emptied to redeem a traitor home?
Shall we buy treason? and indent with fears
When they have lost and forfeited themselves?
No, on the barren mountains let him starve!
For I shall never hold that man my friend
Whose tongue shall ask me for one penny cost
To ransom home revolted Mortimer.

Hotspur. Revolted Mortimer?
He never did fall off, my sovereign liege,
But by the chance of war. To prove that true
Needs no more but one tongue for all those wounds,
Those mouthed wounds, which valiantly he took
When on the gentle Severn's sedgy bank,
In single opposition hand to hand,
He did confound the best part of an hour
In changing hardiment with great Glendower.
Three times they breathed, and three times did they drink,
Upon agreement, of swift Severn's flood;
Who then, affrighted with their bloody looks,
Ran fearfully among the trembling reeds
And hid his crisp head in the hollow bank,
Bloodstained with these valiant cohabitants.
Never did base and rotten policy
Color her working with such deadly wounds;
Nor never could the noble Mortimer
Receive so many, and all willingly.
Then let not him be slandered with revolt.

King. You do belie him, Percy, you do belie him!
He never did encounter with Glendower.
I tell you
He dared as well have met the devil alone

As Owen Glendower for an enemy.
Are you not ashamed? But, sirrah, henceforth
Let me not hear you speak of Mortimer.
Send me your prisoners with the speediest means,
Or you shall hear in such a kind from me
As will displease you. My Lord Northumberland,
We license your departure with your son.—
Send us your prisoners, or you will hear of it.

[*Exit King, Blunt, and others*]

Hotspur. Oh, if the devil come and roar for them,
   I will not send them. I will after straight
   And tell him so; for I will else my heart,
   Albeit I make a hazard of my head.

Northumberland. What, drunk with choler? Stay, and pause awhile.
   Here comes your uncle.

[*Enter Worcester*]

Hotspur. Speak of Mortimer?
   Zounds, I will speak of him, and let my soul
   Want mercy if I do not join with him!
   Yea, on his part I'll empty all these veins,
   And shed my dear blood drop by drop in the dust,
   But I will lift the downtrod Mortimer
   As high in the air as this unthankful King,
   As this ingrate and cankered Bolingbroke.

Northumberland. Brother, the King has made your nephew mad.

Worcester. Who struck this heat up after I was gone?

Hotspur. He will indeed have all my prisoners;
   And when I urged the ransom once again
   Of my wife's brother, then his cheek looked pale,
   And on my face he turned an eye of death,
   Trembling even at the name of Mortimer.

Worcester. I cannot blame him. Was not he proclaimed
   By Richard that dead is, the next of blood?

Northumberland. He was; I heard the proclamation.
   And then it was when the unhappy King,
   Whose wrongs in us God pardon, did set forth
   Upon his Irish expedition;
   From whence he intercepted did return
   To be deposed, and shortly murdered.

Worcester. And for whose death we in the world's wide mouth
   Live scandalized and foully spoken of.

Hotspur. But soft, I pray you. Did King Richard then
   Proclaim my brother Edmund Mortimer
   Heir to the crown?

Northumberland. He did; myself did hear it.

Hotspur. Nay, then I cannot blame his cousin King,
   That wished him on the barren mountains starve.
   But shall it be that you, that set the crown
   Upon the head of this forgetful man,
   And for his sake wear the detested blot
   Of murderous subornation— shall it be
   That you a world of curses undergo,
   Being the agents or base second means,
   The cords, the ladder, or the hangman rather?
   O, pardon me that I descend so low
   To show the line and the predicament
   Wherein you range under this subtle King!
   Shall it for shame be spoken in these days,
   Or fill up chronicles in time to come,
   That men of your nobility and power
   Did gage them both in an unjust behalf,
   As both of you, God pardon it! have done,
   To put down Richard, that sweet lovely rose,
   And plant this thorn, this canker, Bolingbroke?
   And shall it in more shame be further spoken
   That you are fooled, discarded, and shook off
   By him for whom these shames you underwent?
   No! yet time serves wherein you may redeem
   Your banished honors and restore yourselves
   Into the good thoughts of the world again;
   Revenge the jeering and disdained contempt
   Of this proud King, who studies day and night
   To answer all the debt he owes to you
   Even with the bloody payment of your deaths.
   Therefore I say—

Worcester. Peace, cousin, say no more;
   And now, I will unclasp a secret book,
   And to your quick-conceiving discontents
   I'll read you matter deep and dangerous,
   As full of peril and adventurous spirit
   As to overwalk a current roaring loud

On the unsteadfast footing of a spear.

Hotspur. If he fall in, good night, or sink or swim!
   Send danger from the east unto the west,
   So honor cross it from the north to south,
   And let them grapple. O, the blood more stirs
   To rouse a lion than to start a hare!

Northumberland. Imagination of some great exploit
   Drives him beyond the bounds of patience.

Hotspur. By heaven, I think it were an easy leap
   To pluck bright honor from the pale-faced moon,
   Or dive into the bottom of the deep,
   Where fathom line could never touch the ground,
   And pluck up drowned honor by the locks,
   So he that does redeem her thence might wear
   Without co-rival all her dignities;
   But out upon this half-faced fellowship!

Worcester. He apprehends a world of figures here,
   But not the form of what he should attend.
   Good cousin, give me audience for a while.

Hotspur. I cry you mercy.

Worcester. Those same noble Scots
   That are your prisoners—

Hotspur. I'll keep them all.
   By God, he shall not have a Scot of them!
   No, if a Scot would save his soul, he shall not.
   I'll keep them, by this hand!

Worcester. You start away.
   And lend no ear unto my purposes.
   Those prisoners you shall keep.

Hotspur. Nay, I will! That is flat!
   He said he would not ransom Mortimer,
   Forbade my tongue to speak of Mortimer,
   But I will find him when he lies asleep,
   And in his ear I'll holler "Mortimer.'
   Nay;
   I'll have a starling shall be taught to speak
   Nothing but "Mortimer," and give it him
   To keep his anger still in motion.

Worcester. Hear you, cousin, a word.

Hotspur. All studies here I solemnly defy

Save how to gall and pinch this Bolingbroke;
And that same sword-and-buckler Prince of Wales—
But that I think his father loves him not
And would be glad he met with some mischance,
I would have him poisoned with a pot of ale.

Worcester. Farewell, kinsman. I will talk to you
When you are better tempered to attend.

Northumberland. Why, what a wasp-stung and impatient fool
Are you to break into this woman's mood,
Tying your ear to no tongue but your own!

Hotspur. Why, look you, I am whipped and scourged with rods,
Nettled, and stung with pismires when I hear
Of this vile politician, Bolingbroke.
In Richard's time— what do you call the place—
A plague upon it! it is in GIoucestershire—
'Twas where the madcap Duke his uncle kept—
His uncle York— where I first bowed my knee
Unto this king of smiles, this Bolingbroke—
'Sblood!
When you and he came back from Ravenspurgh—

Northumberland. At Berkeley Castle.

Hotspur. You say true.
Why, what a candy deal of courtesy
This fawning greyhound then did proffer me!
Look, "when his infant fortune came to age,"
And "gentle Harry Percy," and "kind cousin"—
O, the devil take such cozeners!— God forgive me!
Good uncle, tell your tale, for I have done.

Worcester. Nay, if you have not, to it again.
We will stay your leisure.

Hotspur. I have done, truly.

Worcester. Then once more to your Scottish prisoners.
Deliver them up without their ransom straight,
And make the Douglas's son your only mean
For powers In Scotland; which, for diverse reasons
Which I shall send you written, be assured
Will easily be granted.
[*To Northumberland*] You, my lord,
Your son in Scotland being thus employed,
Shall secretly into the bosom creep
Of that same noble prelate well-beloved,

The Archbishop.

Hotspur. Of York, is it not?

Worcester. True; who bears hard
  His brother's death at Bristow, the Lord Scroop.
  I speak not this in estimation,
  As what I think might be, but what I know
  Is ruminated, plotted, and set down,
  And only stays but to behold the face
  Of that occasion that shall bring it on.

Hotspur. I smell it. Upon my life, it will do well.

Northumberland. Before the game is afoot you still let it slip.

Hotspur. Why, it cannot choose but be a noble plot.
  And then the power of Scotland and of York
  To join with Mortimer, ha?

Worcester. And so they shall.

Hotspur. In faith, it is exceedingly well aimed.

Worcester. And 'tis no little reason bids us speed,
  To save our heads by raising of a head;
  For, bear ourselves as even as we can,
  The King will always think him in our debt,
  And think we think ourselves unsatisfied,
  Till he has found a time to pay us home.
  And see already how he does begin
  To make us strangers to his looks of love.

Hotspur. He does, he does! We'll be revenged on him.

Worcester. Cousin, farewell. No further go in this
  Than I by letters shall direct your course.
  When time is ripe, which will be suddenly,
  I'll steal to Glendower and Lord Mortimer,
  Where you and Douglas, and our powers at once,
  As I will fashion it, shall happily meet,
  To bear our fortunes in our own strong arms,
  Which now we hold at much uncertainty.

Northumberland. Farewell, good brother. We shall thrive, I trust.

Hotspur. Uncle, adieu. O, let the hours be short
  Till fields and blows and groans applaud our sport!

                    [*Exit All*]

Act Two

1

[*Rochester. An inn yard*]

[*Enter a Carrier with a lantern*]

First Carrier. Heigh-ho! if it be not four by the day, I'll be hanged. Charles' wain is over the new chimney, and yet our horse not packed. What, ostler!

Ostler. [*Within*] Anon, anon.

First Carrier. I tell you, Tom, beat Cut's saddle, put a few flocks in the point; poor jade, is wrung in the withers out of all cess.

[*Enter another Carrier*]

Second Carrier. Peas and beans are as dank here as a dog, and that is the next way to give poor jades the bots. This house is turned upside down since Robin Ostler died.

First Carrier. Poor fellow, never joyed since the price of oats rose; it was the death of him.

Second Carrier. I think this be the most villainous house in all London road for fleas. I am stung like a tench.

First Carrier. Like a tench! by the mass, there is never a king christen could be better bit than I have been since the first cock.

Second Carrier. Why, they will allow us never a jordan, and then we leak in your chimney; and your chamber-lye breeds fleas like a loach.

First Carrier. What, ostler! come away and be hanged! come away.

Second Carrier. I have a gammon of bacon and two razes of ginger, to be delivered as far as Charing Cross.

First Carrier. God's body! the turkeys in my pannier are quite starved. What, ostler! A plague on you! Have you never an eye in your head? Can't you hear? If 'twere not as good deed as drink, to break the pate on you, I am a very villain. Come, and be hanged! Have no faith in you?

[Enter Gadshill]

Gadshill. Good morrow, carriers. What's o'clock?

First Carrier. I think it be two o'clock.

Gadshill. I pray you lend me your lantern, to see my gelding in the stable.

First Carrier. Nay, by God, soft; I know a trick worth two of that, truly.

Gadshill. I pray you, lend me yours.

Second Carrier. Ay, when? can't you tell? Lend me your lantern, quoth he? Indeed, I'll see you hanged first.

Gadshill. Sirrah carrier, what time do you mean to come to London?

Second Carrier. Time enough to go to bed with a candle, I warrant you. Come, neighbor Mugs, we'll call up the gentlemen. they will along with company, for they have great charge.

[Exit All Carriers]

Gadshill. What, ho! chamberlain!

Chamberlain. *[Within]* At hand, quoth pickpurse.

Gadshill. That's even as fair as—at hand, quoth the chamberlain; for you vary no more from picking of purses than giving direction does from laboring; you lay the plot how.

[Enter Chamberlain]

Chamberlain. Good morrow, Master Gadshill. It holds current that I told you yesternight. there's a franklin in the wild of Kent has brought three hundred marks with him in gold. I heard him tell it to one of his company last night at supper; a kind of auditor; one that has abundance of charge too, God knows what. They are up already, and call for eggs and butter; they will away presently.

Gadshill. Sirrah, if they meet not with Saint Nicholas' clerks, I'll give you this neck.

Chamberlain. No, I'll none of it. I pray you, keep that for the hangman; for I know you worship St. Nicholas as truly as a man of falsehood may.

Gadshill. What talk you to me of the hangman? If I hang, I'll make a fat pair of gallows; for if I hang, old Sir John hangs with me, and you know he is no starveling. Tut! there are other Trojans that you dream not of, the which for sport sake are content to do the profession some grace; that would, if matters should be looked into, for their own credit sake, make all whole. I am joined with no foot-land rakers, no long-staff sixpenny strikers, none of these mad mustachio purple-hued malt-worms; but with nobility and tranquillity, burgomasters and great one-yers, such as can hold in, such as will strike sooner than speak, and speak sooner than drink, and drink sooner than pray. and yet, 'zounds, I lie; for they pray continually to their saint, the commonwealth; or rather, not pray to her, but prey on her, for they ride up and down on her and make her their boots.

Chamberlain. What, the commonwealth their boots? will she hold out water in foul way?

Gadshill. She will, she will; justice has liquored her. We steal as in a castle, cock-sure; we have the receipt of fern-seed, we walk invisible.

Chamberlain. Nay, by my faith, I think you are more beholding to the night than to fern-seed for your walking invisible.

Gadshill. Give me your hand. you shall have a share in our purchase, as I am a true man.

Chamberlain. Nay, rather let me have it, as you are a false thief.

Gadshill. Go to; "homo sapiens" is a common name to all men. Bid the ostler bring my gelding out of the stable. Farewell, you muddy knave.

[*Exit All*]

[The highway, near Gad's Hill]

[Enter Prince Henry and Poins]

Poins. Come, shelter, shelter. I have removed Falstaff's horse, and he frets like a gummed velvet.

Prince. Stand close.

[Enter Falstaff]

Falstaff. Poins! Poins, and be hanged! Poins!

Prince. Peace, you fat-kidneyed rascal! What a brawling do you keep!

Falstaff. Where's Poins, Hal?

Prince. He is walked up to the top of the hill. I'll go seek him.

Falstaff. I am accursed to rob in that thief's company. the rascal has removed my horse, and tied him I know not where. If I travel but four foot by the square further afoot, I shall break my wind. Well, I doubt not but to die a fair death for all this, if I escape hanging for killing that rogue. I have forsworn his company hourly any time this two and twenty years, and yet I am bewitched with the rogue's company. If the rascal has not given me medicines to make me love him, I'll be hanged; it could not be else; I have drunk medicines. Poins! Hal! a plague upon you both! Bardolph! Peto! I'll starve before I'll rob a foot further. If 'twere not as good a deed as drink, to turn true man and to leave these rogues, I am the veriest varlet that ever chewed with a tooth. Eight yards of uneven ground is threescore and ten miles afoot with me; and the stony-hearted villains know it well enough. a plague upon it when thieves cannot be true one to another! *[They whistle]* Whew! A plague upon you all! Give me my horse, you rogues; give me my horse, and be hanged!

Prince. Peace, you fat-guts! lie down; lay your ear close to the ground and listen if you can hear the tread of travellers.

Falstaff. Have you any levers to lift me up again, being down? 'Sblood, I'll not bear my own flesh so far afoot again for all the coin in your father's exchequer. What a plague mean you to colt me thus?

Prince. You lie; you are not colted, you are uncolted.

Falstaff. I beg you, good Prince Hal, help me to my horse, good King's son.

Prince. Out, you rogue! Shall I be your ostler?

Falstaff. Go, hang yourself in your own heir-apparent garters! If I be taken, I'll peach for this. If I have not ballads made on you all and sung to filthy tunes, let a cup of sack be my poison. when a jest is so forward, and afoot too! I hate it.

[*Enter Gadshill, Bardolph and Peto with him*]

Gadshill. Stand.

Falstaff. So I do, against my will.

Poins. O, 'tis our setter. I know his voice. Bardolph, what news?

Bardolph. Case you, case you; on with your vizards. there's money of the King's coming down the hill; 'tis going to the King's exchequer.

Falstaff. You lie, you rogue; 'tis going to the King's tavern.

Gadshill. There's enough to make us all.

Falstaff. To be hanged.

Prince. Sirs, you four shall front them in the narrow lane; Ned Poins and I will walk lower. if they escape from your encounter, then they light on us.

Peto. How many be there of them?

Gadshill. Some eight or ten.

Falstaff. 'Zounds, will they not rob us?

Prince. What, a coward, Sir John Paunch?

Falstaff. Indeed, I am not John of Gaunt, your grandfather; but yet no coward, Hal.

Prince. Well, we leave that to the proof.

Poins. Sirrah Jack, your horse stands behind the hedge. when you need him, there you shall find him. Farewell, and stand fast.

Falstaff. Now cannot I strike him, if I should be hanged.

Prince. Ned, where are our disguises?

Poins. Here, hard by. stand close.

[*Exit All Prince and Poins*]

Falstaff. Now, my masters, happy man be his dole, say I. every man to his business.

[*Enter the Travellers*]

First Traveler. Come, neighbor. the boy shall lead our horses down the hill; we'll walk afoot awhile, and ease our legs.

Thieves. Stand!

Travellers. Jesus bless us!

Falstaff. Strike; down with them; cut the villains' throats. ah! whoreson caterpillars! bacon-fed knaves! they hate us youth. down with them. fleece them.

Travellers. O, we are undone, both we and ours forever!

Falstaff. Hang you, gorbellied knaves, are you undone? No, you fat chuffs; I would your store were here! On, bacons, on! What, you knaves! young men must live. You are grand-jurors, are you! we'll jure you, in faith.

[*They rob and tie up the Travellers. Exit All*]

[*Re-enter Prince Henry and Poins*]

Prince. The thieves have bound the true men. Now could you and I rob the thieves and go merrily to London, it would be argument for a week, laughter for a month and a good jest forever.

Poins. Stand close; I hear them coming.

[*Enter the Thieves again*]

Falstaff. Come, my masters, let us share, and then to horse before day. If the Prince and Poins be not two arrant cowards, there's no equity stirring. there's no more valor in that Poins than in a wild-duck.

Prince. Your money!

Poins. Villains!

[*The Prince and Poins set upon the Thieves, who run away*]

[*Falstaff waddles away too, leaving all the booty*]

Prince. Got with much ease. Now merrily to horse.
The thieves are all scattered and possessed with fear
So strongly that they dare not meet each other;
Each takes his fellow for an officer.
Away, good Ned. Falstaff sweats to death,
And lards the lean earth as he walks along.
Were it not for laughing, I should pity him.

Poins. How the rogue roared!

[*Exit All*]

[Warkworth Castle]

[Enter Hotspur]

Hotspur. *[Reading a letter]*

> *But for my own part, my Lord. I could be well*
> *contented to be there, in respect of the love I bear*
> *your house.*

He could be contented: Why is he not then? "In respect of the
love he bears our house." He shows in this, he loves his own
barn better then he loves our house. Let me see some more.

> *The purpose you vndertake is dangerous.*

Why that's certain: 'Tis dangerous to take a cold, to sleep, to
drink—but I tell you, my Lord fool, out of this nettle, Danger,
we pluck this flower, Safety.

> *The purpose you vndertake is dangerous, the friends*
> *you have named vncertain, the time itself unsorted,*
> *and your whole plot too light, for the counterpoise of*
> *so great an opposition.*

Say you so, say you so: I say unto you again, you are a shallow
cowardly hind, and you lie. What a lackbrain is this? I protest,
our plot is as good a plot as ever was laid; our friend true and
constant—A good plot, good friends, and full of expectation.
An excellent plot, very good friends. What a frosty-spirited
rogue is this? Why, my Lord of York commends the plot, and
the general course of the action. By this hand, if I were now by
this rascal, I could brain him with his lady's fan. Is there not my
Father, my Vncle, and my Selfe, Lord Edmund Mortimer, my
Lord of York, and Owen Glendower? Is there not besides, the
Douglas? Have I not all their letters, to meet me in arms by the
ninth of the next Month? And are they not some of them set
forward already? What a pagan rascal is this? An infidel. Ha,
you shall see now in very sincerity of fear and cold heart, will he
to the King, and lay open all our proceedings. O, I could divide
my self, and go to buffets, for moving such a dish of skimmed
milk with so honorable an action. Hang him, let him tell the
King we are prepared. I will set forward tonight.

[Enter his Lady]

How now Kate, I must leave you within these two hours.

Lady Percy. O, my good Lord, why are you thus alone?
For what offense have I this fortnight been
A banished woman from my Harry's bed?
Tell me, sweet Lord, what is it that takes from you
Your stomach, pleasure, and your golden sleep?
Why do you bend your eyes upon the earth?
And start so often when you sit alone?
Why have you lost the fresh blood in your cheeks?
And given my treasures and my rights of you,
To thick-eyed musing, and cursed melancholy?
In my faint-slumbers, I by you have watched,
And heard you murmur tales of Iron Wars:
Speak terms of manage to your bounding steed,
Cry courage to the field. And you have talked
Of sallies, and retires; trenches, tents,
Of palizadoes, frontiers, parapets,
Of basilisks, of cannon, culverin,
Of prisoners' ransom, and of soldiers slain,
And all the current of a heady fight.
Your spirit within you has been so at war,
And thus has so bestirred you in your sleep,
That beads of sweat have stood upon your brow,
Like bubbles in a late-disturbed stream;
And in your face strange motions have appeared,
Such as we see when men restrain their breath
On some great sudden haste. O what portents are these?
Some heavy businesse has my Lord in hand,
And I must know it: else he loves me not.

Hotspur. What ho; is Gilliams with the packet gone?

Servant. He is my Lord, an hour a-gone.

Hotspur. Has Butler brought those horses from the Sheriff?

Servant. One horse, my Lord, he brought even now.

Hotspur. What horse? A roan, a crop ear, is it not?

Servant. It is my Lord.

Hotspur. That Roan shall be my Throne. Well, I will back him
straight. Esperance, bid Butler lead him forth into the Park.

Lady Percy. But hear you, my lord

Hotspur. What say you, my Lady?

Lady Percy. What is it carries you away?

Hotspur. Why, my horse, my love, my horse.

Lady Percy. Out you mad-headed ape, a weasel has not such a deal of spleen, as you are tossed with. In sooth, I'll know your business, Harry, that I will. I fear my brother Mortimer does stir about his title, and has sent for you to line his enterprise. But if you go—

Hotspur. So far afoot, I shall be weary, Love.

Lady Percy. Come, come, you Paraquito, answer me directly unto this question, that I shall ask. Indeed, I'll break your little finger, Harry, if you will not tell me true.

Hotspur. Away, away you trifler. Love, I love you not,
I care not for you, Kate: this is no world
To play with mammets, and to tilt with lips.
We must have bloody noses, and cracked crowns,
And pass them current too. Gods me, my horse.
What say you, Kate? What would you have with me?

Lady Percy. Do you not love me? Do you not, indeed?
Well, do not then. For since you love me not,
I will not love myself. Do you not love me?
Nay, tell me if you speak in jest, or no.

Hotspur. Come, will you see me ride?
And when I am a horseback, I will swear
I love you infinitely. But hark you, Kate,
I must not have you henceforth, question me,
Where I go, nor reason whereabout.
Whether I must, I must. And to conclude,
This evening must I leave you, gentle Kate.
I know you wise, but yet no further wise
Than Harry Percy's wife. Constant you are,
But yet a woman, and for secrecy,
No Lady closer. For I will believe
You will not utter what you do not know,
And so far will I trust you, gentle Kate

Lady Percy. How so far?

Hotspur. Not an inch further. But hark you, Kate,
Where I go, there shall you go too.
Today will I set forth, tomorrow you.
Will this content you, Kate?

Lady Percy. It must of force.

[*Exit All*]

[*The Boar's Head Tavern, Eastcheap*]

[*Enter the Prince, and Poins*]

Prince. Ned, please, come out of that fat room, and lend me your hand to laugh a little.

Poins. Where have you been, Hal?

Prince. With three or four loggersheads among three or four score hogsheads. I have sounded the very base-string of humility. Sirrah, I am sworn brother to a leash of drawers; and can call them all by their christen names, as Tom, Dick, and Francis. They take it already upon their salvation, that though I be but Prince of Wales, yet I am the king of courtesy; and tell me flatly I am no proud Jack, like Falstaff, but a Corinthian, a lad of mettle, a good boy, by the Lord, so they call me, and when I am King of England, I shall command all the good lads in Eastcheap. They call drinking deep, dyeing scarlet; and when you breathe in your watering, they cry "hem!" and bid you play it off. To conclude, I am so good a proficient in one quarter of an hour, that I can drink with any tinker in his own language during my life. I tell you, Ned, you have lost much honor, that you were not with me in this action. But, sweet Ned, I give you this pennyworth of sugar, clapped even now into my hand by an under-skinker, one that never spoke other English in his life than "Eight shillings and sixpence," and "You are welcome," with this shrill addition, "Anon, anon, sir! Score a pint of bastard in the Half-moon," or so. But, Ned, to drive away the time till Falstaff come, I ask, do you stand in some by-room, while I question my puny drawer to what end he gave me the sugar; and do you never leave calling "Francis," that his tale to me may be nothing but "Anon." Step aside, and I'll show you a precedent.

Poins. Francis!

Prince. You are perfect.

Poins. Francis!

[*Exit Poins*]

Francis. Anon, anon, sir. Look down into the Pomgarnet, Ralph.

Prince. Come here, Francis.

Francis. My lord?

Prince. How long have you to serve, Francis?

Francis. Forsooth, five years, and as much as to—

Poins. [*Within*] Francis!

Francis. Anon, anon, sir.

Prince. Five year! by'r lady, a long lease for the clinking of pewter. But, Francis, dare you be so valiant as to play the coward with your indenture and show it a fair pair of heels and run from it?

Francis. O Lord, sir, I'll be sworn upon all the books in England, I could find in my heart.

Poins. [*Within*] Francis!

Francis. Anon, sir.

Prince. How old are you, Francis?

Francis. Let me see—about Michaelmas next I shall be—

Poins. [*Within*] Francis!

Francis. Anon, sir. Pray stay a little, my lord.

Prince. Nay, but hark you, Francis. for the sugar you gave me, 'twas a pennyworth, was it not?

Francis. O Lord, I would it had been two!

Prince. I will give you for it a thousand pound. Ask me when you will, and you shall have it.

Poins. [*Within*] Francis!

Francis. Anon, anon.

Prince. Anon, Francis? No, Francis; but tomorrow, Francis, or, Francis, on Thursday; or indeed, Francis, when you will. But, Francis!

Francis. My lord?

Prince. Will you rob this leathern jerkin, crystal-button, not-pated, agate-ring, puke-stocking, caddis-garter, smooth-tongue, Spanish-pouch—

Francis. O Lord, sir, who do you mean?

Prince. Why, then, your brown bastard is your only drink; for look you, Francis, your white canvas doublet will sully. in Barbary, sir, it cannot come to so much.

Francis. What, sir?

Poins. [*Within*] Francis!

Prince. Away, you rogue! do you not hear them call?

Here they both call him; the drawer stands amazed, not knowing which way to go.

[Enter Vintner]

Vintner. What, stand you still, and hear such a calling? Look to the guests within.

[Exit Francis]

My lord, old Sir John, with half-a-dozen more, are at the door. shall I let them in?

Prince. Let them alone awhile, and then open the door.

[Exit Vintner]

Poins!

[Re-enter Poins]

Poins. Anon, anon, sir.

Prince. Sirrah, Falstaff and the rest of the thieves are at the door. shall we be merry?

Poins. As merry as crickets, my lad. But hark you; what cunning match have you made with this jest of the drawer? Come, what's the issue?

Prince. I am now of all humors that have showed themselves humors since the old days of goodman Adam to the pupil age of this present twelve o'clock at midnight.

[Re-enter Francis]

What's o'clock, Francis?

Francis. Anon, anon, sir.

[Exit Francis]

Prince. That ever this fellow should have fewer words than a parrot, and yet the son of a woman! His industry is upstairs and downstairs; his eloquence the parcel of a reckoning. I am not yet of Percy's mind, the Hotspur of the north; he that kills me some six or seven dozen of Scots at a breakfast, washes his hands, and says to his wife "Fie upon this quiet life! I want work." "O my sweet Harry," says she, "how many have you killed today?" "Give my roan horse a drench," says he; and answers "Some fourteen," an hour after; "a trifle, a trifle." I say, call in Falstaff. I'll play Percy, and that damed brawn shall play Dame Mortimer his wife. "Rivo!" says the drunkard. Call in ribs, call in tallow.

[Enter Falstaff, Gadshill, Bardolph, and Peto; Francis
with wine]

Poins. Welcome, Jack. where have you been?

Falstaff. A plague of all cowards, I say, and a vengeance too! Indeed, and amen! Give me a cup of sack, boy. Before I lead this life long, I'll sew nether stocks and mend them and foot them too. A plague of all cowards! Give me a cup of sack, rogue. Is there no virtue extant? [*He drinks*]

Prince. Did you never see Titan kiss a dish of butter? Pitiful-hearted Titan, that melted at the sweet tale of the sun's! If you did, then behold that compound.

Falstaff. You rogue, here's lime in this sack too. there is nothing but roguery to be found in villainous man. yet a coward is worse than a cup of sack with lime in it. A villainous coward! Go your ways, old Jack; die when you will, if manhood, good manhood, be not forgot upon the face of the earth, then am I a shotten herring. There live not three good men unhanged in England; and one of them is fat and grows old. God help the while! A bad world, I say, I would I were a weaver; I could sing psalms or anything. A plague of all cowards, I say still.

Prince. How now, wool-sack! what mutter you?

Falstaff. A King's son! If I do not beat you out of your kingdom with a dagger of lath, and drive all your subjects afore you like a flock of wild geese, I'll never wear hair on my face more. You Prince of Wales!

Prince. Why, you whoreson round man, what's the matter?

Falstaff. Are not you a coward? answer me to that. and Poins there?

Poins. 'Zounds, you fat paunch, if you call me coward, by the Lord, I'll stab you.

Falstaff. I call you coward! I'll see you damned before I call you coward. but I would give a thousand pound I could run as fast as you can. You are straight enough in the shoulders, you care not who sees your back. call you that backing of your friends? A plague upon such backing! I give me them that will face me. Give me a cup of sack. I am a rogue, if I drunk today.

Prince. O villain! your lips are scarce wiped since you drank last.

Falstaff. All's one for that. [*He drinks*] A plague of all cowards, still say I.

Prince. What's the matter?

Falstaff. What's the matter! there be four of us here have taken a thousand pound this day morning.

Prince. Where is it, Jack? where is it?

Falstaff. Where is it! taken from us it is. A hundred upon poor four of us.

Prince. What, a hundred, man?

Falstaff. I am a rogue, if I were not at half-sword with a dozen of them two hours together. I have escaped by miracle. I am eight times thrust through the doublet, four through the hose; my buckler cut through and through; my sword hacked like a hand-saw—ecce signum! I never dealt better since I was a man. all would not do. A plague of all cowards! Let them speak. if they speak more or less than truth, they are villains and the sons of darkness.

Prince. Speak, sirs; how was it?

Gadshill. We four set upon some dozen—

Falstaff. Sixteen at least, my lord.

Gadshill. And bound them.

Peto. No, no, they were not bound.

Falstaff. You rogue, they were bound, every man of them; or I am a Jew else, an Ebrew Jew.

Gadshill. As we were sharing, some six or seven fresh men set upon us—

Falstaff. And unbound the rest, and then come in the other.

Prince. What, fought you with them all?

Falstaff. All! I know not what you call all; but if I fought not with fifty of them, I am a bunch of radish. if there were not two or three and fifty upon poor old Jack, then am I no two-legged creature.

Prince. Pray God you have not murdered some of them.

Falstaff. Nay, that's past praying for. I have peppered two of them; two I am sure I have paid, two rogues in buckram suits. I tell you what, Hal, if I tell you a lie, spit in my face, call me horse. You know my old ward; here I lay, and thus I bore my point. Four rogues in buckram let drive at me—

Prince. What, four? you said but two even now.

Falstaff. Four, Hal; I told you four.

Poins. Ay, ay, he said four.

Falstaff. These four came all a-front, and mainly thrust at me. I made me no more ado but took all their seven points in my target, thus.

Prince. Seven? why, there were but four even now.

Falstaff. In buckram?

Poins. Ay, four, in buckram suits.

Falstaff. Seven, by these hilts, or I am a villain else.

Prince. Please, let him alone; we shall have more anon.

Falstaff. Do you hear me, Hal?

Prince. Ay, and mark you too, Jack.

Falstaff. Do so, for it is worth the listening to. These nine in buckram that I told you of—

Prince. So, two more already.

Falstaff. Their points being broken—

Poins. Down fell their hose.

Falstaff. Began to give me ground. but I followed me close, came in foot and hand; and with a thought seven of the eleven I paid.

Prince. O monstrous! eleven buckram men grown out of two!

Falstaff. But, as the devil would have it, three misbegotten knaves in Kendal green came at my back and let drive at me; for it was so dark, Hal, that you could not see your hand.

Prince. These lies are like their father that begets them; gross as a mountain, open, palpable. Why, you clay-brained guts, you knotty-pated fool, you whoreson, obscene, greasy tallow-catch—

Falstaff. What, are you mad? are you mad? is not the truth the truth?

Prince. Why, how could you know these men in Kendal green, when it was so dark you could not see your hand? Come, tell us your reason. what say you to this?

Poins. Come, your reason, Jack, your reason.

Falstaff. What, upon compulsion? 'Zounds, if I were at the strappado, or all the racks in the world, I would not tell you on compulsion. Give you a reason on compulsion! if reasons were as plentiful as blackberries, I would give no man a reason upon compulsion, I.

Prince. I'll be no longer guilty of this sin; this sanguine coward, this bed-presser, this horseback-breaker, this huge hill of flesh—

Falstaff. 'Sblood, you starveling, you elf-skin, you dried neat's tongue, you bull's pizzle, you stock-fish! O for breath to utter what is like you! you tailor's-yard, you sheath, you bow-case, you vile standing-tuck—

Prince. Well, breathe awhile, and then to it again. and when you have tired yourself in base comparisons, hear me speak but this.

Poins. Mark, Jack.

Prince. We two saw you four set on four and bound them, and were masters of their wealth. Mark now, how a plain tale shall put you down. Then did we two set on you four; and, with a word, out-faced you from your prize, and have it; yea, and can show it you here in the house. and, Falstaff, you carried your guts away as nimbly, with as quick dexterity, and roared for mercy and still run and roared, as ever I heard bull-calf. What a slave are you, to hack your sword as you have done, and then say it was in fight! What trick, what device, what starting-hole, can you not find out to hide you from this open and apparent shame?

Poins. Come, let's hear, Jack; what trick have you now?

Falstaff. By the Lord, I knew you as well as he that made you. Why, hear you, my masters. Was it for me to kill the heir apparent? Should I turn upon the true Prince? why, you know I am as valiant as Hercules. but beware instinct; the lion will not touch the true Prince. Instinct is a great matter; I was now a coward on instinct. I shall think the better of myself and you during my life; I for a valiant lion, and you for a true Prince. But, by the Lord, lads, I am glad you have the money. Hostess, clap to the doors. watch tonight, pray tomorrow. Gallants, lads, boys, hearts of gold, all the titles of good fellowship come to you! What, shall we be merry! shall we have a play extempore?

Prince. Content; and the argument shall be your running away.

Falstaff. Ah, no more of that, Hal, if you love me!

[*Enter Hostess*]

Hostess. O Jesu, my lord the Prince!

Prince. How now, my lady the hostess! what say you to me?

Hostess. Well, my lord, there is a nobleman of the court at door would speak with you. He says he comes from your father.

Prince. Give him as much as will make him a royal man, and send him back again to my mother.

Falstaff. What manner of man is he?

Hostess. An old man.

Falstaff. What does gravity out of his bed at midnight? Shall I give him his answer?

Prince. Please do, Jack.

Falstaff. Faith, and I'll send him packing.

[*Exit Falstaff*]

Prince. Now, sirs. by'r lady, you fought fair; so did you, Peto; so did you, Bardolph. you are lions too, you ran away upon instinct, you will not touch the true Prince; no, fie!

Bardolph. Faith, I ran when I saw others run.

Prince. Faith, tell me now in earnest, how came Falstaff's sword so hacked?

Peto. Why, he hacked it with his dagger, and said he would swear truth out of England but he would make you believe it was done in fight, and persuaded us to do the like.

Bardolph. Yea, and to tickle our noses with spear-grass to make them bleed, and then to beslubber our garments with it and swear it was the blood of true men. I did that I did not this seven year before, I blushed to hear his monstrous devices.

Prince. O villain, you stole a cup of sack eighteen years ago, and were taken with the manner, and ever since you have blushed extempore. You had fire and sword on your side, and yet you ran away. what instinct had you for it?

Bardolph. My lord, do you see these meteors? Do you behold these exhalations?

Prince. I do.

Bardolph. What think you they portend?

Prince. Hot livers and cold purses.

Bardolph. Choler, my lord, if rightly taken.

Prince. No, if rightly taken, halter.

[*Re-enter Falstaff*]

Here comes lean Jack, here comes bare-bone. How now, my sweet creature of bombast! How long is it ago, Jack, since you saw your own knee?

Falstaff. My own knee! when I was about your years, Hal, I was not an eagle's talon in the waist; I could have crept into any alderman's thumb-ring. a plague of sighing and grief! it blows a man up like a bladder. There's villainous news abroad. here was Sir John Bracy from your father; you must to the court in the morning. That same mad fellow of the north, Percy, and he of Wales, that gave Amamon the bastinado and made Lucifer cuckold and swore the devil his true liegeman upon the cross of a Welsh hook—what a plague call you him?

Poins. O, Glendower.

Falstaff. Owen, Owen, the same; and his son-in-law Mortimer, and old Northumberland, and that sprightly Scot of Scots, Douglas, that runs on horseback up a hill perpendicular—

Prince. He that rides at high speed and with his pistol kills a sparrow flying.

Falstaff. You have hit it.

Prince. So did he never the sparrow.

Falstaff. Well, that rascal has good mettle in him; he will not run.

Prince. Why, what a rascal are you then, to praise him so for running!

Falstaff. On horseback, you cuckoo; but afoot he will not budge a foot.

Prince. Yes, Jack, upon instinct.

Falstaff. I grant you, upon instinct. Well, he is there too, and one Mordake, and a thousand blue-caps more. Worcester is stolen away tonight; your father's beard is turned white with the news. you may buy land now as cheap as stinking mackerel.

Prince. Why, then, it is like, if there come a hot June and this civil buffeting hold, we shall buy maidenheads as they buy hob-nails, by the hundreds.

Falstaff. By the mass, lad, you say true; it is like we shall have good trading that way. But tell me, Hal, are not you horrible afeard? you being heir apparent, could the world pick you out three such enemies again as that fiend Douglas, that spirit Percy, and that devil Glendower? Are you not horribly afraid? Does not your blood thrill at it?

Prince. Not a whit, truly; I lack some of your instinct.

Falstaff. Well, you will be horribly chid tomorrow when you come to your father. if you love me, practice an answer.

Prince. Do you stand for my father, and examine me upon the particulars of my life.

Falstaff. Shall I? Content. This chair shall be my state, this dagger my scepter, and this cushion my crown.

Prince. Your state is taken for a joined-stool, your golden scepter for a leaden dagger, and your precious rich crown for a pitiful bald crown!

Falstaff. Well, if the fire of grace be not quite out of you, now shall you be moved. Give me a cup of sack to make my eyes look red, that it may be thought I have wept; for I must speak in passion, and I will do it in King Cambyses' vein.

Prince. Well, here is my leg.

Falstaff. And here is my speech. Stand aside, nobility.

Hostess. O Jesu, this is excellent sport, indeed!

Falstaff. Weep not, sweet queen; for trickling tears are vain.

Hostess. O, the father, how he holds his countenance!

Falstaff. For God's sake, lords, convey my tristful queen;
For tears do stop the flood-gates of her eyes.

Hostess. O Jesu, he does it as like one of these harlotry players as ever I see!

Falstaff. Peace, good pint-pot; peace, good tickle-brain. Harry, I do not only marvel where you spend your time, but also how you are accompanied. for though the camomile, the more it is trodden on, the faster it grows—yet youth, the more it is wasted the sooner it wears. That you are my son, I have partly your mother's word, partly my own opinion, but chiefly a villainous trick of your eye and a foolish hanging of your nether lip, that does warrant me. If then you be son to me, here lies the point. Why, being son to me, are you so pointed at? Shall the blessed sun of heaven prove a micher and eat blackberries? A question not to be asked. Shall the son of England prove a thief and take purses? —a question to be asked. There is a thing, Harry, which you have often heard of and it is known to many in our land by the name of pitch. this pitch, as ancient writers do report, does defile; so does the company you keep. for, Harry, now I do not speak to you in drink but in tears, not in pleasure but in passion, not in words only, but in woes also. and yet there is a virtuous man whom I have often noted in your company, but I know not his name.

Prince. What manner of man, if it like your majesty?

Falstaff. A goodly portly man, indeed, and a corpulent; of a cheerful look, a pleasing eye and a most noble carriage; and, as I think, his age some fifty, or, by'r lady, inclining to three score; and now I remember me, his name is Falstaff. if that man should be lewdly given, he deceives me; for, Harry, I see virtue in his looks. If then the tree may be known by the fruit, as the fruit by the tree, then, peremptorily I speak it, there is virtue in that Falstaff.

him keep with, the rest banish. And tell me now, you naughty varlet, tell me, where have you been this month?

Prince. Do you speak like a King? Do you stand for me, and I'll play my father.

Falstaff. Depose me? if you do it half so gravely, so majestically, both in word and matter, hang me up by the heels for a rabbit-sucker or a poulter's hare.

Prince. Well, here I am set.

Falstaff. And here I stand. Judge, my masters.

Prince. Now, Harry, whence come you?

Falstaff. My noble lord, from Eastcheap.

Prince. The complaints I hear of you are grievous.

Falstaff. 'Sblood, my lord, they are false. nay, I'll tickle you for a young Prince, truly.

Prince. Swear you, ungracious boy? Henceforth never look on me. You are violently carried away from grace. there is a devil haunts you in the likeness of an old fat man; a tun of man is your companion. Why do you converse with that trunk of humors, that bolting-hutch of beastliness, that swollen parcel of dropsies, that huge bombard of sack, that stuffed cloak-bag of guts, that roasted Manningtree ox with the pudding in his belly, that reverend vice, that grey iniquity, that father ruffian, that vanity in years? Wherein is he good, but to taste sack and drink it? Wherein neat and cleanly, but to carve a capon and eat it? Wherein cunning, but in craft? Wherein crafty, but in villainy? Wherein villainous, but in all things? Wherein worthy, but in nothing?

Falstaff. I would your grace would take me with you. Whom means your grace?

Prince. That villainous abominable misleader of youth, Falstaff, that old white-bearded Satan.

Falstaff. My lord, the man I know.

Prince. I know you do.

Falstaff. But to say I know more harm in him than in myself, were to say more than I know. That he is old, the more the pity, his white hairs do witness it; but that he is, saving your reverence, a whoremaster, that I utterly deny. If sack and sugar be a fault, God help the wicked! If to be old and merry be a sin, then many an old host that I know is damned. If to be fat be to be hated, then Pharaoh's lean kine are to be loved. No, my good lord; banish Peto, banish Bardolph, banish Poins. but for sweet Jack Falstaff, kind Jack Falstaff, true Jack Falstaff, valiant Jack Falstaff, and therefore more valiant, being, as he is, old Jack Falstaff, banish not him your Harry's company, banish not him your Harry's company. Banish plumb Jack, and banish all the world.

Prince. I do, I will.

[A knocking heard]

[Exit All Hostess, Francis, and Bardolph. Re-enter Bardolph, running]

Bardolph. O, my lord, my lord! the sheriff with a most monstrous watch is at the door.

Falstaff. Out, you rogue! Play out the play. I have much to say in behalf of that Falstaff.

[Re-enter the Hostess]

Hostess. O Jesu, my lord, my lord!

Prince. Heigh, heigh! the devil rides upon a fiddlestick. what's the matter?

Hostess. The sheriff and all the watch are at the door; they are come to search the house. Shall I let them in?

Falstaff. Do you hear, Hal? Never call a true piece of gold a counterfeit. you are essentially mad, without seeming so.

Prince. And you a natural coward, without instinct.

Falstaff. I deny your major. If you will deny the sheriff, so; if not, let him enter; if I become not a cart as well as another man, a plague on my bringing up! I hope I shall as soon be strangled with a halter as another.

Prince. Go, hide you behind the arras. the rest walk up above. Now, my masters, for a true face and good conscience.

Falstaff. Both which I have had. But their date is out, and therefore I'll hide me.

Prince. Call in the sheriff.

[Exit all except the Prince and Peto]

[Enter Sheriff and the Carrier]

Now, master sheriff, what is your will with me?

Sheriff. First, pardon me, my lord. A hue and cry
Has followed certain men unto this house.

Prince. What men?

Sheriff. One of them is well known, my gracious lord,
A gross fat man.

Carrier. As fat as butter.

Prince. The man, I do assure you, is not here;
For I myself at this time have employed him.
And, sheriff, I will engage my word to you
That I will, by tomorrow dinnertime,
Send him to answer you, or any man,
For anything he shall be charged withal.
And so let me entreat you, leave the house.

Sheriff. I will, my lord. There are two gentlemen
Have in this robbery lost three hundred marks.

Prince. It may be so. If he have robbed these men,
He shall be answerable; and so farewell.

Sheriff. Good night, my noble lord.

Prince. I think it is good morrow, is it not?

Sheriff. Indeed, my lord, I think it be two o'clock.

[Exit All Sheriff and Carrier]

Prince. This oily rascal is known as well as Paul's. Go, call him
forth.

Peto. Falstaff!—Fast asleep behind the arras, and snorting like a
horse.

Prince. Hark, how hard he fetches breath. Search his pockets.

[He searches his pockets, and finds certain papers]

What have you found?

Peto. Nothing but papers, my lord.

Prince. Let's see what they be. Read them.

Peto. [*Reads*]

Item, A capon.....2 shillings. 2 pence.

Item, Sauce.....4 shillings.

Item, Sack, two gallons.....5 shillings. 8 pence.

Item, Anchovies and sack after supper.....2 shillings. 6 pence.

Item, Bread.....obolus.

Prince. O monstrous! but one half-pennyworth of bread to this intolerable deal of sack! What there is else, keep close; we'll read it at more advantage. there let him sleep till day. I'll to the court in the morning. We must all to the wars, and your place shall be honorable. I'll procure this fat rogue a charge of foot; and I know his death will be a march of twelve-score. The money shall be paid back again with advantage. Be with me betimes in the morning; and so, good morrow, Peto.

[*Exit All*]

Act Three

1

[*Bangor. The Archdeacon's house*]

[*Enter Hotspur, Worcester, Lord Mortimer, Owen Glendower*]

Mortimer. These promises are fair, the parties sure,
  And our induction full of prosperous hope.

Hotspur. Lord Mortimer, and cousin Glendower,
  Will you sit down?
  And uncle Worcester. A plague upon it!
  I have forgot the map.

Glendower. No, here it is.
  Sit, cousin Percy; sit, good cousin Hotspur,
  For by that name as oft as Lancaster
  Does speak of you, his cheek looks pale, and with
  A rising sigh he wishes you in heaven.

Hotspur. And you in hell, as oft as he hears
  Owen Glendower spoke of.

Glendower. I cannot blame him. At my nativity
  The front of heaven was full of fiery shapes
  Of burning cressets, and at my birth
  The frame and huge foundation of the earth
  Shaked like a coward.

Hotspur. Why, so it would have done at the same season, if your
  mother's cat had but kittened, though yourself had never been
  born.

Glendower. I say the earth did shake when I was born.

Hotspur. And I say the earth was not of my mind,
  If you suppose as fearing you it shook.

Glendower. The heavens were all on fire, the earth did tremble.

Hotspur. O, then the earth shook to see the heavens on fire,
And not in fear of your nativity.
Diseased nature oftentimes breaks forth
In strange eruptions; oft the teeming earth
Is with a kind of colic pinched and vexed
By the imprisoning of unruly wind
Within her womb, which, for enlargement striving,
Shakes the old beldame earth and topples down
Steeples and mossgrown towers. At your birth
Our grandam earth, having this distemp'rature,
In passion shook.

Glendower. Cousin, of many men
I do not bear these crossings. Give me leave
To tell you once again that at my birth
The front of heaven was full of fiery shapes,
The goats ran from the mountains, and the herds
Were strangely clamorous to the frighted fields.
These signs have marked me extraordinary,
And all the courses of my life do show
I am not in the roll of common men.
Where is he living, clipped in with the sea
That chides the banks of England, Scotland, Wales,
Which calls me pupil or has read to me?
And bring him out that is but woman's son
Can trace me in the tedious ways of art
And hold me pace in deep experiments.

Hotspur. I think there's no man speaks better Welsh. I'll to
dinner.

Mortimer. Peace, cousin Percy; you will make him mad.

Glendower. I can call spirits from the vasty deep.

Hotspur. Why, so can I, or so can any man;
But will they come when you do call for them?

Glendower. Why, I can teach you, cousin, to command the devil.

Hotspur. And I can teach you, coz, to shame the devil—
By telling truth. Tell truth and shame the devil.
If you have power to raise him, bring him here,
And I'll be sworn I have power to shame him hence.
O, while you live, tell truth and shame the devil!

Mortimer. Come, come, no more of this unprofitable chat.

Glendower. Three times has Henry Bolingbroke made head

Against my power; thrice from the banks of Wye
And sandy-bottomed Severn have I sent him
Bootless home and weather-beaten back.

Hotspur. Home without boots, and in foul weather too?
How scapes he agues, in the devil's name

Glendower. Come, here's the map. Shall we divide our right
According to our threefold order taken?

Mortimer. The Archdeacon has divided it
Into three limits very equally.
England, from Trent and Severn hereto,
By south and east is to my part assigned;
All westward, Wales beyond the Severn shore,
And all the fertile land within that bound,
To Owen Glendower; and, dear coz, to you
The remnant northward lying off from Trent.
And our indentures tripartite are drawn;
Which being sealed interchangeably,
A business that this night may execute),
To-morrow, cousin Percy, you and I
And my good Lord of Worcester will set forth
To meet your father and the Scottish bower,
As is appointed us, at Shrewsbury.
My father Glendower is not ready yet,
Nor shall we need his help these fourteen days.
[*To Glendower*] Within that space you may have drawn together
Your tenants, friends, and neighboring gentlemen.

Glendower. A shorter time shall send me to you, lords;
And in my conduct shall your ladies come,
From whom you now must steal and take no leave,
For there will be a world of water shed
Upon the parting of your wives and you.

Hotspur. Methinks my moiety, north from Burton here,
In quantity equals not one of yours.
See how this river comes me cranking in
And cuts me from the best of all my land
A huge half-moon, a monstrous cantle out.
I'll have the current ill this place dammed up,
And here the smug and sliver Trent shall run
In a new channel fair and evenly.
It shall not wind with such a deep indent
To rob me of so rich a bottom here.

Glendower. Not wind? It shall, it must! You see it doth.

Mortimer. Yea, but
Mark how he bears his course, and runs me up
With like advantage on the other side,
Gelding the opposed continent as much
As on the other side it takes from you.

Worcester. Yea, but a little charge will trench him here
And on this north side win this cape of land;
And then he runs straight and even.

Hotspur. I'll have it so. A little charge will do it.

Glendower. I will not have it alt'red.

Hotspur. Will not you?

Glendower. No, nor you shall not.

Hotspur. Who shall say me nay?

Glendower. No, that will I.

Hotspur. Let me not understand you then; speak it in Welsh.

Glendower. I can speak English, lord, as well as you;
For I was trained up in the English court,
Where, being but young, I framed to the harp
Many an English ditty lovely well,
And gave the tongue a helpful ornament—
A virtue that was never seen in you.

Hotspur. Marry,
And I am glad of it with all my heart!
I had rather be a kitten and cry mew
Than one of these same metre ballet-mongers.
I had rather hear a brazen canstick turned
Or a dry wheel grate on the axletree,
And that would set my teeth nothing on edge,
Nothing so much as mincing poetry.
'Tis like the forced gait of a shuffling nag,

Glendower. Come, you shall have Trent turned.

Hotspur. I do not care. I'll give thrice so much land
To any well-deserving friend;
But in the way of bargain, mark you me,
I'll cavil on the ninth part of a hair
Are the indentures drawn? Shall we be gone?

Glendower. The moon shines fair; you may away by night.
I'll haste the writer, and withal

Break with your wives of your departure hence.
I am afraid my daughter will run mad,
So much she dotes on her Mortimer.

[*Exit Glendower*]

Mortimer. Fie, cousin Percy! how you cross my father!

Hotspur. I cannot choose. Sometimes he angers me
  With telling me of the moldwarp and the ant,
  Of the dreamer Merlin and his prophecies,
  And of a dragon and a finless fish,
  A clip-winged griffin and a moulten raven,
  A couching lion and a ramping cat,
  And such a deal of skimble-skamble stuff
  As puts me from my faith. I tell you what—
  He held me last night at least nine hours
  In reckoning up the several devils' names
  That were his lackeys. I cried "hum," and "Well, go to!"
  But marked him not a word. O, he is as tedious
  As a tired horse, a railing wife;
  Worse than a smoky house. I had rather live
  With cheese and garlic in a windmill far
  Than feed on cates and have him talk to me
  In any summer house in Christendom).

Mortimer. In faith, he is a worthy gentleman,
  Exceedingly well read, and profited
  In strange concealments, valiant as a lion,
  And wondrous affable, and as bountiful
  As mines of India. Shall I tell you, cousin?
  He holds your temper in a high respect
  And curbs himself even of his natural scope
  When you come 'cross his humor. Faith, he does.
  I warrant you that man is not alive
  Might so have tempted him as you have done
  Without the taste of danger and reproof.
  But do not use it oft, let me entreat you.

Worcester. In faith, my lord, you are too willful-blame,
  And since your coming here have done enough
  To put him quite besides his patience.
  You must needs learn, lord, to amend this fault.
  Though sometimes it show greatness, courage, blood—
  And that's the dearest grace it renders you—
  Yet oftentimes it does present harsh rage,

Defect of manners, want of government,
Pride, haughtiness, opinion, and disdain;
The least of which haunting a nobleman
Loses men's hearts, and leaves behind a stain
Upon the beauty of all parts besides,
Beguiling them of commendation.

Hotspur. Well, I am schooled. Good manners be your speed!
Here come our wives, and let us take our leave.

[*Enter Glendower with the Ladies*]

Mortimer. This is the deadly spite that angers me—
My wife can speak no English, I no Welsh.

Glendower. My daughter weeps; she will not part with you;
She'll be a soldier too, she'll to the wars.

Mortimer. Good father, tell her that she and my aunt Percy
Shall follow in your conduct speedily.

[*Glendower and his wife discuss in Welsh*]

Glendower. She is desperate here. A peevish self-willed harlotry,
One that no persuasion can do good upon.

[*The Lady speaks in Welsh*]

Mortimer. I understand your looks. That pretty Welsh
Which you pour down from these swelling heavens
I am too perfect in; and, but for shame,
In such a Barley should I answer you.

[*The Lady again in Welsh*]

I understand your kisses, and you mine,
And that's a feeling disputation.
But I will never be a truant, love,
Till I have learnt your language. for your tongue
Makes Welsh as sweet as ditties highly penned,
Sung by a fair queen in a summer's bower,
With ravishing division, to her lute.

Glendower. Nay, if you melt, then will she run mad.

[*The Lady speaks again in Welsh*]

Mortimer. O, I am ignorance itself in this!

Glendower. She bids you on the wanton rushes lay you down
And rest your gentle head upon her lap,
And she will sing the song that pleases you

And on your eyelids crown the god of sleep,
Charming your blood with pleasing heaviness,
Making such difference between wake and sleep
As is the difference between day and night
The hour before the heavenly-harnessed team
Begins his golden progress in the East.

Mortimer. With all my heart I'll sit and hear her sing.
By that time will our book, I think, be drawn.

Glendower. Do so,
And those musicians that shall play to you
Hang in the air a thousand leagues from hence,
And straight they shall be here. Sit, and attend.

Hotspur. Come, Kate, you are perfect in lying down. Come, quick,
quick, that I may lay my head in your lap.

Lady Percy. Go, you giddy goose.

[*The music plays*]

Hotspur. Now I perceive the devil understands Welsh;
And 'tis no marvel, be is so humorous.
By'r lady, he is a good musician.

Lady Percy. Then should you be nothing but musical; for you are
altogether governed by humors. Lie still, you thief, and hear
the lady sing in Welsh.

Hotspur. I had rather hear Lady, my brach, howl in Irish.

Lady Percy. Wouldst you have your head broken?

Hotspur. No.

Lady Percy. Then be still.

Hotspur. Neither! 'tis a woman's fault.

Lady Percy. Now God help you!

Hotspur. To the Welsh lady's bed.

Lady Percy. What's that?

Hotspur. Peace! she sings.

[*Here the Lady sings a Welsh song*]

Come, Kate, I'll have your song too.

Lady Percy. Not mine, in good sooth.

Hotspur. Not yours, in good sooth? Heart! you swear like a
comfit-maker's wife. "Not you, in good sooth!" and "as true
as I live!" and "as God shall mend me!" and "as sure as day!"

And give such sarcenet surety for your oaths
As if you never walk'st further than Finsbury.
Swear me, Kate, like a lady as you art,
A good mouth-filling oath; and leave "in sooth"
And such protest of pepper gingerbread
To velvet guards and Sunday citizens. Come, sing.

Lady Percy. I will not sing.

Hotspur. 'Tis the next way to turn tailor or be redbreast-teacher. If
the indentures be drawn, I'll away within these two hours; and
so come in when you will.

[*Exit Hotspur*]

Glendower. Come, come, Lord Mortimer. You are as slow
As hot Lord Percy is on fire to go.
By this our book is drawn; we'll but seal,
And then to horse immediately.

Mortimer. With all my heart.

[*Exit All*]

[*London. The Palace*]

[*Enter the King, Prince of Wales, and others*]

King. Lords, give us leave. The Prince of Wales and I
  Must have some private conference; but be near at hand,
  For we shall presently have need of you.

[*Exit All Lords*]

  I know not whether God will have it so,
  For some displeasing service I have done,
  That, in his secret doom, out of my blood
  He'll breed revengement and a scourge for me;
  But you do in your passages of life
  Make me believe that you are only marked
  For the hot vengeance and the rod of heaven
  To punish my mistreadings. Tell me else,
  Could such inordinate and low desires,
  Such poor, such bare, such lewd, such mean attempts,
  Such barren pleasures, rude society,
  As you are matched withal and grafted to,
  Accompany the greatness of your blood
  And hold their level with your princely heart?

Prince. So please your Majesty, I would I could
  Quit all offenses with as clear excuse
  As well as I am doubtless I can purge
  Myself of many I am charged withal.
  Yet such extenuation let me beg
  As, in reproof of many tales devised,
  Which oft the ear of greatness needs must bear
  By, smiling pickthanks and base newsmongers,
  I may, for some things true wherein my youth
  Has faulty wand'red and irregular,
  And pardon on lily true submission.

King. God pardon you! Yet let me wonder, Harry,
  At your affections, which do hold a wing,
  Quite from the flight of all your ancestors.
  Your place in Council you have rudely lost,
  Which by your younger brother is supplied,

And are almost an alien to the hearts
Of all the court and Princes of my blood.
The hope and expectation of your time
Is ruined, and the soul of every man
Prophetically do forethink your fall.
Had I so lavish of my presence been,
So common-hackneyed in the eyes of men,
So stale and cheap to vulgar company,
Opinion, that did help me to the crown,
Had still kept loyal to possession
And left me in reputeless banishment,
A fellow of no mark nor likelihood.
By being seldom seen, I could not stir
But, like a comet, I was wondered at;
That men would tell their children, "This is he!"
Others would say, "Where? Which is Bolingbroke?"
And then I stole all courtesy from heaven,
And dressed myself in such humility
That I did pluck allegiance from men's hearts,
Loud shouts and salutations from their mouths
Even in the presence of the crowned King.
Thus did I keep my person fresh and new,
My presence, like a robe pontifical,
Never seen but wondered at; and so my state,
Seldom but sumptuous, showed like a feast
And won by rareness such solemnity.
The skipping King, he ambled up and down
With shallow jesters and rash bavin wits,
Soon kindled and soon burnt; carded his state;
Mingled his royalty with cap'ring fools;
Had his great name profaned with their scorns
And gave his countenance, against his name,
To laugh at gibing boys and stand the push
Of every beardless vain comparative;
Grew a companion to the common streets,
Enfeoffed himself to popularity;
That, being dally swallowed by men's eyes,
They surfeited with honey and began
To loathe the taste of sweetness, whereof a little
More than a little is by much too much.
So, when he had occasion to be seen,
He was but as the cuckoo is in June,
Heard, not regarded— seen, but with such eyes

As, sick and blunted with community,
Afford no extraordinary gaze,
Such as is bent on unlike majesty
When it shines seldom in admiring eyes;
But rather drowsed and hung their eyelids down,
Slept in his face, and rend'red such aspect
As cloudy men use to their adversaries,
Being with his presence glutted, gorged, and full.
And in that very line, Harry, stand thou;
For you have lost your princely privilege
With vile participation. Not an eye
But is aweary of your common sight,
Save mine, which has desired to see you more;
Which now does that I would not have it do—
Make blind itself with foolish tenderness.

Prince. I shall hereafter, my thrice-gracious lord,
Be more myself.

King. For all the world,
As you are to this hour, was Richard then
When I from France set foot at Ravenspurgh;
And even as I was then is Percy now.
Now, by my scepter, and my soul to boot,
He has more worthy inter to the state
Than you, the shadow of succession;
For of no right, nor color like to right,
He does fill fields with harness in the realm,
Turns head against the lion's armed jaws,
And, Being no more in debt to years than you,
Leads ancient lords and reverend Bishops on
To bloody battles and to bruising arms.
What never-dying honor has he got
Against renowned Douglas! whose high deeds,
Whose hot incursions and great name in arms
Holds from all soldiers chief majority
And military title capital
Through all the kingdoms that acknowledge Christ.
Thrice has this Hotspur, Mars in swathling clothes,
This infant warrior, in his enterprises
Discomfited great Douglas; taken him once,
Enlarged him, and made a friend of him,
To fill the mouth of deep defiance up
And shake the peace and safety of our throne.

And what say you to this? Percy, Northumberland,
The Archbishop's Grace of York, Douglas, Mortimer
Capitulate against us and are up.
But wherefore do I tell these news to you
Why, Harry, do I tell you of my foes,
Which are my nearest and dearest enemy
You that are like enough, through vassal fear,
Base inclination, and the start of spleen,
To fight against me under Percy's pay,
To dog his heels and curtsy at his frowns,
To show how much you are degenerate.

Prince. Do not think so. You shall not find it so.
And God forgive them that so much have swayed
Your Majesty's good thoughts away from me!
I will redeem all this on Percy's head
And, in the closing of some glorious day,
Be bold to tell you that I am your son,
When I will wear a garment all of blood,
And stain my favors in a bloody mask,
Which, washed away, shall scour my shame with it.
And that shall be the day, whene'er it lights,
That this same child of honor and renown,
This gallant Hotspur, this all-praised knight,
And your unthought of Harry chance to meet.
For every honor sitting on his helm,
Would they were multitudes, and on my head
My shames redoubled! For the time will come
That I shall make this Northern youth exchange
His glorious deeds for my indignities.
Percy is but my factor, good my lord,
To engross up glorious deeds on my behalf;
And I will call hall to so strict account
That he shall render every glory up,
Yea, even the slightest worship of his time,
Or I will tear the reckoning from his heart.
This in the name of God I promise here;
The which if he be pleased I shall perform,
I do beseech your Majesty may salve
The long-grown wounds of my intemperance.
If not, the end of life cancels all bands,
And I will die a hundred thousand deaths
Before break the smallest parcel of this vow.

King. A hundred thousand rebels die in this!
You shall have charge and sovereign trust herein.

[*Enter Blunt*]

How now, good Blunt? Your looks are full of speed.

Blunt. So has the business that I come to speak of.
Lord Mortimer of Scotland has sent word
That Douglas and the English rebels met
The eleventh of this month at Shrewsbury.
A mighty and a fearful head they are,
If promises be kept oil every hand,
As ever off'red foul play in a state.

King. The Earl of Westmoreland set forth today;
With him my son, Lord John of Lancaster;
For this advertisement is five days old.
On Wednesday next, Harry, you shall set forward;
On Thursday we ourselves will march. Our meeting
Is Bridgenorth; and, Harry, you shall march
Through Gloucestershire; by which account,
Our business valued, some twelve days hence
Our general forces at Bridgenorth shall meet.
Our hands are full of business. Let's away.
Advantage feeds him fat while men delay.

[*Exit All*]

3

[Eastcheap. The Boar's Head Tavern]

[Enter Falstaff and Bardolph]

Falstaff. Bardolph, am I not fallen away vilely since this last action? Do I not bate? Do I not dwindle? Why, my skin hangs about me like an old lady's loose gown! I am withered like an old apple-john. Well, I'll repent, and that suddenly, while I am in some liking. I shall be out of heart shortly, and then I shall have no strength to repent. If I have not forgotten what the inside of a church is made of, I am a peppercorn, a brewer's horse. The inside of a church! Company, villainous company, has been the spoil of me.

Bardolph. Sir John, you are so fretful you cannot live long.

Falstaff. Why, there is it! Come, sing me a bawdy song; make me merry. I was as virtuously given as a gentleman need to be, virtuous enough. swore little, diced not above seven times a week, went to a bawdy house not above once in a quarter of an hour, paid money that I borrowed— three or four times, lived well, and in good compass; and now I live out of all order, out of all compass.

Bardolph. Why, you are so fat, Sir John, that you must needs be out of all compass— out of all reasonable compass, Sir John.

Falstaff. Do you amend your face, and I'll amend my life. You are our admiral, you bear the lantern in the poop— but 'tis in the nose of you. You are the Knight of the Burning Lamp.

Bardolph. Why, Sir John, my face does you no harm.

Falstaff. No, I'll be sworn. I make as good use of it as many a man does of a death's-head or a memento mori. I never see your face but I think upon hellfire and Dives that lived in purple; for there he is in his robes, burning, burning. if you were any way given to virtue, I would swear by your face; my oath should be "By this fire, that's God's angel." But you are altogether given over, and were indeed, but for the light in your face, the son of utter darkness. When you ran'st up Gad's Hill. in the night to catch my horse, if I did not think you had been an ignis fatuus or a ball of wildfire, there's no purchase in money. O, you are a perpetual triumph, an everlasting bonfire-light! You have saved me a thousand marks in links and torches, walking with you in the night between tavern and tavern; but the sack that you have drunk me would have bought me lights as good cheap at the dearest chandler's in Europe. I have maintained that salamander of yours with fire any time this two-and-thirty years. God reward me for it!

Bardolph. 'Sblood, I would my face were in your belly!

Falstaff. God-a-mercy! so should I be sure to be heart-burned.

[*Enter Hostess*]

How now, Dame Partlet the hen? Have you enquired yet who picked my pocket?

Hostess. Why, Sir John, what do you think, Sir John? Do you think I keep thieves in my house? I have searched, I have enquired, so has my husband, man by man, boy by boy, servant by servant. The tithe of a hair was never lost in my house before.

Falstaff. Ye lie, Hostess. Bardolph was shaved and lost many a hair, and I'll be sworn my pocket was picked. Go to, you are a woman, go!

Hostess. Who, I? No; I defy you! God's light, I was never called so in my own house before!

Falstaff. Go to, I know you well enough.

Hostess. No, Sir John; you do not know me, Sir John. I know you, Sir John. You owe me money, Sir John, and now you pick a quarrel to beguile me of it. I bought you a dozen of shirts to your back.

Falstaff. Dowlas, filthy dowlas! I have given them away to bakers' wives; they have made bolters of them.

Hostess. Now, as I am a true woman, holland of eight shillings an ell. You owe money here besides, Sir John, for your diet and by-drinkings, and money lent you, four-and-twenty pound.

Falstaff. He had his part of it; let him pay.

Hostess. He? Alas, he is poor; he has nothing.

Falstaff. How? Poor? Look upon his face. What call you rich? Let them coin his nose, let them coin his cheeks. I'll not pay a denier. What, will you make a younker of me? Shall I not take my ease in my inn but I shall have my pocket picked? I have lost a seal-ring of my grandfather's worth forty mark.

Hostess. O Jesu, I have heard the Prince tell him, I know not how oft, that that ring was copper!

Falstaff. How? the Prince is a Jack, a sneak-cup. 'Sblood, if he were here, I would cudgel him like a dog if he would say so.

[*Enter the Prince and Poins, marching*]

[*Falstaff plays on an imaginary fife*]

How now, lad? Is the wind in that door, truly? Must we all march?

Bardolph. Yea, two and two, Newgate fashion.

Hostess. My lord, I pray you hear me.

Prince. What say you, Mistress Quickly? How does your husband? I love him well; he is an honest man.

Hostess. Good my lord, hear me.

Falstaff. Please let her alone and list to me.

Prince. What say you, Jack?

Falstaff. The other night I fell asleep here behind the arras and had my pocket picked. This house is turned bawdy house; they pick pockets.

Prince. What did you lose, Jack?

Falstaff. Will you believe me, Hal? Three or four bonds of forty pound apiece and a seal-ring of my grandfather's.

Prince. A trifle, some eightpenny matter.

Hostess. So I told him, my lord, and I said I heard your Grace say so; and, my lord, he speaks most vilely of you, like a foul-mouthed man as he is, and said he would cudgel you.

Prince. What! he did not?

Hostess. There's neither faith, truth, nor womanhood in me else.

Falstaff. There's no more faith in you than in a stewed prune, nor no more truth in you than in a drawn fox; and for woman-hood, Maid Marian may be the deputy's wife of the ward to you. Go, you thing, go!

Hostess. Say, what thing? What thing?

Falstaff. What thing? Why, a thing to thank God on.

Hostess. I am no thing to thank God on, I would you should know it! I am an honest man's wife, and, setting your knighthood aside, you are a knave to call me so.

Falstaff. Setting your womanhood aside, you are a beast to say otherwise.

Hostess. Say, what beast, you knave, you?

Falstaff. What beast? Why, an otter.

Prince. An otter, Sir John? Why an otter?

Falstaff. Why, she's neither fish nor flesh; a man knows not where to have her.

Hostess. You are an unjust man in saying so. You or any man knows where to have me, you knave, thou!

Prince. You say true, hostess, and he slanders you most grossly.

Hostess. So he does you, my lord, and said this other day you ought him a thousand pound.

Prince. Sirrah, do I owe you a thousand pound?

Falstaff. A thousand pound, Hal? A million! Your love is worth a million; you owe me your love.

Hostess. Nay, my lord, he called you Jack and said he would cudgel you.

Falstaff. Did I, Bardolph?

Bardolph. Indeed, Sir John, you said so.

Falstaff. Yea. if he said my ring was copper.

Prince. I say, 'tis copper. Dare you be as good as your word now?

Falstaff. Why, Hal, you know, as you are but man, I dare; but as you are Prince, I fear you as I fear the roaring of the lion's whelp.

Prince. And why not as the lion?

Falstaff. The King himself is to be feared as the lion. Do you think I'll fear you as I fear your father? Nay, if I do, I pray God my girdle break.

Prince. O, if it should, how would your guts fall about your knees! But, sirrah, there's no room for faith, truth, nor honesty in this bosom of yours. It is all filled up with guts and midriff. Charge an honest woman with picking your pocket? Why, you whoreson, impudent, embossed rascal, if there were anything in your pocket but tavern reckonings, memorandums of bawdy houses, and one poor pennyworth of sugar candy to make you long-winded— if your pocket were enriched with any other injuries but these, I am a villain. And yet you will stand to it; you will not pocket up wrong. Are you not ashamed?

Falstaff. Do you hear, Hal? You know in the state of innocency Adam fell; and what should poor Jack Falstaff do in the days of villany? You see I have more flesh than another man, and therefore more frailty. You confess then, you picked my pocket?

Prince. It appears so by the story.

Falstaff. Hostess, I forgive you. Go make ready breakfast. Love your husband, look to your servants, cherish your guests. You shall

find me tractable to any honest reason. You see I am pacified.
—Still?— Nay, please be gone.

[*Exit Hostess*]

Now, Hal, to the news at court. For the robbery, lad— how is
that answered?

Prince. O my sweet beef, I must still be good angel to you. The
money is paid back again.

Falstaff. O, I do not like that paying back! 'tis a double labor.

Prince. I am good friends with my father, and may do anything.

Falstaff. Rob me the exchequer the first thing you doest, and do it
with unwashed hands too.

Bardolph. Do, my lord.

Prince. I have procured you, Jack, a charge of foot.

Falstaff. I would it had been of horse. Where shall I find one that
can steal well? O for a fine thief of the age of two-and-twenty or
thereabouts! I am heinously unprovided. Well, God be thanked
for these rebels. They offend none but the virtuous. I laud them,
I praise them.

Prince. Bardolph!

Bardolph. My lord?

Prince. Go bear this letter to Lord John of Lancaster, To my brother
John; this to my Lord of Westmoreland.

[*Exit Bardolph*]

Go, Poins, to horse, to horse; for you and I
Have thirty miles to ride yet before dinner time.

[*Exit Poins*]

Jack, meet me tomorrow in the Temple Hall
At two o'clock in the afternoon.
There shall you know your charge. And there receive
Money and order for their furniture.
The land is burning; Percy stands on high;
And either they or we must lower lie.

[*Exit Prince Hal*]

Falstaff. Rare words! brave world! Hostess, my breakfast, come. O,
I could wish this tavern were my drum!

[*Exit Falstaff*]

Act Four

1

[*The rebel camp near Shrewsbury*]

[*Enter Harry Hotspur, Worcester, and Douglas*]

Hotspur. Well said, my noble Scot. If speaking truth
   In this fine age were not thought flattery,
   Such attribution should the Douglas have
   As not a soldier of this season's stamp
   Should go so general current through the world.
   By God, I cannot flatter, I defy
   The tongues of soothers! but a braver place
   In my heart's love has no man than yourself.
   Nay, task me to my word; approve me, lord.

Douglas. You are the King of honor.
   No man so potent breathes upon the ground
   But I will beard him.

[*Enter Messenger*]

Hotspur. Do so, and 'tis well.—
   What letters have you there?— I can but thank you.

Messenger. These letters come from your father.

Hotspur. Letters from him? Why comes he not himself?

Messenger. He cannot come, my lord; he is grievous sick.

Hotspur. Zounds! how has he the leisure to be sick
   In such a justling time? Who leads his power?
   Under whose government come they along?

Messenger. His letters bears his mind, not I, my lord.

Worcester. I beg you tell me, does he keep his bed?

Messenger. He did, my lord, four days before I set forth,
   And at the time of my departure thence
   He was much feared by his physicians.

Worcester. I would the state of time had first been whole
   Before he by sickness had been visited.
   His health was never better worth than now.

Hotspur. Sick now? droop now? This sickness does infect
   The very lifeblood of our enterprise.
   'Tis catching here, even to our camp.
   He writes me here that inward sickness—
   And that his friends by deputation could not
   So soon be drawn; no did he think it meet
   To lay so dangerous and dear a trust
   On any soul removed but on his own.
   Yet does he give us bold advertisement,
   That with our small conjunction we should on,
   To see how fortune is disposed to us;
   For, as he writes, there is no quailing now,
   Because the King is certainly possessed
   Of all our purposes. What say you to it?

Worcester. Your father's sickness is a maim to us.

Hotspur. A perilous gash, a very limb lopped off.
   And yet, in faith, it is not! His present want
   Seems more than we shall find it. Were it good
   To set the exact wealth of all our states
   All at one cast? to set so rich a man
   On the nice hazard of one doubtful hour?
   It were not good; for therein should we read
   The very bottom and the soul of hope,
   The very list, the very utmost bound
   Of all our fortunes.

Douglas. Faith, and so we should;
   Where now remains a sweet reversion.
   We may boldly spend upon the hope of what
   Is to come in.
   A comfort of retirement lives in this.

Hotspur. A rendezvous, a home to fly unto,
   If that the devil and mischance look big
   Upon the maidenhead of our affairs.

Worcester. But yet I would your father had been here.
   The quality and hair of our attempt
   Brooks no division. It will be thought
   By some that know not why he is away,
   That wisdom, loyalty, and mere dislike

Of our proceedings kept the Earl from hence.
And think how such an apprehension
May turn the tide of fearful faction
And breed a kind of question in our cause.
For well you know we of the off'ring side
Must keep aloof from strict arbitrement,
And stop all sight-holes, every loop from whence
The eye of reason may pry in upon us.
This absence of your father's draws a curtain
That shows the ignorant a kind of fear
Before not dreamt of.

Hotspur. You strain too far.
I rather of his absence make this use.
It lends a lustre and more great opinion,
A larger dare to our great enterprise,
Than if the Earl were here; for men must think,
If we, without his help, can make a head
To push against a kingdom, with his help
We shall overturn it topsy-turvy down.
Yet all goes well; yet all our joints are whole.

Douglas. As heart can think. There is not such a word
Spoke of in Scotland as this term of fear.

[Enter Sir Richard Vernon]

Hotspur. My cousin Vernon! welcome, by my soul.

Vernon. Pray God my news be worth a welcome, lord.
The Earl of Westmoreland, seven thousand strong,
Is marching herewards; with him Prince John.

Hotspur. No harm. What more?

Vernon. And further, I have learned
The King himself in person is set forth,
Or herewards intended speedily,
With strong and mighty preparation.

Hotspur. He shall be welcome too. Where is his son,
The nimble-footed madcap Prince of Wales,
And his comrades, that daffed the world aside
And bid it pass?

Vernon. All furnished, all in arms;
All plumed like estridges that with the wind
Bated like eagles having lately bathed;
Glittering in golden coats like images;

As full of spirit as the month of May
And gorgeous as the sun at midsummer;
Wanton as youthful goats, wild as young bulls.
I saw young Harry with his beaver on
His cushes on his thighs, gallantly armed,
Rise from the ground like feathered Mercury,
And vaulted with such ease into his seat
As if an angel dropped down from the clouds
To turn and wind a fiery Pegasus
And witch the world with noble horsemanship.

Hotspur. No more, no more! Worse than the sun in March,
This praise does nourish agues. Let them come.
They come like sacrifices in their trim,
And to the fire-eyed maid of smoky war
All hot and bleeding Will we offer them.
The mailed Mars Shall on his altar sit
Up to the ears in blood. I am on fire
To hear this rich reprisal is so nigh,
And yet not ours. Come, let me taste my horse,
Who is to bear me like a thunderbolt
Against the bosom of the Prince of Wales.
Harry to Harry shall, hot horse to horse,
Meet, and never part till one drop down a corpse.
that Glendower were come!

Vernon. There is more news.
I learned in Worcester, as I rode along,
He cannot draw his power this fourteen days.

Douglas. That's the worst tidings that I hear of yet.

Worcester. Ay, by my faith, that bears a frosty sound.

Hotspur. What may the King's whole battle reach unto?

Vernon. To thirty thousand.

Hotspur. Forty let it be.
My father and Glendower being both away,
The powers of us may serve so great a day.
Come, let us take a muster speedily.
Doomsday is near. Die all, die merrily.

Douglas. Talk not of dying. I am out of fear
Of death or death's hand for this one half-year.

[Exit All]

[*A public road near Coventry*]

[*Enter Falstaff and Bardolph*]

Falstaff. Bardolph, get you before to Coventry; fill me a bottle of sack. Our soldiers shall march through. We'll to Sutton Co'fil' tonight.

Bardolph. Will you give me money, Captain?

Falstaff. Lay out, lay out.

Bardolph. This bottle makes an angel.

Falstaff. And if it do, take it for your labor; if it make twenty, take them all; I'll answer the coinage. Bid my lieutenant Peto meet me at town's end.

Bardolph. I will, Captain. Farewell.

[*Exit Bardolph*]

Falstaff. If I be not ashamed of my soldiers, I am a soused gurnet. I have misused the King's press damnably. I have got in exchange of a hundred and fifty soldiers, three hundred and odd pounds. I press me none but good householders, yeomen's sons; inquire me out contracted bachelors, such as had been asked twice on the banes— such a commodity of warm slaves as had as lieve hear the devil as a drum; such as fear the report of a caliver worse than a struck fowl or a hurt wild duck. I pressed me none but such toasts-and-butter, with hearts in their bellies no bigger than pins' heads, and they have bought out their services; and now my whole charge consists of ancients, corporals, lieutenants, gentlemen of companies— slaves as ragged as Lazarus in the painted cloth, where the glutton's dogs licked his sores; and such as indeed were never soldiers, but discarded unjust serving-men, younger sons to Younger brothers, revolted tapsters, and ostlers trade-fallen; the cankers of a calm world and a long peace; ten times more dishonorable ragged than an old faced ancient; and such have I to fill up the rooms of them that have bought out their services that you would think that I had a hundred and fifty tattered Prodigals lately come from swine-keeping, from eating draff and husks. A mad fellow met me on the way, and told me I had unloaded all the gibbets and pressed the dead bodies. No eye has seen such scarecrows. I'll not march through Coventry with them, that's flat. Nay, and the villains march wide between the legs, as if they had gyves on; for indeed

I had the most of them out of prison. There's but a shirt and a half in all my company; and the half-shirt is two napkins tacked together and thrown over the shoulders like a herald's coat without sleeves; and the shirt, to say the truth, stolen from my host at Saint Alban's, or the red-nose innkeeper of Daventry. But that's all one; they'll find linen enough on every hedge.

[*Enter the Prince and the Lord of Westmoreland*]

Prince. How now, blown Jack? How now, quilt?

Falstaff. What, Hal? How now, mad wag? What a devil do you in Warwickshire? My good Lord of Westmoreland, I cry you mercy. I thought your honor had already been at Shrewsbury.

Westmoreland. Faith, Sir John, 'tis more than time that I were there, and you too; but my powers are there already. The King, I can tell you, looks for us all. We must away all, tonight.

Falstaff. Tut, never fear me. I am as vigilant as a cat to steal cream.

Prince. I think, to steal cream indeed, for your theft has already made you butter. But tell me, Jack, whose fellows are these that come after?

Falstaff. Mine, Hal, mine.

Prince. I did never see such pitiful rascals.

Falstaff. Tut, tut! good enough to toss; food for powder, food for powder. They'll fill a pit as well as better. Tush, man, mortal men, mortal men.

Westmoreland. Ay, but, Sir John, I think they are exceeding poor and bare— too beggarly.

Falstaff. Faith, for their poverty, I know, not where they had that; and for their bareness, I am surd they never learned that of me.

Prince. No, I'll be sworn, unless you call three fingers on the ribs bare. But, sirrah, make haste. Percy's already in the field.

[*Exit Prince Hal*]

Falstaff. What, is the King encamped?

Westmoreland. He is, Sir John. I fear we shall stay too long.

[*Exit*]

Falstaff. Well,
To the latter end of a fray and the beginning of a feast
Fits a dull fighter and a keen guest.

[*Exit All*]

[*The rebel camp near Shrewsbury*]

[*Enter Hotspur, Worcester, Douglas, Vernon*]

Hotspur. We'll fight with him tonight.

Worcester. It may not be.

Douglas. You give him then advantage.

Vernon. Not a whit.

Hotspur. Why say you so? Looks he no for supply?

Vernon. So do we.

Hotspur. His is certain, ours's doubtful.

Worcester. Good cousin, be advised; stir not tonight.

Vernon. Do not, my lord.

Douglas. You do not counsel well.
    You speak it out of fear and cold heart.

Vernon. Do me no slander, Douglas. By my life—
    And I dare well maintain it with my life—
    If well-respected honor bid me on
    I hold as little counsel with weak fear
    As you, my lord, or any Scot that this day lives.
    Let it be seen tomorrow in the battle
    Which of us fears.

Douglas. Yea, or tonight.

Vernon. Content.

Hotspur. To-night, say I.
    Come, come, it may not be. I wonder much,
    Being men of such great leading as you are,
    That you foresee not what impediments
    Drag back our expedition. Certain horse
    Of my cousin Vernon's are not yet come up.
    Your uncle Worcester's horse came but today;
    And now their pride and mettle is asleep,
    Their courage with hard labor tame and dull,
    That not a horse is half the half of himself.

Hotspur. So are the horses of the enemy,
    In general journey-bated and brought low.
    The better part of ours are full of rest.

Worcester. The number of the King exceeds ours.
For God's sake, cousin, stay till all come in.

[*The trumpet sounds a parley*]

[*Enter Sir Walter Blunt*]

Blunt. I come with gracious offers from the King,
If you vouchsafe me hearing and respect.

Hotspur. Welcome, Sir Walter Blunt, and would to God
You were of our determination!
Some of us love you well; and even those some
Envy your great deservings and good name,
Because you are not of our quality,
But stand against us like an enemy.

Blunt. And God defend but still I should stand so,
So long as out of limit and true rule
You stand against anointed majesty!
But to my charge. The King has sent to know
The nature of your griefs; and whereupon
You conjure from the breast of civil peace
Such bold hostility, teaching his duteous land
Audacious cruelty. If that the King
Have any way your good deserts forgot,
Which he confesses to be manifold,
He bids you name your griefs, and with all speed
You shall have your desires with interest,
And pardon absolute for yourself and these
Herein misled by your suggestion.

Hotspur. The King is kind; and well we know the King
Knows at what time to promise, when to pay.
My father and my uncle and myself
Did give him that same royalty he wears;
And when he was not six-and-twenty strong,
Sick in the world's regard, wretched and low,
A poor unminded outlaw sneaking home,
My father gave him welcome to the shore;
And when he heard him swear and vow to God
He came but to be Duke of Lancaster,
To sue his livery and beg his peace,
With tears of innocency and terms of zeal,
My father, in kind heart and pity moved,
Swore him assistance, and performed it too.

Now, when the lords and barons of the realm
Perceived Northumberland did lean to him,
The more and less came in with cap and knee;
Met him on boroughs, cities, villages,
Attended him on bridges, stood in lanes,
Laid gifts before him, proffered him their oaths,
Give him their heirs as pages, followed him
Even at the heels in golden multitudes.
He presently, as greatness knows itself,
Steps me a little higher than his vow
Made to my father, while his blood was poor,
Upon the naked shore at Ravenspurgh;
And now, forsooth, takes on him to reform
Some certain edicts and some strait decrees
That lie too heavy on the commonwealth;
Cries out upon abuses, seems to weep
Over his country's wrongs; and by this face,
This seeming brow of justice, did he win
The hearts of all that he did angle for;
Proceeded further— cut me off the heads
Of all the favorites that the absent King
In deputation left behind him here
When he was personal in the Irish war.

Blunt. Tut! I came not to hear this.

Hotspur. Then to the point.
In short time after lie deposed the King;
Soon after that deprived him of his life;
And in the neck of that tasked the whole state;
To make that worse, suff'red his kinsman March,
Who is, if every owner were well placid,
Indeed his King, to be engaged in Wales,
There without ransom to lie forfeited;
Disgraced me in my happy victories,
Sought to entrap me by intelligence;
Rated my uncle from the Council board;
In rage dismissed my father from the court;
Broke an oath on oath, committed wrong on wrong;
And in conclusion drove us to seek out
This head of safety, and withal to pry
Into his title, the which we find
Too indirect for long continuance.

Blunt. Shall I return this answer to the King?

Hotspur. Not so, Sir Walter. We'll withdraw awhile.
　　Go to the King; and let there be impawned
　　Some surety for a safe return again,
　　And In the morning early shall my uncle
　　Bring him our purposes; and so farewell.

Blunt. I would you would accept of grace and love.

Hotspur. And may be so we shall.

Blunt. Pray God you do.

[Exit All]

[*York. The Archbishop's Palace*]

[*Enter the Archbishop of York and Sir Michael*]

Archbishop. Hie, good Sir Michael; bear this sealed brief
  With winged haste to the Lord Marshal;
  This to my cousin Scroop; and all the rest
  To whom they are directed. If you knew
  How much they do import, you would make haste.
Sir Michael. My good lord,
  I guess their tenor.
Archbishop. Like enough you do.
  Tomorrow, good Sir Michael, is a day
  Wherein the fortune of ten thousand men
  Must bide the touch; for, sir, at Shrewsbury,
  As I am truly given to understand,
  The King with mighty and quick-raised power
  Meets with Lord Harry; and I fear, Sir Michael,
  What with the sickness of Northumberland,
  Whose power was in the first proportion,
  And what with Owen Glendower's absence thence,
  Who with them was a rated sinew too
  And comes not in, overruled by prophecies—
  I fear the power of Percy is too weak
  To wage an instant trial with the King.
Sir Michael. Why, my good lord, you need not fear;
  There is Douglas and Lord Mortimer.
Archbishop. No, Mortimer is not there.
Sir Michael. But there is Mordake, Vernon, Lord Harry Percy,
  And there is my Lord of Worcester, and a head
  Of gallant warriors, noble gentlemen.
Archbishop. And so there is; but yet the King has drawn
  The special head of all the land together—
  The Prince of Wales, Lord John of Lancaster,
  The noble Westmoreland and warlike Blunt,
  And many moe corrivals and dear men
  Of estimation and command in arms.
Sir Michael. Doubt not, my lord, they shall be well opposed.

Archbishop. I hope no less, yet needful 'tis to fear;
   And, to prevent the worst, Sir Michael, speed.
   For if Lord Percy thrive not, before the King
   Dismiss his power, he means to visit us,
   For he has heard of our confederacy,
   And 'tis but wisdom to make strong against him.
   Therefore make haste. I must go write again
   To other friends; and so farewell, Sir Michael.

                    [*Exit All*]

Act Five

1

[The King's camp near Shrewsbury]

*[Enter the King, Prince of Wales, Lord John of
Lancaster, Sir Walter Blunt, Falstaff]*

King. How bloodily the sun begins to peer
    Above yon busky hill! The day looks pale
    At his distemperature.

Prince. The southern wind
    Does play the trumpet to his purposes
    And by his hollow whistling in the leaves
    Foretells a tempest and a blustering day.

King. Theft with the losers let it sympathize,
    For nothing can seem foul to those that win.

      The trumpet sounds. Enter Worcester [and Vernon].

    How, now, my Lord of Worcester? 'tis not well
    That you and I should meet upon such terms
    As now we meet. You have deceived our trust
    And made us doff our easy robes of peace
    To crush our old limbs in ungentle steel.
    This is not well, my lord; this is not well.
    What say you to it? Will you again unknit
    This churlish knot of all-abhorred war,
    And move in that obedient orb again
    Where you did give a fair and natural light,
    And be no more an exhaled meteor,
    A prodigy of fear, and a portent
    Of broached mischief to the unborn times?

Worcester. Hear me, my liege.
    For my own part, I could be well content
    To entertain the lag-end of my life
    With quiet hours; for I do protest

I have not sought the day of this dislike.

King. You have not sought it! How comes it then,

Falstaff. Rebellion lay in his way, and he found it.

Prince. Peace, chewet, peace!

Worcester. It pleased your Majesty to turn your looks
    Of favor from myself and all our house;
    And yet I must remember you, my lord,
    We were the first and dearest of your friends.
    For you my staff of office did I break
    In Richard's time, and posted day and night
    To meet you on the way and kiss your hand
    When yet you were in place and in account
    Nothing so strong and fortunate as I.
    It was myself, my brother, and his son
    That brought you home and boldly did outdare
    The dangers of the time. You swore to us,
    And you did swear that oath at Doncaster,
    That you did nothing purpose against the state,
    Nor claim no further than your new-fallen right,
    The seat of Gaunt, dukedom of Lancaster.
    To this we swore our aid. But in short space
    It it rained down fortune showering on your head,
    And such a flood of greatness fell on you—
    What with our help, what with the absent King,
    What with the injuries of a wanton time,
    The seeming sufferances that you had borne,
    And the contrarious winds that held the King
    So long in his unlucky Irish wars
    That all in England did repute him dead—
    And from this swarm of fair advantages
    You took occasion to be quickly wooed
    To gripe the general sway into your hand;
    Forgot your oath to us at Doncaster;
    And, being fed by us, you used us so
    As that ungentle gull, the cuckoo's bird,
    Uses the sparrow— did oppress our nest;
    Grew, by our feeding to so great a bulk
    That even our love thirst not come near your sight
    For fear of swallowing; but with nimble wing
    We were enforced for safety sake to fly
    Out of your sight and raise this present head;
    Whereby we stand opposed by such means

As you yourself have forged against yourself
By unkind usage, dangerous countenance,
And violation of all faith and troth
Sworn to tis in your younger enterprise.

King. These things, indeed, you have articulate,
Proclaimed at market crosses, read in churches,
To face the garment of rebellion
With some fine color that may please the eye
Of fickle changelings and poor discontents,
Which gape and rub the elbow at the news
Of hurlyburly innovation.
And never yet did insurrection want
Such water colors to impaint his cause,
Nor moody beggars, starving for a time
Of pell-mell havoc and confusion.

Prince. In both our armies there is many a soul
Shall pay full dearly for this encounter,
If once they join in trial. Tell your nephew
The Prince of Wales does join with all the world
In praise of Henry Percy. By my hopes,
This present enterprise set off his head,
I do not think a braver gentleman,
More active-valiant or more valiant-young,
More daring or more bold, is now alive
To grace this latter age with noble deeds.
For my part, I may speak it to my shame,
I have a truant been to chivalry;
And so I hear he does account me too.
Yet this before my father's Majesty—
I am content that he shall take the odds
Of his great name and estimation,
And will to save the blood on either side,
Try fortune with him in a single fight.

King. And, Prince of Wales, so dare we venture you,
Albeit considerations infinite
Do make against it. No, good Worcester, no!
We love our people well; even those we love
That are misled upon your cousin's part;
And, will they take the offer of our grace,
Both he, and they, and you, yea, every man
Shall be my friend again, and I'll be his.
So tell your cousin, and bring me word

What he will do. But if he will not yield,
Rebuke and dread correction wait on us,
And they shall do their office. So be gone.
We will not now be troubled with reply.
We offer fair; take it advisedly.

[*Exit Worcester and Vernon*]

Prince. It will not be accepted, on my life.
The Douglas and the Hotspur both together
Are confident against the world in arms.

King. Hence, therefore, every leader to his charge;
For, on their answer, will we set on them,
And God befriend us as our cause is just!

[*Exit All except Prince Hal and Falstaff*]

Falstaff. Hal, if you see me down in the battle and bestride me, so!
'tis a point of friendship.

Prince. Nothing but a Colossus can do you that friendship. Say your
prayers, and farewell.

Falstaff. I would 'twere bedtime, Hal, and all well.

Prince. Why, you owe God a death.

[*Exit Prince Hal*]

Falstaff. 'Tis not due yet. I would be loath to pay him before his
day. What need I be so forward with him that calls not on me?
Well, 'tis no matter; honor pricks me on. Yea, but how if honor
prick me off when I come on? How then? Can honor set to a
leg? No. Or an arm? No. Or take away the grief of a wound?
No. Honour has no skill in surgery then? No. What is honor?
A word. What is that word honor? Air. A trim reckoning! Who
has it? He that died a Wednesday. Does he feel it? No. Does be
bear it? No. 'Tis insensible then? Yea, to the dead. But will it
not live with the living? No. Why? Detraction will not suffer it.
Therefore I'll none of it. Honour is a mere scutcheon— and so
ends my catechism.

[*Exit Falstaff*]

[*The rebel camp*]

[*Enter Worcester and Sir Richard Vernon*]

Worcester. O no, my nephew must not know, Sir Richard,
  The liberal and kind offer of the King.

Vernon. 'Twere best he did.

Worcester. Then are we all undone.
  It is not possible, it cannot be
  The King should keep his word in loving us.
  He will suspect us still and find a time
  To punish this offense in other faults.
  Suspicion all our lives shall be stuck full of eyes;
  For treason is but trusted like the fox
  Who, never so tame, so cherished and locked up,
  Will have a wild trick of his ancestors.
  Look how we can, or sad or merrily,
  Interpretation will misquote our looks,
  And we shall feed like oxen at a stall,
  The better cherished, still the nearer death.
  My nephew's trespass may be well forgot;
  It has the excuse of youth and heat of blood,
  And an adopted name of privilege—
  A hare-brained Hotspur governed by a spleen.
  All his offenses live upon my head
  And on his father's. We did train him on;
  And, his corruption being taken from us,
  We, as the spring of all, shall pay for all.
  Therefore, good cousin, let not Harry know,
  In any case, the offer of the King.

[*Enter Hotspur and Douglas*]

Vernon. Deliver what you will, I'll say 'tis so.
  Here comes your cousin.

Hotspur. My uncle is returned.
  Deliver up my Lord of Westmoreland. Uncle, what news?

Worcester. The King will bid you battle presently.

Douglas. Defy him by the Lord Of Westmoreland.

Hotspur. Lord Douglas, go you and tell him so.

Douglas. Well, and shall, and very willingly.

[Exit Douglas]

Worcester. There is no seeming mercy in the King.

Hotspur. Did you beg any, God forbid!

Worcester. I told him gently of our grievances,
Of his oath-breaking; which he mended thus,
By now forswearing that he is forsworn.
He calls us rebels, traitors, aid will scourge
With haughty arms this hateful name in us.

[Re-enter Douglas]

Douglas. Arm, gentlemen! to arms! for I have thrown
A brave defiance in King Henry's teeth,
And Westmoreland, that was engaged, did bear it;
Which cannot choose but bring him quickly on.

Worcester. The Prince of Wales stepped forth before the King
And, nephew, challenged you to single fight.

Hotspur. O, would the quarrel lay upon our heads,
And that no man might draw short breath today
But I and Harry Monmouth! Tell me, tell me,
How showed his tasking? Seemed it in contempt?

Vernon. No, by my soul. I never in my life
Did hear a challenge urged more modestly,
Unless a brother should a brother dare
To gentle exercise and proof of arms.
He gave you all the duties of a man;
Trimmed up your praises with a princely tongue;
Spoke your deservings like a chronicle;
Making you ever better than his praise
By still dispraising praise valued with you;
And, which became him like a Prince indeed,
He made a blushing cital of himself,
And chid his truant youth with such a grace
As if lie mastered there a double spirit
Of teaching and of learning instantly.
There did he pause; but let me tell the world,
If he outlive the envy of this day,
England did never owe so sweet a hope,
So much misconstrued in his wantonness.

Hotspur. Cousin, I think you are enamoured

Upon his follies. Never did I hear
Of any Prince so wild a libertine.
But be he as he will, yet once before night
I will embrace him with a soldier's arm,
That he shall shrink under my courtesy.
Arm, arm with speed! and, fellows, soldiers, friends,
Better consider what you have to do
Than I, that have not well the gift of tongue,
Can lift your blood up with persuasion.

[*Enter a Messenger*]

Messenger. My lord, here are letters for you.

Hotspur. I cannot read them now.—
O gentlemen, the time of life is short!
To spend that shortness basely were too long
If life did ride upon a dial's point,
Still ending at the arrival of an hour.
If we live, we live to tread on kings;
If die, brave death, when princes die with us!
Now for our consciences, the arms are fair,
When the intent of bearing them is just.

[*Enter another Messenger*]

Messenger. My lord, prepare. The King comes on apace.

Hotspur. I thank him that he cuts me from my tale,
For I profess not talking. Only this—
Let each man do his best; and here draw I
A sword whose temper I intend to stain
With the best blood that I can meet withal
In the adventure of this perilous day.
Now, Esperance! Percy! and set on.
Sound all the lofty instruments of war,
And by that music let us all embrace;
For, heaven to earth, some of us never shall
A second time do such a courtesy.

[*The rebels embrace*]

[*The trumpets sound*]

[*Exit All*]

[*Plain between the camps*]

[*Alarum to the battle*]

[*The King enters with his retinue. Shortly after enter
Douglas and Sir Walter Blunt*]

Blunt. What is your name, that in the battle thus
You cross me? What honor do you seek
Upon my head?

Douglas. Know then my name is Douglas,
And I do haunt you in the battle thus
Because some tell me that you are a King.

Blunt. They tell you true.

Douglas. The Lord of Stafford dear today has bought
Your likeness; for instead of you, King Harry,
This sword has ended him. So shall it you,
Unless you yield you as my prisoner.

Blunt. I was not born a yielder, you proud Scot;
And you shall find a King that will revenge
Lord Stafford's death.

They fight. Douglas kills Blunt. Then enter Hotspur.

Hotspur. O Douglas, had you fought at Holmedon thus,
I never had triumphed upon a Scot.

Douglas. All's done, all's won. Here breathless lies the King.

Hotspur. Where?

Douglas. Here.

Hotspur. This, Douglas? No. I know this face full well.
A gallant knight he was, his name was Blunt;
Semblably furnished like the King himself.

Douglas. A fool go with your soul, where it goes!
A borrowed title have you bought too dear.
Why did you tell me that you were a King?

Hotspur. The King has many marching in his coats.

Douglas. Now, by my sword, I will kill all his coats;
I'll murder all his wardrop, piece by piece,
Until I meet the King.

Hotspur. Up and away!
Our soldiers stand full fairly for the day.

[*Exit All*]

[*Alarum*]

[*Enter Falstaff alone*]

Falstaff. Though I could escape shot-free at London, I fear the shot
here. Here's no scoring but upon the pate. Soft! who are you?
Sir Walter Blunt. There's honor for you! Here's no vanity! I am
as hot as molten lead, and as heavy too. God keep lead out of
me! I need no more weight than my own bowels. I have led my
rag-of-muffins where they are peppered. There's not three of my
hundred and fifty left alive; and they are for the town's end, to
beg during life. But who comes here?

[*Enter the Prince*]

Prince. What, stand you idle here? Lend me your sword.
Many a nobleman lies stark and stiff
Under the hoofs of vaunting enemies,
Whose deaths are yet unrevenged. I beg you
Rend me your sword.

Falstaff. O Hal, I beg you give me leave to breathe awhile. Turk
Gregory never did such deeds in arms as I have done this day. I
have paid Percy; I have made him sure.

Prince. He is indeed, and living to kill you.
I ask you lend me your sword.

Falstaff. Nay, before God, Hal, if Percy be alive, you get not my
sword; but take my pistol, if you wilt.

Prince. Give it me. What, is it in the case?

Falstaff. Ay, Hal. 'Tis hot, 'tis hot. There's that will sack a city.

[*The Prince draws out a bottle of sack*]

Prince. What, is it a time to jest and dally now?

[*Hal throws the bottle at Falstaff*]

[*Exit*]

Falstaff. Well, if Percy be alive, I'll pierce him. If he do come in my
way, so; if he do not, if I come in his willingly, let him make a
carbonado of me. I like not such grinning honor as Sir Walter

has. Give me life; which if I can save, so; if not, honor comes unlooked for, and there's an end.

[*Exit Falstaff*]

[Another part of the field]

[Alarum. Excursions]

[Enter the King, the Prince, Lord John of Lancaster, Earl of Westmoreland]

King. I beg you,
   Harry, withdraw yourself; you bleed too much.
   Lord John of Lancaster, go you unto him.

Lord John. Not I, my lord, unless I did bleed too.

Prince. I do beseech your Majesty make up,
   Lest Your retirement do amaze your friends.

King. I will do so.
   My Lord of Westmoreland, lead him to his tent.

Westmoreland. Come, my lord, I'll lead you to your tent.

Prince. Lead me, my lord, I do not need your help;
   And God forbid a shallow scratch should drive
   The Prince of Wales from such a field as this,
   Where stained nobility lies trodden on,
   And rebels' arms triumph in massacres!

Lord John. We breathe too long. Come, cousin Westmoreland,
   Our duty this way lies. For God's sake, come.

[Exit All Prince John and Westmoreland]

Prince. By God, you have deceived me, Lancaster!
   I did not think you lord of such a spirit.
   Before, I loved you as a brother, John;
   But now, I do respect you as my soul.

King. I saw him hold Lord Percy at the point
   With lustier maintenance than I did look for
   Of such an ungrown warrior.

Prince. O, this boy
   Lends mettle to us all!

[Exit All]

[Enter Douglas]

Douglas. Another King? They grow like Hydra's heads.

I am the Douglas, fatal to all those
That wear those colors on them. What are thou
That counterfeit the person of a King?

King. The King himself, who, Douglas, grieves at heart
So many of his shadows you have met,
And not the very King. I have two boys
Seek Percy and yourself about the field;
But, seeing you fall on me so luckily,
I will assay you. So defend yourself.

Douglas. I fear you are another counterfeit;
And yet, in faith, you bear you like a King.
But mine I am sure you art, whoever you be,
And thus I win you.

[*They fight, the King is being overpowered*]

[*Enter Prince of Wales*]

Prince. Hold up your head, vile Scot, or you are like
Never to hold it up again! The spirits
Of valiant Shirley, Stafford, Blunt are in my arms.
It is the Prince of Wales that threatens you,
Who never promises but he means to pay.

[*They fight*]

[*Douglas flees*]

Cheerly, my lord. How fares your Grace?
Sir Nicholas Gawsey has for succour sent,
And so has Clifton. I'll to Clifton straight.

King. Stay and breathe awhile.
You have redeemed your lost opinion,
And showed you make some tender of my life,
In this fair rescue you have brought to me.

Prince. O God! they did me too much injury
That ever said I hearkened for your death.
If it were so, I might have let alone
The insulting hand of Douglas over you,
Which would have been as speedy in your end
As all the poisonous potions in the world,
And saved the treacherous labor of your son.

King. Make up to Clifton; I'll to Sir Nicholas Gawsey.

[*Exit King*]

Enter Hotspur.

Hotspur. If I mistake not, you are Harry Monmouth.

Prince. You speak as if I would deny my name.

Hotspur. My name is Harry Percy.

Prince. Why, then I see
    A very valiant rebel of the name.
    I am the Prince of Wales; and think not, Percy,
    To share with me in glory any more.
    Two stars keep not their motion in one sphere,
    Nor can one England brook a double reign
    Of Harry Percy and the Prince of Wales.

Hotspur. Nor shall it, Harry; for the hour is come
    To end the one of us and would to God
    Your name in arms were now as great as mine!

Prince. I'll make it greater before I part from you,
    And all the budding honors on your crest
    I'll crop to make a garland for my head.

Hotspur. I can no longer brook your vanities.

[They fight]

[Enter Falstaff]

Falstaff. Well said, Hal! to it, Hal! Nay, you shall find no boy's play
    here, I can tell you.

[Enter Douglas]

[Douglas fights with Falstaff, who falls to the ground]

[Exit Douglas]

[The Prince kills Percy]

Hotspur. O Harry, you have robbed me of my youth!
    I better brook the loss of brittle life
    Than those proud titles you have won of me.
    They wound my thoughts worse than your sword my flesh.
    But thoughts the slave, of life, and life time's fool,
    And time, that takes survey of all the world,
    Must have a stop. O, I could prophesy,
    But that the earthy and cold hand of death
    Lies on my tongue. No, Percy, you are dust,
    And food for—

[*Dies*]

Prince. For worms, brave Percy. Fare you well, great heart!
Ill-weaved ambition, how much are you shrunk!
When that this body did contain a spirit,
A kingdom for it was too small a bound;
But now two paces of the vilest earth
Is room enough. This earth that bears you dead
Bears not alive so stout a gentleman.
If you were sensible of courtesy,
I should not make so dear a show of zeal.
But let my favors hide your mangled face;
And, even in your behalf, I'll thank myself
For doing these fair rites of tenderness.
Adieu, and take your praise with you to heaven!
Your ignominy sleep with you in the grave,
But not remembered in your epitaph!

[*Hal spots Falstaff on the ground*]

What, old acquaintance? Could not all this flesh
Keep in a little life? Poor Jack, farewell!
I could have better spared a better man.
O, I should have a heavy miss of you
If I were much in love with vanity!
Death has not struck so fat a deer today,
Though many dearer, in this bloody fray.
Embowelled will I see you by-and-by;
Till then in blood by noble Percy lie.

[*Exit Prince*]

[*Falstaff rises up*]

Falstaff. Embowelled? If you embowel me today, I'll give you leave
to powder me and eat me too tomorrow. 'Sblood, 'twas time
to counterfeit, or that hot termagant Scot had paid me scot
and lot too. Counterfeit? I lie; I am no counterfeit. To die is
to be a counterfeit; for he is but the counterfeit of a man who
has not the life of a man; but to counterfeit dying when a man
thereby liveth, is to be no counterfeit, but the true and perfect
image of life indeed. The better part of valor is discretion; in
the which better part I have saved my life. Zounds, I am afraid
of this gunpowder Percy, though he be dead. How if he should
counterfeit too, and rise? By my faith, I am afraid he would
prove the better counterfeit. Therefore I'll make him sure; yea,

and I'll swear I killed him. Why may not he rise as well as I? Nothing confutes me but eyes, and nobody sees me. Therefore, sirrah [stabs him], with a new wound in your thigh, come you along with me.

[*He hoists Hotspur onto his back*]

[*Enter Prince and John of Lancaster*]

Prince. Come, brother John; full bravely have you fleshed
Your maiden sword.

Lord John. But, soft! whom have we here?
Did you not tell me this fat man was dead?

Prince. I did; I saw him dead,
Breathless and bleeding on the ground. Are you alive,
Or is it fantasy that plays upon our eyesight?
I tell you speak. We will not trust our eyes
Without our ears. You are not what you seem.

Falstaff. No, that's certain! I am not a double man; but if I be not Jack Falstaff, then am I a Jack. There's Percy. If your father will do me any honor, so; if not, let him kill the next Percy himself. I look to be either earl or duke, I can assure you.

Prince. Why, Percy I killed myself, and saw you dead!

Falstaff. Did you? Lord, Lord, how this world is given to lying! I grant you I was down, and out of breath, and so was he; but we rose both at an instant and fought a long hour by Shrewsbury clock. If I may be believed, so; if not, let them that should reward valor bear the sin upon their own heads. I'll take it upon my death, I gave him this wound in the thigh. If the man were alive and would deny it, zounds! I would make him eat a piece of my sword.

Lord John. This is the strangest tale that ever I heard.

Prince. This is the strangest fellow, brother John.
Come, bring your luggage nobly on your back.
For my part, if a lie may do you grace,
I'll gild it with the happiest terms I have.

[*A retreat is sounded*]

The trumpet sounds retreat; the day is ours.
Come, brother, let's to the highest of the field,
To see what friends are living, who are dead.

[*Exit Prince Henry and Prince John*]

Falstaff. I'll follow, as they say, for reward. He that rewards me,
God reward him! If I do grow great, I'll grow less; for I'll purge,
and leave sack, and live cleanly, as a nobleman should do.

[*Exit Falstaff, carrying off the body of Hotspur*]

[*Another part of the field*]

[*The trumpets sound*]

[*Enter the King, Prince of Wales, Lord John of Lancaster, Earl of Westmoreland, guards leading Worcester and Vernon as prisoners*]

King. Thus ever did rebellion find rebuke.
    Ill-spirited Worcester! did not we send grace,
    Pardon, and terms of love to all of you?
    And would you turn our offers contrary?
    Misuse the tenor of your kinsman's trust?
    Three knights upon our party slain today,
    A noble earl, and many a creature else
    Had been alive this hour,
    If like a Christian you had truly borne
    Between our armies true intelligence.

Worcester. What I have done my safety urged me to;
    And I embrace this fortune patiently,
    Since not to be avoided it fails on me.

King. Bear Worcester to the death, and Vernon too;
    Other offenders we will pause upon.

            [*Exit All Worcester and Vernon, guarded*]

    How goes the field?

Prince. The noble Scot, Lord Douglas, when he saw
    The fortune of the day quite turned from him,
    The Noble Percy slain and all his men
    Upon the foot of fear, fled with the rest;
    And falling from a hill, he was so bruised
    That the pursuers took him. At my tent
    The Douglas is, and I beseech Your Grace
    I may dispose of him.

King. With all my heart.

Prince. Then brother John of Lancaster, to you
    This honorable bounty shall belong.
    Go to the Douglas and deliver him
    Up to his pleasure, ransomless and free.
    His valor shown upon our crests today

Has taught us how to cherish such high deeds,
Even in the bosom of our adversaries.

Lord John. I thank your Grace for this high courtesy,
Which I shall give away immediately.

King. Then this remains, that we divide our power.
You, son John, and my cousin Westmoreland,
Towards York shall bend you with your dearest speed
To meet Northumberland and the prelate Scroop,
Who, as we hear, are busily in arms.
Myself and you, son Harry, will towards Wales
To fight with Glendower and the Earl of March.
Rebellion in this laud shall lose his sway,
Meeting the check of such another day;
And since this business so fair is done,
Let us not leave till all our own be won.

[*Exit All*]

THE END

Henry IV, Part One

Henry IV, Part Two

The Merry Wives of Windsor

Henry V

Induction

[*Warkworth. Before the castle*]

[*Enter Rumor*]

Rumor. Open your ears; for which of you will stop
   The vent of hearing when loud Rumor speaks?
   I, from the orient to the drooping west,
   Making the wind my post-horse, still unfold
   The acts commenced on this ball of earth.
   Upon my tongues continual slanders ride,
   The which in every language I pronounce,
   Stuffing the ears of men with false reports.
   I speak of peace, while covert emnity
   Under the smile of safety wounds the world.
   And who but Rumor, who but only I,
   Make fearful musters and prepared defense,
   While the big year, swollen with some other grief,
   Is thought with child by the stern tyrant war,
   And no such matter? Rumor is a pipe
   Blown by surmises, jealousies, conjectures,
   And of so easy and so plain a stop
   That the blunt monster with uncounted heads,
   The still-discordant wavering multitude,
   Can play upon it. But what need I thus
   My well-known body to anatomize
   Among my household? Why is Rumor here?
   I run before King Harry's victory;
   Who in a bloody field by Shrewsbury
   Has beaten down young Hotspur and his troops,
   Quenching the flame of bold rebellion
   Even with the rebels' blood. But what mean I
   To speak so true at first? my office is

To noise abroad that Harry Monmouth fell
Under the wrath of noble Hotspur's sword,
And that the King before the Douglas' rage
Stooped his anointed head as low as death.
This have I rumored through the peasant towns
Between that royal field of Shrewsbury
And this worm-eaten hold of ragged stone,
Where Hotspur's father, old Northumberland,
Lies crafty-sick. the posts come tiring on,
And not a man of them brings other news
Than they have learned of me. from Rumor's tongues
They bring smooth comforts false, worse than true wrongs.

[Exit Rumor]

Act One

1

[*Warkworth. Before the castle*]

[*Enter Lord Bardolph*]

Lord Bardolph. Who keeps the gate here, ho?

[*The Porter opens the gate*]

Where is the earl?

Porter. What shall I say you are?

Lord Bardolph. Tell you the Earl
That the Lord Bardolph does attend him here.

Porter. His lordship is walked forth into the orchard.
Please it your honor, knock but at the gate,
And he himself will answer.

[*Enter Northumberland*]

Lord Bardolph. Here comes the Earl.

[*Exit Porter*]

Northumberland. What news, Lord Bardolph? Every minute now
Should be the father of some stratagem.
The times are wild; contention, like a horse
Full of high feeding, madly has broke loose
And bears down all before him.

Lord Bardolph. Noble earl,
I bring you certain news from Shrewsbury.

Northumberland. Good, if God will!

Lord Bardolph. As good as heart can wish.
The King is almost wounded to the death;
And, in the fortune of my lord your son,
Prince Harry slain outright; and both the Blunts
Killed by the hand of Douglas; young Prince John,

And Westmoreland and Stafford fled the field.
And Harry Monmouth's brawn, the hulk Sir John,
Is prisoner to your son. O, such a day,
So fought, so followed and so fairly won,
Came not till now to dignify the times,
Since Caesar's fortunes!

Northumberland. How is this derived?
Saw you the field? Came you from Shrewsbury?

Lord Bardolph. I spake with one, my lord, that came from thence,
A gentleman well-bred and of good name,
That freely rendered me these news for true.

Northumberland. Here comes my servant Travers, whom I sent
On Tuesday last to listen after news.

[*Enter Travers*]

Lord Bardolph. My lord, I over-rode him on the way;
And he is furnished with no certainties
More than he haply may retail from me.

Northumberland. Now, Travers, what good tidings comes with you?

Travers. My lord, Sir John Umfrevile turned me back
With joyful tidings; and, being better horsed,
Out-rode me. After him came spurring hard
A gentleman, almost forspent with speed,
That stopped by me to breathe his bloodied horse.
He asked the way to Chester; and of him
I did demand what news from Shrewsbury.
He told me that rebellion had bad luck
And that young Harry Percy's spur was cold.
With that, he gave his able horse the head,
And bending forward struck his armed heels
Against the panting sides of his poor jade
Up to the rowel-head, and starting so
He seemed in running to devour the way,
Staying no longer question.

Northumberland. Ha! Again.
Said he young Harry Percy's spur was cold?
Of Hotspur Coldspur? that rebellion
Had met ill luck?

Lord Bardolph. My lord, I'll tell you what;
If my young lord your son have not the day,
Upon my honor, for a silken point

I'll give my barony. never talk of it.

Northumberland. Why should that gentleman that rode by Travers
Give then such instances of loss?

Lord Bardolph. Who, he?
He was some hilding fellow that had stolen
The horse he rode on, and, upon my life,
Spoke at a venture. Look, here comes more news.

[*Enter Morton*]

Northumberland. Yea, this man's brow, like to a title-leaf,
Foretells the nature of a tragic volume.
So looks the strand whereon the imperious flood
Has left a witnessed usurpation.
Say, Morton, did you come from Shrewsbury?

Morton. I ran from Shrewsbury, my noble lord;
Where hateful death put on his ugliest mask
To fright our party.

Northumberland. How does my son and brother?
You tremble; and the whiteness in your cheek
Is apter than your tongue to tell your errand.
Even such a man, so faint, so spiritless,
So dull, so dread in look, so woe-begone,
Drew Priam's curtain in the dead of night,
And would have told him half his Troy was burnt;
But Priam found the fire before he his tongue,
And I my Percy's death before you report it.
This you would say. "Your son did thus and thus;
Your brother thus. So fought the noble Douglas"—
Stopping my greedy ear with their bold deeds.
But in the end, to stop my ear indeed,
You have a sigh to blow away this praise,
Ending with "Brother, son, and all are dead."

Morton. Douglas is living, and your brother, yet.
But, for my lord your son—

Northumberland. Why, he is dead.
See what a ready tongue suspicion has!
He that but fears the thing he would not know
Has by instinct knowledge from others' eyes
That what he feared is chanced. Yet speak, Morton;
Tell you an Earl his divination lies,
And I will take it as a sweet disgrace

And make you rich for doing me such wrong.

Morton. You are too great to be by me gainsaid.
Your spirit is too true, your fears too certain.

Northumberland. Yet, for all this, say not that Percy's dead.
—I see a strange confession in your eye;
You shake your head and hold it fear or sin
To speak a truth. If he be slain, say so;
The tongue offends not that reports his death.
And he does sin that does belie the dead,
Not he which says the dead is not alive
Yet the first bringer of unwelcome news
Has but a losing office, and his tongue
Sounds ever after as a sullen bell,
Remembered tolling a departing friend.

Lord Bardolph. I cannot think, my lord, your son is dead.

Morton. I am sorry I should force you to believe
That which I would to God I had not seen;
But these my eyes saw him in bloody state,
Rendering faint quittance, wearied and outbreathed,
To Harry Monmouth; whose swift wrath beat down
The never-daunted Percy to the earth,
From whence with life he never more sprung up.
In few, his death, whose spirit lent a fire
Even to the dullest peasant in his camp,
Being bruited once, took fire and heat away
From the best-tempered courage in his troops;
For from his mettle was his party steeled;
Which once in him abated, all the rest
Turned on themselves, like dull and heavy lead.
And as the thing that's heavy in itself,
Upon enforcement flies with greatest speed,
So did our men, heavy in Hotspur's loss,
Lend to this weight such lightness with their fear
That arrows fled not swifter toward their aim
Than did our soldiers, aiming at their safety,
Fly from the field. Then was that noble Worcester
Too soon taken prisoner; and that furious Scot,
The bloody Douglas, whose well-laboring sword
Had three times slain the appearance of the King,
Began vail his stomach and did grace the shame
Of those that turned their backs, and in his flight,
Stumbling in fear, was took. The sum of all

Is that the King has won, and has sent out
A speedy power to encounter you, my lord,
Under the conduct of young Lancaster
And Westmoreland. This is the news at full.

Northumberland. For this I shall have time enough to mourn.
In poison there is physic; and these news,
Having been well, that would have made me sick,
Being sick, have in some measure made me well.
And as the wretch, whose fever-weakened joints,
Like strengthless hinges, buckle under life,
Impatient of his fit, breaks like a fire
Out of his keeper's arms, even so my limbs,
Weakened with grief, being now enraged with grief,
Are thrice themselves. Hence, therefore, you nice crutch!
A scaly gauntlet now with joints of steel
Must glove this hand. And hence, you sickly quoif!
You are a guard too wanton for the head
Which princes, fleshed with conquest, aim to hit.
Now bind my brows with iron; and approach
The raggedest hour that time and spite dare bring
To frown upon the enraged Northumberland!
Let heaven kiss earth! now let not Nature's hand
Keep the wild flood confined! let order die!
And let this world no longer be a stage
To feed contention in a lingering act;
But let one spirit of the first-born Cain
Reign in all bosoms, that, each heart being set
On bloody courses, the rude scene may end,
And darkness be the burier of the dead!

Travers. This strained passion does you wrong, my lord.

Lord Bardolph. Sweet Earl, divorce not wisdom from your honor.

Morton. The lives of all your loving complices
Lean on your health; the which, if you give over
To stormy passion, must perforce decay.
You cast the event of war, my noble lord,
And summed the account of chance, before you said
"Let us make head." It was your presurmise,
That, in the dole of blows, your son might drop.
You knew he walked over perils, on an edge,
More likely to fall in than to get over;
You were advised his flesh was capable
Of wounds and scars and that his forward spirit
Would lift him where most trade of danger ranged.

Yet did you say "Go forth"—and none of this,
Though strongly apprehended, could restrain
The stiff-borne action. What has then befallen,
Or what has this bold enterprise brought forth,
More than that being which was like to be?

Lord Bardolph. We all that are engaged to this loss
Knew that we ventured on such dangerous seas
That if we wrought out life 'twas ten to one;
And yet we ventured, for the gain proposed
Choked the respect of likely peril feared;
And since we are overset, venture again.
Come, we will put forth, body and goods.

Morton. 'Tis more than time. and, my most noble lord,
I hear for certain, and dare speak the truth.
The gentle Archbishop of York is up
With well-appointed powers. He is a man
Who with a double surety binds his followers.
My lord, your son had only but the corpse,
But shadows and the shows of men, to fight;
For that same word, rebellion, did divide
The action of their bodies from their souls;
And they did fight with queasiness, constrained,
As men drink potions, that their weapons only
Seemed on our side; but, for their spirits and souls,
This word, rebellion, it had froze them up,
As fish are in a pond. But now the Bishop
Turns insurrection to religion.
Supposed sincere and holy in his thoughts,
He's followed both with body and with mind;
And does enlarge his rising with the blood
Of fair King Richard, scraped from Pomfret stones;
Derives from heaven his quarrel and his cause;
Tells them he does bestride a bleeding land,
Gasping for life under great Bolingbroke;
And more and less do flock to follow him.

Northumberland. I knew of this before; but, to speak truth,
This present grief had wiped it from my mind.
Go in with me; and counsel every man
The aptest way for safety and revenge.
Get posts and letters, and make friends with speed.
Never so few, and never yet more need.

[*Exit All*]

[London. A street]

[Enter Falstaff and his Page]

Falstaff. Sirrah, you giant, what says the doctor to my water?

Page. He said, sir, the water itself was a good healthy water; but, for the party that owed it, he might have more diseases than he knew for.

Falstaff. Men of all sorts take a pride to gird at me. The brain of this foolish-compounded clay, man, is not able to invent anything that tends to laughter, more than I invent or is invented on me. I am not only witty in myself, but the cause that wit is in other men. I do here walk before you like a sow that has overwhelmed all her litter but one. If the Prince put you into my service for any other reason than to set me off, why then I have no judgment. You whoreson mandrake, you are fitter to be worn in my cap than to wait at my heels. I was never manned with an agate till now. but I will inset you neither in gold nor silver, but in vile apparel, and send you back again to your master, for a jewel—the juvenile, the Prince your master, whose chin is not yet fledged. I will sooner have a beard grow in the palm of my hand than he shall get one on his cheek; and yet he will not stick to say his face is a face-royal. God may finish it when he will, 'tis not a hair amiss yet. He may keep it still at a face-royal, for a barber shall never earn sixpence out of it; and yet he'll be crowing as if he had writ man ever since his father was a bachelor. He may keep his own grace, but he's almost out of mine, I can assure him. What said Master Dombledon about the satin for my short cloak and my slops?

Page. He said, sir, you should procure him better assurance than Bardolph. He would not take his band and yours; he liked not the security.

Falstaff. Let him be damned, like the glutton! Pray God his tongue be hotter! A whoreson Achitophel! a rascally yea-forsooth knave! To bear a gentleman in hand, and then stand upon security! The whoreson smooth-pates do now wear nothing but high shoes, and bunches of keys at their girdles; and if a man is through with them in honest taking up, then they must stand upon security. I had as lief they would put ratsbane in my mouth as offer to stop it with security. I looked 'a should have sent me two and twenty yards of satin, as I am a true knight, and he sends me security. Well, he may sleep in security; for he has the horn of abundance, and the lightness of his wife shines through it. and yet cannot he see, though he have his own lantern to light him. Where's Bardolph?

Page. He's gone into Smithfield to buy your worship a horse.

Falstaff. I bought him in Paul's, and he'll buy me a horse in Smithfield. If I could get me but a wife in the stews, I were manned, horsed, and wived.

[Enter the Lord Chief Justice and Servant]

Page. Sir, here comes the nobleman that committed the Prince for striking him about Bardolph.

Falstaff. Wait close; I will not see him.

Chief Justice. What's he that goes there?

Servant. Falstaff, if it please your lordship.

Chief Justice. He that was in question for the robbery?

Servant. He, my lord; but he has since done good service at Shrewsbury; and, as I hear, is now going with some charge to the Lord John of Lancaster.

Chief Justice. What, to York? Call him back again.

Servant. Sir John Falstaff!

Falstaff. Boy, tell him I am deaf.

Page. You must speak louder; my master is deaf.

Chief Justice. I am sure he is, to the hearing of anything good. Go, pluck him by the elbow; I must speak with him.

Servant. Sir John!

Falstaff. What! a young knave, and begging! Is there not wars? Is there not employment? Does not the King lack subjects? Do not the rebels need soldiers? Though it be a shame to be on any side but one, it is worse shame to beg than to be on the worst side, were it worse than the name of rebellion can tell how to make it.

Servant. You mistake me, sir.

Falstaff. Why, sir, did I say you were an honest man? Setting my knighthood and my soldiership aside, I had lied in my throat, if I had said so.

Servant. I pray you, sir, then set your knighthood and your soldiership aside; and give me leave to tell you, you lie in your throat, if you say I am any other than an honest man.

Falstaff. I give you leave to tell me so! I lay aside that which grows to me! If you get any leave of me, hang me; if you take leave, you were better be hanged. You hunt counter. Hence! Avaunt!

Servant. Sir, my lord would speak with you.

Chief Justice. Sir John Falstaff, a word with you.

Falstaff. My good lord! God give your lordship good time of day. I am glad to see your lordship abroad. I heard say your lordship was sick. I hope your lordship goes abroad by advice. Your lordship, though not clean past your youth, has yet some smack of age in you, some relish of the saltness of time; and I most humbly beseech your lordship to have a reverend care of your health.

Chief Justice. Sir John, I sent for you before your expedition to Shrewsbury.

Falstaff. If it please your lordship, I hear his majesty is returned with some discomfort from Wales.

Chief Justice. I talk not of his majesty. You would not come when I sent for you.

Falstaff. And I hear, moreover, his highness is fallen into this same whoreson apoplexy.

Chief Justice. Well God mend him! I pray you, let me speak with you.

Falstaff. This apoplexy is, as I take it, a kind of lethargy, if it please your lordship; a kind of sleeping in the blood, a whoreson tingling.

Chief Justice. What tell you me of it? Be it as it is.

Falstaff. It has its original from much grief, from study and perturbation of the brain. I have read the cause of his effects in Galen. It is a kind of deafness.

Chief Justice. I think you are fallen into the disease, for you hear not what I say to you.

Falstaff. Very well, my lord, very well. rather, if it please you, it is the disease of not listening, the malady of not marking, that I am troubled withal.

Chief Justice. To punish you by the heels would amend the attention of your ears; and I care not if I do become your physician.

Falstaff. I am as poor as Job, my lord, but not so patient. Your lordship may minister the potion of imprisonment to me in respect of poverty; but how I should be your patient to follow your prescriptions, the wise may make some dram of a scruple, or indeed a scruple itself.

Chief Justice. I sent for you, when there were matters against you for your life, to come speak with me.

Falstaff. As I was then advised by my learned counsel in the laws of this land-service, I did not come.

Chief Justice. Well, the truth is, Sir John, you live in great infamy.

Falstaff. He that buckles himself in my belt cannot live in less.

Chief Justice. Your means are very slender, and your waste is great.

Falstaff. I would it were otherwise; I would my means were greater, and my waist slenderer.

Chief Justice. You have misled the youthful Prince.

Falstaff. The young Prince has misled me. I am the fellow with the great belly, and he my dog.

Chief Justice. Well, I am loath to gall a new-healed wound. Your day's service at Shrewsbury has a little gilded over your night's exploit on Gad's-hill. You may thank the unquiet time for your quiet over-posting that action.

Falstaff. My lord?

Chief Justice. But since all is well, keep it so. Wake not a sleeping wolf.

Falstaff. To wake a wolf is as bad as smell a fox.

Chief Justice. What! You are as a candle, the better part burnt out.

Falstaff. A wassail candle, my lord, all tallow. if I did say of wax, my growth would approve the truth.

Chief Justice. There is not a white hair in your face but should have his effect of gravity.

Falstaff. His effect of gravy, gravy, gravy.

Chief Justice. You follow the young Prince up and down, like his ill angel.

Falstaff. Not so, my lord; your ill angel is light. But I hope he that looks upon me will take me without weighing. and yet, in some respects, I grant, I cannot go. I cannot tell. Virtue is of so little regard in these costermonger times that true valor is turned bear-herd; pregnancy is made a tapster, and has his quick wit wasted in giving reckonings. all the other gifts appertinent to man, as the malice of this age shapes them, are not worth a gooseberry. You that are old consider not the capacities of us that are young; you do measure the heat of our livers with the bitterness of your galls. and we that are in the vaward of our youth, I must confess, are wags too.

Chief Justice. Do you set down your name in the scroll of youth, that are written down old with all the characters of age? Have you not a moist eye? A dry hand? A yellow cheek? A white beard? A decreasing leg? An increasing belly? Is not your voice broken? Your wind short? Your chin double? Your wit single? And every part about you blasted with antiquity? And will you yet call yourself young? Fie, fie, fie, Sir John!

Falstaff. My lord, I was born about three of the clock in the afternoon, with a white head and something a round belly. For my voice, I have lost it with halloing and singing of anthems. To approve my youth further, I will not. The truth is, I am only old in judgment and understanding; and he that will caper with me for a thousand marks, let him lend me the money, and have at him! For the box of the ear that the Prince gave you, he gave it like a rude Prince, and you took it like a sensible lord. I have checked him for it, and the young lion repents; indeed, not in ashes and sackcloth, but in new silk and old sack.

Chief Justice. Well, God send the Prince a better companion!

Falstaff. God send the companion a better Prince! I cannot rid my hands of him.

Chief Justice. Well, the King has severed you and Prince Harry. I hear you are going with Lord John of Lancaster against the Archbishop and the Earl of Northumberland.

Falstaff. Yea; I thank your pretty sweet wit for it. But look you pray, all you that kiss my Lady Peace at home, that our armies join not in a hot day; for, by the Lord, I take but two shirts out with me, and I mean not to sweat extraordinarily. if it be a hot day, and I brandish anything but a bottle, I would I might never spit white again. There is not a dangerous action can peep out his head but I am thrust upon it. Well, I cannot last ever. But it was alway yet the trick of our English nation, if they have a good thing, to make it too common. If you will needs say I am an old man, you should give me rest. I would to God my name were not so terrible to the enemy as it is. I were better to be eaten to death with a rust than to be scoured to nothing with perpetual motion.

Chief Justice. Well, be honest, be honest; and God bless your expedition!

Falstaff. Will your lordship lend me a thousand pound to furnish me forth?

Chief Justice. Not a penny, not a penny; you are too impatient to bear crosses. Fare you well. commend me to my cousin Westmoreland.

[Exit Chief Justice and Servant]

Falstaff. If I do, fillip me with a three-man beetle. A man can no more separate age and covetousness than 'a can part young limbs and lechery—but the gout galls the one, and the pox pinches the other; and so both the degrees prevent my curses. Boy!

Page. Sir?

Falstaff. What money is in my purse?

Page. Seven groats and two pence.

Falstaff. I can get no remedy against this consumption of the purse. borrowing only lingers and lingers it out, but the disease is incurable. Go bear this letter to my Lord of Lancaster; this to the Prince; this to the Earl of Westmoreland; and this to old Mistress Ursula, whom I have weekly sworn to marry since I perceived the first white hair of my chin. About it. You know where to find me.

[Exit Page]

A pox of this gout! or, a gout of this pox! for the one or the other plays the rogue with my great toe. 'Tis no matter if I do halt; I have the wars for my color, and my pension shall seem the more reasonable. A good wit will make use of anything. I will turn diseases to commodity.

[Exit Falstaff]

[*York. The Archbishop's palace*]

[*Enter the Archbishop, the Lords Hastings, Mowbray, Bardolph*]

Archbishop. Thus have you heard our cause and known our means;
And, my most noble friends, I pray you all,
Speak plainly your opinions of our hopes.
And first, Lord Marshal, what say you to it?

Mowbray. I well allow the occasion of our arms;
But gladly would be better satisfied
How in our means we should advance ourselves
To look with forehead bold and big enough
Upon the power and puissance of the King.

Hastings. Our present musters grow upon the file
To five and twenty thousand men of choice;
And our supplies live largely in the hope
Of great Northumberland, whose bosom burns
With an incensed fire of injuries.

Lord Bardolph. The question then, Lord Hastings, stands thus.
Whether our present five and twenty thousand
May hold up head without Northumberland?

Hastings. With him, we may.

Lord Bardolph. Yea, well, there's the point.
But if without him we be thought too feeble,
My judgment is, we should not step too far
Till we had his assistance by the hand;
For in a theme so bloody-faced as this
Conjecture, expectation, and surmise
Of aids uncertain should not be admitted.

Archbishop. 'Tis very true, Lord Bardolph; for indeed
It was young Hotspur's case at Shrewsbury.

Lord Bardolph. It was, my lord; who lined himself with hope,
Eating the air on promise of supply,
Flattering himself in project of a power
Much smaller than the smallest of his thoughts.
And so, with great imagination
Proper to madmen, led his powers to death
And, winking, leaped into destruction.

Hastings. But, by your leave, it never yet did hurt
 To lay down likelihoods and forms of hope.

Lord Bardolph. Yes, if this present quality of war,
 Indeed the instant action. a cause on foot
 Lives so in hope as in an early spring
 We see the appearing buds; which to prove fruit,
 Hope gives not so much warrant as despair
 That frosts will bite them. When we mean to build,
 We first survey the plot, then draw the model;
 And when we see the figure of the house,
 Then we must rate the cost of the erection;
 Which if we find outweighs ability,
 What do we then but draw anew the model
 In fewer offices, or at least desist
 To build at all? Much more, in this great work,
 Which is almost to pluck a kingdom down
 And set another up, should we survey
 The plot of situation and the model,
 Consent upon a sure foundation,
 Question surveyors, know our own estate,
 How able such a work to undergo,
 To weigh against his opposite; or else
 We fortify in paper and in figures,
 Using the names of men instead of men;
 Like one that draws the model of a house
 Beyond his power to build it; who, half through,
 Gives over and leaves his part-created cost
 A naked subject to the weeping clouds
 And waste for churlish winter's tyranny.

Hastings. Grant that our hopes, yet likely of fair birth,
 Should be still-born, and that we now possessed
 The utmost man of expectation,
 I think we are a body strong enough,
 Even as we are, to equal with the King.

Lord Bardolph. What, is the King but five and twenty thousand?

Hastings. To us no more; nay, not so much, Lord Bardolph.
 For his divisions, as the times do brawl,
 Are in three heads. one power against the French,
 And one against Glendower; perforce a third
 Must take up us. so is the unfirm King
 In three divided; and his coffers sound
 With hollow poverty and emptiness.

Archbishop. That he should draw his several strengths together
And come against us in full puissance,
Need not be dreaded.

Hastings. If he should do so,
He leaves his back unarmed, the French and Welsh
Baying him at the heels. never fear that.

Lord Bardolph. Who is it like should lead his forces here?

Hastings. The Duke of Lancaster and Westmoreland;
Against the Welsh, himself and Harry Monmouth.
But who is substituted against the French,
I have no certain notice.

Archbishop. Let us on,
And publish the occasion of our arms.
The commonwealth is sick of their own choice;
Their over-greedy love has surfeited.
An habitation giddy and unsure
Has he that builds on the vulgar heart.
O you fond many, with what loud applause
Did you beat heaven with blessing Bolingbroke,
Before he was what you would have him be!
And being now trimmed in your own desires,
You, beastly feeder, are so full of him,
That you provoke yourself to cast him up.
So, so, you common dog, did you disgorge
Your glutton bosom of the royal Richard;
And now you would eat your dead vomit up,
And howl to find it. What trust is in these times?
They that, when Richard lived, would have him die,
Are now become enamoured on his grave.
You that threw dust upon his goodly head
When through proud London he came sighing on
After the admired heels of Bolingbroke,
Cry now "O earth, yield us that King again,
And take you this!" O thoughts of men accursed!
Past and to come seems best; things present worst.

Mowbray. Shall we go draw our numbers, and set on?

Hastings. We are time's subjects, and time bids be gone.

[*Exit All*]

Act Two

1

[London. A street]

[Enter Hostess, Fang and his Boy, and Snare]

Hostess. Master Fang, have you entered the action?

Fang. It is entered.

Hostess. Where's your yeoman? Is it a lusty yeoman? will 'a stand to it?

Fang. Sirrah, where's Snare?

Hostess. O Lord, ay! good Master Snare.

Snare. Here, here.

Fang. Snare, we must arrest Sir John Falstaff.

Hostess. Yea, good Master Snare; I have entered him and all.

Snare. It may chance cost some of our lives, for he will stab.

Hostess. Alas the day! Take heed of him; he stabbed me in my own house, and that most beastly. in good faith, he cares not what mischief he does, if his weapon be out. he will foin like any devil; he will spare neither man, woman, nor child.

Fang. If I can close with him, I care not for his thrust.

Hostess. No, nor I neither. I'll be at your elbow.

Fang. If I but fist him once; if 'a come but within my vice—

Hostess. I am undone by his going; I warrant you, he's an infinitive thing upon my score. Good Master Fang, hold him sure. Good Master Snare, let him not escape. A' comes continuantly to Pie-corner—saving your manhoods—to buy a saddle; and he is indited to dinner to the Lubber's-head in Lumbert Street, to Master Smooth's the silkman. I pray you, since my exion is entered and my case so openly known to the world, let him be brought in to his answer. A hundred mark is a long one for a poor lone woman to bear. And I have borne, and borne, and borne; and have been fubbed off, and fubbed off, and fubbed

off, from this day to that day, that it is a shame to be thought
on. There is no honesty in such dealing; unless a woman
should be made an ass and a beast, to bear every knave's
wrong. Yonder he comes; and that arrant malmsey-nose knave,
Bardolph, with him. Do your offices, do your offices, Master
Fang and Master Snare, do me, do me, do me your offices.

[*Enter Falstaff, Page, and Bardolph*]

Falstaff. How now! Whose mare's dead? What's the matter?

Fang. Sir John, I arrest you at the suit of Mistress Quickly.

Falstaff. Away, varlets! Draw, Bardolph. Cut me off the villain's
head. Throw the quean in the channel.

Hostess. Throw me in the channel! I'll throw you in the channel.
Will you? Will you? you bastardly rogue! Murder, murder! Ah,
you honey-suckle villain! Will you kill God's officers and the
King's? Ah, you honey-seed rogue! you are a honey-seed, a man-
queller, and a woman-queller.

Falstaff. Keep them off, Bardolph.

Fang. A rescue! a rescue!

Hostess. Good people, bring a rescue or two. You wo't, wo't you?
you wo't, wo't ta? Do, do, you rogue! Do, you hemp-seed!

Page. Away, you scullion! you rampallian! you fustilarian! I'll tickle
your catastrophe.

[*Enter the Lord Chief Justice, and his men*]

Chief Justice. What is the matter? Keep the peace here, ho!

Hostess. Good my lord, be good to me. I beseech you, stand to me.

Chief Justice. How now, Sir John! what are you brawling here?
Does this become your place, your time and business? You
should have been well on your way to York. Stand from him,
fellow. Wherefore hang you upon him?

Hostess. O my most worshipful lord, if it please your grace, I am a
poor widow of Eastcheap, and he is arrested at my suit.

Chief Justice. For what sum?

Hostess. It is more than for some, my lord; it is for all, all I have.
He has eaten me out of house and home; he has put all my
substance into that fat belly of his. But I will have some of it out
again, or I will ride you o' nights like the mare.

Falstaff. I think I am as like to ride the mare, if I have any vantage
of ground to get up.

Chief Justice. How comes this, Sir John? Fie! What man of good
   temper would endure this tempest of exclamation? Are you not
   ashamed to enforce a poor widow to so rough a course to come
   by her own?

Falstaff. What is the gross sum that I owe you?

Hostess. Well, if you were an honest man, yourself and the money
   too. You did swear to me upon a parcel-gilt goblet, sitting in my
   Dolphin-chamber, at the round table, by a sea-coal fire, upon
   Wednesday in Wheeson week, when the Prince broke your head
   for liking his father to a singing-man of Windsor, you did swear
   to me then, as I was washing your wound, to marry me and
   make me my lady your wife. Can you deny it? Did not goodwife
   Keech, the butcher's wife, come in then and call me Gossip
   Quickly? Coming in to borrow a mess of vinegar; telling us she
   had a good dish of prawns, whereby you did desire to eat some,
   whereby I told you they were ill for green wound? And did you
   not, when she was gone down stairs, desire me to be no more
   so familiarity with such poor people; saying that before long
   they should call me madam? And did you not kiss me, and bid
   me fetch you thirty shillings? I put you now to your book-oath.
   deny it, if you can.

Falstaff. My lord, this is a poor mad soul; and she says up and down
   the town that her eldest son is like you. She has been in good
   case, and the truth is, poverty has distracted her. But for these
   foolish officers, I beseech you I may have redress against them.

Chief Justice. Sir John, Sir John, I am well acquainted with your
   manner of wrenching the true cause the false way. It is not a
   confident brow, nor the throng of words that come with such
   more than impudent sauciness from you, can thrust me from
   a level consideration. You have, as it appears to me, practiced
   upon the easy-yielding spirit of this woman, and made her serve
   your uses both in purse and in person.

Hostess. Yea, in truth, my lord.

Chief Justice. Pray you, peace. Pay her the debt you owe her, and
   unpay the villainy you have done her. The one you may do with
   sterling money, and the other with current repentance.

Falstaff. My lord, I will not undergo this sneap without reply. You
   call honorable boldness impudent sauciness. If a man will
   make courtesy and say nothing, he is virtuous. no, my lord, my
   humble duty remembered, I will not be your suitor. I say to you,
   I do desire deliverance from these officers, being upon hasty

employment in the King's affairs.

Chief Justice. You speak as having power to do wrong. but answer in the effect of your reputation, and satisfy the poor woman.

Falstaff. Come here, Hostess.

[*Enter Gower*]

Chief Justice. Now, Master Gower, what news?

Gower. The King, my lord, and Harry Prince of Wales
Are near at hand. The rest the paper tells.

Falstaff. As I am a gentleman...

Hostess. Faith, you said so before.

Falstaff. As I am a gentleman. Come, no more words of it.

Hostess. By this heavenly ground I tread on, I must be fain to pawn both my plate and the tapestry of my dining-chambers.

Falstaff. Glasses, glasses, is the only drinking. And for your walls, a pretty slight drollery, or the story of the Prodigal, or the German hunting in water-work, is worth a thousand of these bed-hangings and these fly-bitten tapestries. Let it be ten pound, if you can. Come, if 'twere not for your humors, there's not a better wench in England. Go, wash your face, and draw the action. Come, you must not be in this humor with me; do not know me? Come, come, I know you were set on to this.

Hostess. Pray you, Sir John, let it be but twenty nobles. Truly, I am loath to pawn my plate, so God save me, la!

Falstaff. Let it alone; I'll make other shift. You'll be a fool still.

Hostess. Well, you shall have it, though I pawn my gown. I hope you'll come to supper. You'll pay me all together?

Falstaff. Will I live?

[*To Bardolph*] Go, with her, with her; hook on, hook on.

Hostess. Will you have Doll Tearsheet meet you at supper?

Falstaff. No more words; let's have her.

[*Exit All Hostess, Bardolph, Officers, and Boy*]

Chief Justice. I have heard better news.

Falstaff. What's the news, my lord?

Chief Justice. Where lay the King last night?

Gower. At Basingstoke, my lord.

Falstaff. I hope, my lord, all's well. what is the news, my lord?

Chief Justice. Come all his forces back?

Gower. No; fifteen hundred foot, five hundred horse,
Are marched up to my Lord of Lancaster,
Against Northumberland and the Archbishop.

Falstaff. Comes the King back from Wales, my noble lord?

Chief Justice. You shall have letters of me presently.
Come, go along with me, good Master Gower.

Falstaff. My lord!

Chief Justice. What's the matter?

Falstaff. Master Gower, shall I entreat you with me to dinner?

Gower. I must wait upon my good lord here; I thank you, good Sir John.

Chief Justice. Sir John, you loiter here too long, being you are to take soldiers up in counties as you go.

Falstaff. Will you sup with me, Master Gower?

Chief Justice. What foolish master taught you these manners, Sir John?

Falstaff. Master Gower, if they become me not, he was a fool that taught them me. This is the right fencing grace, my lord; tap for tap, and so part fair.

Chief Justice. Now the Lord lighten you! You are a great fool.

[*Exit All*]

[*London. Another street*]

[*Enter Prince Henry and Poins*]

Prince. Before God, I am exceeding weary.

Poins. Is it come to that? I had thought weariness dared not have attached one of so high blood.

Prince. Indeed, it does me; though it discolors the complexion of my greatness to acknowledge it. Does it not show vilely in me to desire small beer?

Poins. Why, a Prince should not be so loosely studied as to remember so weak a composition.

Prince. Belike then my appetite was not princely got; for, by my troth, I do now remember the poor creature, small beer. But, indeed, these humble considerations make me out of love with my greatness. What a disgrace is it to me to remember your name! Or to know your face tomorrow! Or to take note how many pair of silk stockings you have, such as these, and those that were your peach-colored ones! Or to bear the inventory of your shirts, as, one for superfluity, and another for use! But that the tennis-court-keeper knows better than I; for it is a low ebb of linen with you when you keep not racket there; as you have not done a great while, because the rest of your low countries have made a shift to eat up your holland. And God knows, whether those that bawl out of the ruins of your linen shall inherit his kingdom. But the midwives say the children are not in the fault; whereupon the world increases, and kindreds are mightily strengthened.

Poins. How ill it follows, after you have labored so hard, you should talk so idly! Tell me, how many good young princes would do so, their fathers being so sick as yours at this time is?

Prince. Shall I tell you one thing, Poins?

Poins. Yes, do; and let it be an excellent good thing.

Prince. It shall serve among wits of no higher breeding than yours.

Poins. Go to; I stand the push of your one thing that you will tell.

Prince. Well, I tell you it is not meet that I should be sad, now my father is sick. Albeit I could tell to you, as to one it pleases me, for fault of a better, to call my friend, I could be sad, and sad indeed too.

Poins. Very hardly upon such a subject.

Prince. By this hand, you think me as far in the devil's book as you and Falstaff for obduracy and persistency. let the end try the man. But I tell you, my heart bleeds inwardly that my father is so sick. and keeping such vile company as you are has in reason taken from me all ostentation of sorrow.

Poins. The reason?

Prince. What would you think of me, if I should weep?

Poins. I would think you a most princely hypocrite.

Prince. It would be every man's thought; and you are a blessed fellow to think as every man thinks. never a man's thought in the world keeps the road-way better than yours. every man would think me an hypocrite indeed. And what accites your most worshipful thought to think so?

Poins. Why, because you have been so lewd and so much engraffed to Falstaff.

Prince. And to you.

Poins. By this light, I am well spoke on; I can hear it with my own ears. the worst that they can say of me is that I am a second brother and that I am a proper fellow of my hands; and those two things, I confess, I cannot help. By the mass, here comes Bardolph.

[Enter Bardolph and Page]

Prince. And the boy that I gave Falstaff. 'a had him from me Christian; and look, if the fat villain have not transformed him ape.

Bardolph. God save your grace!

Prince. And yours, most noble Bardolph!

Poins. Come, you virtuous ass, you bashful fool, must you be blushing? wherefore blush you now? What a maidenly man-at-arms are you become! Is it such a matter to get a pottle-pot's maidenhead?

Page. 'A calls me e'en now, my lord, through a red lattice, and I could discern no part of his face from the window. at last I spied his eyes, and methought he had made two holes in the ale-wife's new petticoat and so peeped through.

Prince. Has not the boy profited?

Bardolph. Away, you whoreson upright rabbit, away!

Page. Away, you rascally Althaea's dream, away!

Prince. Instruct us, boy; what dream, boy?

Page. Well, my lord, Althaea dreamt she was delivered of a fire-brand; and therefore I call him her dream.

Prince. A crown's worth of good interpretation. There 'tis, boy.

Poins. O, that this blossom could be kept from cankers! Well, there is sixpence to preserve you.

Bardolph. If you do not make him hanged among you, the gallows shall have wrong.

Prince. And how does your master, Bardolph?

Bardolph. Well, my lord. He heard of your grace's coming to town. there's a letter for you.

Poins. Delivered with good respect. And how does the martlemas, your master?

Bardolph. In bodily health, sir.

Poins. Well, the immortal part needs a physician; but that moves not him. Though that be sick, it dies not.

Prince. I do allow this wen to be as familiar with me as my dog; and he holds his place; for look you how he writes.

Poins. [*Reads*] "John Falstaff, knight,"—every man must know that, as oft as he has occasion to name himself. Even like those that are kin to the King; for they never prick their finger but they say, "There's some of the King's blood spilled." "How comes that?" says he, that takes upon him not to conceive. The answer is as ready as a borrower's cap, "I am the King's poor cousin, sir."

Prince. Nay, they will be kin to us, or they will fetch it from Japhet. But to the letter.

Poins. [*Reads*] "Sir John Falstaff, knight, to the son of the King, nearest his father, Harry Prince of Wales, greeting." Why, this is a certificate.

Prince. Peace!

Poins. [*Reads*] "I will imitate the honorable Romans in brevity." He sure means brevity in breath, short-winded. "I commend me to you, I commend you, and I leave you. Be not too familiar with Poins; for he misuses your favors so much, that he swears you are to marry his sister Nell. Repent at idle times as you may; and so, farewell. "Yours, by yea and no, which is as much as to say, as you use him, JACK FALSTAFF with my familiars, JOHN with my brothers and sisters, and SIR JOHN with all Europe." My lord, I'll steep this letter in sack and make him eat it.

Prince. That's to make him eat twenty of his words. But do you use me thus, Ned? Must I marry your sister?

Poins. God send the wench no worse fortune! But I never said so.

Prince. Well, thus we play the fools with the time, and the spirits of the wise sit in the clouds and mock us. Is your master here in London?

Bardolph. Yea, my lord.

Prince. Where sups he? Does the old boar feed in the old frank?

Bardolph. At the old place, my lord, in Eastcheap.

Prince. What company?

Page. Ephesians, my lord, of the old church.

Prince. Sup any women with him?

Page. None, my lord, but old Mistress Quickly and Mistress Doll Tearsheet.

Prince. What pagan may that be?

Page. A proper gentlewoman, sir, and a kinswoman of my master's.

Prince. Even such kin as the parish heifers are to the town bull. Shall we steal upon them, Ned, at supper?

Poins. I am your shadow, my lord; I'll follow you.

Prince. Sirrah, you boy, and Bardolph, no word to your master that I am yet come to town. there's for your silence.

Bardolph. I have no tongue, sir.

Page. And for mine, sir, I will govern it.

Prince. Fare you well; go.

[*Exit Bardolph and Page*]

This Doll Tearsheet should be some road.

Poins. I warrant you, as common as the way between Saint Alban's and London.

Prince. How might we see Falstaff bestow himself tonight in his true colors, and not ourselves be seen?

Poins. Put on two leathern jerkins and aprons, and wait upon him at his table as drawers.

Prince. From a God to a bull? A heavy descension! it was Jove's case. From a Prince to a prentice? a low transformation! That shall be mine; for in everything the purpose must weigh with the folly. Follow me, Ned.

[*Exit All*]

[*Warkworth. Before the castle*]

[*Enter Northumberland, Lady Northumberland, and
Lady Percy*]

Northumberland. I pray you, loving wife, and gentle daughter,
  Give even way unto my rough affairs;
  Put not you on the visage of the times
  And be like them to Percy, troublesome.

Lady Northumberland. I have given over, I will speak no more.
  Do what you will; your wisdom be your guide.

Northumberland. Alas, sweet wife, my honor is at pawn;
  And, but my going, nothing can redeem it.

Lady Percy. O yet, for God's sake, go not to these wars!
  The time was, father, that you broke your word,
  When you were more endeared to it than now!
  When your own Percy, when my heart's dear Harry,
  Threw many a northward look to see his father
  Bring up his powers; but he did long in vain.
  Who then persuaded you to stay at home?
  There were two honors lost, yours and your son's.
  For yours, the God of heaven brighten it!
  For his, it stuck upon him as the sun
  In the grey vault of heaven; and by his light
  Did all the chivalry of England move
  To do brave acts. he was indeed the glass
  Wherein the noble youth did dress themselves.
  He had no legs that practiced not his gait;
  And speaking thick, which nature made his blemish,
  Became the accents of the valiant;
  For those who could speak low and tardily
  Would turn their own perfection to abuse,
  To seem like him. so that in speech, in gait,
  In diet, in affections of delight,
  In military rules, humors of blood,
  He was the mark and glass, copy and book,
  That fashioned others. And him, O wondrous him!
  O miracle of men! Him did you leave,
  Second to none, unseconded by you,
  To look upon the hideous god of war

In disadvantage; to abide a field
Where nothing but the sound of Hotspur's name
Did seem defensible. so you left him.
Never, O never, do his ghost the wrong
To hold your honor more precise and nice
With others than with him! Let them alone.
The Marshal and the Archbishop are strong.
Had my sweet Harry had but half their numbers,
Today might I, hanging on Hotspur's neck,
Have talked of Monmouth's grave.

Northumberland. Beshrew your heart,
Fair daughter, you do draw my spirits from me
With new lamenting ancient oversights.
But I must go and meet with danger there,
Or it will seek me in another place,
And find me worse provided.

Lady Northumberland. O, fly to Scotland,
Till that the nobles and the armed commons
Have of their puissance made a little taste.

Lady Percy. If they get ground and vantage of the King,
Then join you with them, like a rib of steel,
To make strength stronger; but, for all our loves,
First let them try themselves. So did your son;
He was so suffered. So came I a widow;
And never shall have length of life enough
To rain upon remembrance with my eyes,
That it may grow and sprout as high as heaven,
For recordation to my noble husband.

Northumberland. Come, come, go in with me. 'Tis with my mind
As with the tide swelled up unto his height,
That makes a still-stand, running neither way.
Fain would I go to meet the Archbishop,
But many thousand reasons hold me back.
I will resolve for Scotland. there am I,
Till time and vantage crave my company.

[*Exit All*]

4

[*London. The Boar's-head Tavern in Eastcheap*]

[*Enter two Drawers*]

First Drawer. What the devil have you brought there? Apple-johns? You know Sir John cannot endure an apple-john.

Second Drawer. Mass, you say true. The Prince once set a dish of apple-johns before him, and told him there were five more Sir Johns, and, putting off his hat, said "I will now take my leave of these six dry, round, old, withered knights." It angered him to the heart. But he has forgot that.

First Drawer. Why, then, cover, and set them down. and see if you can find out Sneak's noise; Mistress Tearsheet would fain hear some music. Dispatch. The room where they supped is too hot; they'll come in straight.

Second Drawer. Sirrah, here will be the Prince and Master Poins anon; and they will put on two of our jerkins and aprons; and Sir John must not know of it. Bardolph has brought word.

First Drawer. By the mass, here will be old utis. It will be an excellent stratagem.

Second Drawer. I'll see if I can find out Sneak.

[*Exit Second Drawer*]

[*Enter Hostess and Doll Tearsheet*]

Hostess. Truly, sweetheart, I think now you are in an excellent good temperality. your pulsidge beats as extraordinarily as heart would desire; and your color, I warrant you, is as red as any rose, in good truth, la! But, truly, you have drunk too much canaries; and that's a marvellous searching wine, and it perfumes the blood before one can say "What's this?" How do you now?

Doll Tearsheet. Better than I was. Hem!

Hostess. Why, that's well said; a good heart's worth gold. Lo, here comes Sir John.

[*Enter Falstaff*]

Falstaff. [*Singing*] "When Arthur first in court" —Empty the jordan.

[Exit First Drawer]

[Singing] "And was a worthy King."
How now, Mistress Doll!

Hostess. Sick of a calm; yea, good faith.

Falstaff. So is all her sect; if they be once in a calm, they are sick.

Doll Tearsheet. You muddy rascal, is that all the comfort you give me?

Falstaff. You make fat rascals, Mistress Doll Tearsheet.

Doll Tearsheet. I make them! Gluttony and diseases make them; I make them not.

Falstaff. If the cook help to make the gluttony, you help to make the diseases, Doll. We catch of you, Doll, we catch of you; grant that, my poor virtue, grant that.

Doll Tearsheet. Yea, joy, our chains and our jewels.

Falstaff. "Your brooches, pearls, and gew-gaws." For to serve bravely is to come halting off, you know. To come off the breach with his pike bent bravely, and to surgery bravely; to venture upon the charged chambers bravely—

Doll Tearsheet. Hang yourself, you muddy conger, hang yourself!

Hostess. By my troth, this is the old fashion; you two never meet but you fall to some discord. You are both, in good truth, as rheumatic as two dry toasts; you cannot one bear with another's confirmities. What the good-year! One must bear, and that *[To Doll Tearsheet]* must be you. You are the weaker vessel, as as they say, the emptier vessel.

Doll Tearsheet. Can a weak empty vessel bear such a huge full hogshead? There's a whole merchant's venture of Bourdeaux stuff in him; you have not seen a hulk better stuffed in the hold. Come, I'll be friends with you, Jack. You are going to the wars; and whether I shall ever see you again or no, there is nobody cares.

[Re-enter First Drawer]

First Drawer. Sir, Ancient Pistol's below, and would speak with you.

Doll Tearsheet. Hang him, swaggering rascal! Let him not come here. It is the foul-mouthedest rogue in England.

Hostess. If he swagger, let him not come here. No, by my faith; I must live among my neighbors; I'll no swaggerers. I am in good name and fame with the very best. shut the door; there comes no swaggerers here. I have not lived all this while, to have swaggering now. shut the door, I pray you.

Falstaff. Do you hear, hostess?

Hostess. Pray you, pacify yourself, Sir John. there comes no swaggerers here.

Falstaff. Do you hear? It is my ancient.

Hostess. Tilly-fally, Sir John, never tell me. Your ancient swaggerer comes not in my doors. I was before Master Tisick, the debuty, t'other day; and, as he said to me, 'twas no longer ago than Wednesday last, "In good faith, neighbor Quickly," says he; Master Dumbe, our minister, was by then; "Neighbor Quickly," says he, "receive those that are civil; for," said he "you are in an ill name." Now a' said so, I can tell whereupon. "For," says he, "You are an honest woman, and well thought on; therefore take heed what guests you receive. Receive," says he, "no swaggering companions." There comes none here. You would bless you to hear what he said. No, I'll no swaggerers.

Falstaff. He's no swaggerer, hostess; a tame cheater, 'tis true; you may stroke him as gently as a puppy greyhound. He'll not swagger with a Barbary hen, if her feathers turn back in any show of resistance. Call him up, drawer.

[*Exit First Drawer*]

Hostess. Cheater, call you him? I will bar no honest man my house, nor no cheater. but I do not love swaggering, by my troth; I am the worse, when one says swagger. Feel, masters, how I shake; look you, I warrant you.

Doll Tearsheet. So you do, Hostess.

Hostess. Do I? yea, in very truth, do I, if 'twere an aspen leaf. I cannot abide swaggerers.

[*Enter Pistol, Bardolph, and Page*]

Pistol. God save you, Sir John!

Falstaff. Welcome, Ancient Pistol. Here, Pistol, I charge you with a cup of sack. Do you discharge upon my hostess.

Pistol. I will discharge upon her, Sir John, with two bullets.

Falstaff. She is pistol-proof, sir; you shall hardly offend her.

Hostess. Come, I'll drink no proofs nor no bullets. I'll drink no more than will do me good, for no man's pleasure, I.

Pistol. Then to you, Mistress Dorothy; I will charge you.

Doll Tearsheet. Charge me! I scorn you, scurvy companion. What! You poor, base, rascally, cheating, lack-linen mate! Away, you moldy rogue, away! I am meat for your master.

Pistol. I know you, Mistress Dorothy.

Doll Tearsheet. Away, you cut-purse rascal! You filthy bung, away! By this wine, I'll thrust my knife in your moldy chaps, if you play the saucy cuttle with me. Away, you bottle-ale rascal! You basket-hilt stale juggler, you! Since when, I pray you, sir? God's light, with two points on your shoulder? Much!

Pistol. God let me not live, but I will murder your ruff for this.

Falstaff. No more, Pistol; I would not have you go off here. Discharge yourself of our company, Pistol.

Hostess. No, good Captain Pistol; not here, sweet captain.

Doll Tearsheet. Captain! you abominable damned cheater, are you not ashamed to be called captain? If captains were of my mind, they would truncheon you out, for taking their names upon you before you have earned them. You a captain! You slave, for what? For tearing a poor whore's ruff in a bawdy-house? He a captain! hang him, rogue! He lives upon moldy stewed prunes and dried cakes. A captain! God's light, these villains will make the word as odious as the word "occupy"; which was an excellent good word before it was ill sorted. therefore captains had need look to it.

Bardolph. Pray you, go down, good ancient.

Falstaff. Hark you here, Mistress Doll Tearsheet.

Pistol. Not I. I tell you what, Corporal Bardolph, I could tear her. I'll be revenged of her.

Page. Pray you go down.

Pistol. I'll see her damned first; to Pluto's damned lake, by this hand, to the infernal deep, with Erebus and tortures vile also. Hold hook and line, say I. Down, down, dogs! down, faitors! Have we not Hiren here?

Hostess. Good Captain Peesel, be quiet; 'tis very late, i' faith. I beseek you now, aggravate your choler.

Pistol. These be good humors, indeed! Shall packhorses
    And hollow pampered jades of Asia,
    Which cannot go but thirty mile a-day,
    Compare with Caesars, and with Cannibals,
    And Trojan Greeks? Nay, rather damn them with
    King Cerberus; and let the welkin roar.

Shall we fall foul for toys?

Hostess. By my troth, captain, these are very bitter words.

Bardolph. Be gone, good ancient. This will grow to a brawl anon.

Pistol. Die men like dogs! Give crowns like pins! Have we not Hiren
here?

Hostess. On my word, captain, there's none such here. What the
good-year! Do you think I would deny her? For God's sake, be
quiet.

Pistol. Then feed, and be fat, my fair Calipolis.
Come, give's some sack.
"Si fortune me tormente, sperato me contento."
Fear we broadsides? No, let the fiend give fire.
Give me some sack; and, sweetheart, lie you there.

[*Laying down his sword*]

Come we to full points here, and are etceteras nothing?

Falstaff. Pistol, I would be quiet.

Pistol. Sweet knight, I kiss your neif. What! We have seen the seven
stars.

Doll Tearsheet. For God's sake, thrust him down stairs. I cannot
endure such a fustian rascal.

Pistol. Thrust him down stairs! Know we not Galloway nags?

Falstaff. Quoit him down, Bardolph, like a shove-groat shilling.
Nay, if a' do nothing but speak nothing, a' shall be nothing here.

Bardolph. Come, get you down stairs.

Pistol. What! shall we have incision? Shall we imbrue?

[*Snatching up his sword*]

Then death rock me asleep, abridge my doleful days!
Why, then, let grievous, ghastly, gaping wounds
Untwine the Sisters Three! Come, Atropos, I say!

Hostess. Here's goodly stuff toward!

Falstaff. Give me my rapier, boy.

Doll Tearsheet. I pray you, Jack, I pray you, do not draw.

Falstaff. Get you down stairs.

[*Drawing his sword, and driving Pistol out*]

Hostess. Here's a goodly tumult! I'll forswear keeping house, afore
I'll be in these tirrits and frights. So; murder, I warrant now. Alas,
alas! put up your naked weapons, put up your naked weapons.

[Exit Pistol and Bardolph]

Doll Tearsheet. I pray you, Jack, be quiet; the rascal's gone. Ah, you whoreson little valiant villain, you!

Hostess. Are you not hurt i' the groin? I thought a' made a shrewd thrust at your belly.

[Re-enter Bardolph]

Falstaff. Have you turned him out o' doors?

Bardolph. Yea, sir. The rascal's drunk. You have hurt him, sir, in the shoulder.

Falstaff. A rascal! To brave me!

Doll Tearsheet. Ah, you sweet little rogue, you! Alas, poor ape, how you sweat! Come, let me wipe your face; come on, you whoreson chops. Ah, rogue! i' faith, I love you. You are as valorous as Hector of Troy, worth five of Agamemnon, and ten times better than the Nine Worthies. Ah, villain!

Falstaff. A rascally slave! I will toss the rogue in a blanket.

Doll Tearsheet. Do, if you dare for your heart. If you do, I'll canvass you between a pair of sheets.

[Enter Music]

Page. The music is come, sir.

Falstaff. Let them play. Play, sirs. Sit on my knee, Doll. A rascal bragging slave! The rogue fled from me like quicksilver.

Doll Tearsheet. Truly, and you followed him like a church. You whoreson little tidy Bartholomew boar-pig, when will you leave fighting o' days and foining o' nights, and begin to patch up your old body for heaven?

[Enter, behind, Prince Henry and Poins, disguised as barkeeps]

Falstaff. Peace, good Doll! do not speak like a death's-head; do not bid me remember my end.

Doll Tearsheet. Sirrah, what humor's the Prince of?

Falstaff. A good shallow young fellow. 'a would have made a good pantler; a' would ha' chipped bread well.

Doll Tearsheet. They say Poins has a good wit.

Falstaff. He a good wit! Hang him, baboon! His wit's as thick as Tewksbury mustard; there's no more conceit in him than is in a mallet.

Doll Tearsheet. Why does the Prince love him so, then?

Falstaff. Because their legs are both of a bigness, and a' plays at quoits well, and eats conger and fennel, and drinks off candles' ends for flap-dragons, and rides the wild-mare with the boys, and jumps upon joined-stools, and swears with a good grace, and wears his boots very smooth, like unto the sign of the leg, and breeds no bate with telling of discreet stories; and such other gambol faculties a' has, that show a weak mind and an able body, for the which the Prince admits him. For the Prince himself is such another; the weight of a hair will turn the scales between their avoirdupois.

Prince. [*Aside to Poins*] Would not this nave of a wheel have his ears cut off?

Poins. [*Aside to Prince Hal*] Let's beat him before his whore.

Prince. Look, whether the withered elder has not his poll clawed like a parrot.

Poins. Is it not strange that desire should so many years outlive performance?

Falstaff. Kiss me, Doll Tearsheet.

Prince. [*Aside to Poins*] Saturn and Venus this year in conjunction! what says the almanac to that?

Poins. [*Aside to Prince Hal*] And, look, whether the fiery Trigon, his man, be not lisping to his master's old tables, his note-book, his counsel-keeper.

Falstaff. You do give me flattering busses.

Doll Tearsheet. By my troth, I kiss you with a most constant heart.

Falstaff. I am old, I am old.

Doll Tearsheet. I love you better than I love ever a scurvy young boy of them all.

Falstaff. What stuff will have a kirtle of? I shall receive money on Thursday; shall have a cap tomorrow. A merry song, come. It grows late; we'll to bed. You'll forget me when I am gone.

Doll Tearsheet. By my troth, you'll set me a-weeping, if you say so. Prove that ever I dress myself handsome till your return. Well, hearken at the end.

Falstaff. Some sack, Francis.

Prince and Poins. Anon, anon, sir.

[*Coming forward*]

Falstaff. Ha! a bastard son of the King's? And are you not Poins his brother?

Prince. Why, you globe of sinful continents, what a life do you lead!

Falstaff. A better than you. I am a gentleman; you are a drawer.

Prince. Very true, sir; and I come to draw you out by the ears.

Hostess. O, the Lord preserve your grace! By my troth, welcome to London. Now, the Lord bless that sweet face of yours! O Jesu, are you come from Wales?

Falstaff. You whoreson mad compound of majesty, by this light flesh and corrupt blood, you are welcome.

Doll Tearsheet. How, you fat fool! I scorn you.

Poins. My lord, he will drive you out of your revenge and turn all to a merriment, if you take not the heat.

Prince. You whoreson candle-mine, you, how vilely did you speak of me even now before this honest, virtuous, civil gentlewoman!

Hostess. God's blessing of your good heart! And so she is, by my troth.

Falstaff. Did you hear me?

Prince. Yea, and you knew me, as you did when you ran away by Gad's-Hill. you knew I was at your back, and spoke it on purpose to try my patience.

Falstaff. No, no, no; not so; I did not think you were within hearing.

Prince. I shall drive you then to confess the willful abuse; and then I know how to handle you.

Falstaff. No abuse, Hal, o' my honor; no abuse.

Prince. Not to dispraise me, and call me pantler and bread-chipper and I know not what!

Falstaff. No abuse, Hal.

Poins. No abuse!

Falstaff. No abuse, Ned, in the world; honest Ned, none. I dispraised him before the wicked, that the wicked might not fall in love with him; in which doing, I have done the part of a careful friend and a true subject, and your father is to give me thanks for it. No abuse, Hal. none, Ned, none. No, faith, boys, none.

Prince. See now, whether pure fear and entire cowardice does not make you wrong this virtuous gentlewoman to close with us. Is she of the wicked? Is your hostess here of the wicked? Or is your boy of the wicked? Or honest Bardolph, whose zeal burns in his nose, of the wicked?

Poins. Answer, you dead elm, answer.

Falstaff. The fiend has pricked down Bardolph irrecoverable; and his face is Lucifer's privy-kitchen, where he does nothing but roast malt-worms. For the boy, there is a good angel about him; but the devil outbids him too.

Prince. For the women?

Falstaff. For one of them, she is in hell already, and burns poor souls. For the other, I owe her money; and whether she be damned for that, I know not.

Hostess. No, I warrant you.

Falstaff. No, I think you are not; I think you are quit for that. Well, there is another indictment upon you, for suffering flesh to be eaten in your house, contrary to the law; for the which I think you will howl.

Hostess. All victuallers do so. what's a joint of mutton or two in a whole Lent?

Prince. You, gentlewoman—

Doll Tearsheet. What says your grace?

Falstaff. His grace says that which his flesh rebels against.

[*Knocking within*]

Hostess. Who knocks so loud at door? Look to the door there, Francis.

[*Enter Peto*]

Prince. Peto, how now! what news?

Peto. The King your father is at Westminster;
And there are twenty weak and wearied posts
Come from the north. and, as I came along,
I met and overtook a dozen captains,
Bare-headed, sweating, knocking at the taverns,
And asking every one for Sir John Falstaff.

Prince. By heaven, Poins, I feel me much to blame,
So idly to profane the precious time,
When tempest of commotion, like the south
Borne with black vapor, does begin to melt
And drop upon our bare unarmed heads.
Give me my sword and cloak. Falstaff, good night.

[Exit All Prince, Poins, Peto, and Bardolph]

Falstaff. Now comes in the sweetest morsel of the night, and we must hence, and leave it unpicked.

[Knocking within]

More knocking at the door!

[Re-enter Bardolph]

How now! what's the matter?

Bardolph. You must away to court, sir, presently;
A dozen captains stay at door for you.

Falstaff. *[To the Page]* Pay the musicians, sirrah.

Farewell, hostess; farewell, Doll Tearsheet. You see, my good wenches, how men of merit are sought after. the undeserver may sleep, when the man of action is called on. Farewell, good wenches. if I be not sent away post, I will see you again before I go.

Doll Tearsheet. I cannot speak; if my heart be not ready to burst— well, sweet Jack, have a care of yourself.

Falstaff. Farewell, farewell.

[Exit All Falstaff and Bardolph]

Hostess. Well, fare you well. I have known you these twenty-nine years, come peascod-time; but an honester and truer-hearted man— well, fare you well.

Bardolph. *[Within]* Mistress Tearsheet!

Hostess. What's the matter?

Bardolph. *[Within]* Bid Mistress Tearsheet come to my master.

Hostess. O, run, Doll, run; run, good Doll. Come.

[Doll comes, blubbering]

Yea, will you come, Doll?

[Exit All]

Act Three

1

[*Westminster. The palace*]

[*Enter the King in nightclothes, and a Page*]

King. Go call the Earls of Surrey and of Warwick;
But, before they come, bid them over-read these letters,
And well consider of them. Make good speed.

[*Exit Page*]

How many thousands of my poorest subjects
Are at this hour asleep! O sleep, O gentle sleep,
Nature's soft nurse, how have I frighted you,
That you no more will weigh my eyelids down
And steep my senses in forgetfulness?
Why rather, sleep, lie you in smoky cribs,
Upon uneasy pallets stretching you
And hushed with buzzing night-flies to your slumber
Than in the perfumed chambers of the great,
Under the canopies of costly state,
And lulled with sound of sweetest melody?
O you dull god, why lie you with the vile
In loathsome beds, and leave the kingly couch
A watch-case or a common alarm-bell?
Will you upon the high and giddy mast
Seal up the ship-boy's eyes, and rock his brains
In cradle of the rude imperious surge
And in the visitation of the winds,
Who take the ruffian billows by the top,
Curling their monstrous heads and hanging them
With deafening clamor in the slippery clouds,
That, with the hurly, death itself awakes?
Can you, O partial sleep, give your repose
To the wet sea-boy in an hour so rude;
And in the calm and most still night,

With all appliances and means to boot,
Deny it to a King? Then happy low, lie down!
Uneasy lies the head that wears a crown.

[*Enter Warwick and Surrey*]

Warwick. Many good morrows to your majesty!

King. Is it good morrow, lords?

Warwick. 'Tis one o'clock, and past.

King. Why then, good morrow to you all, my lords.
Have you read over the letters that I sent you?

Warwick. We have, my liege.

King. Then you perceive the body of our kingdom
How foul it is; what rank diseases grow,
And with what danger, near the heart of it.

Warwick. It is but as a body yet distempered;
Which to his former strength may be restored
With good advice and little medicine.
My Lord Northumberland will soon be cooled.

King. O God! That one might read the book of fate,
And see the revolution of the times
Make mountains level, and the continent,
Weary of solid firmness, melt itself
Into the sea! And, other times, to see
The beachy girdle of the ocean
Too wide for Neptune's hips; how chances mock,
And changes fill the cup of alteration
With diverse liquors! O, if this were seen,
The happiest youth, viewing his progress through,
What perils past, what crosses to ensue,
Would shut the book, and sit him down and die.
'Tis not ten years gone
Since Richard and Northumberland, great friends,
Did feast together, and in two years after
Were they at wars. It is but eight years since
This Percy was the man nearest my soul,
Who like a brother toiled in my affairs
And laid his love and life under my foot,
Yea, for my sake, even to the eyes of Richard
Gave him defiance. But which of you was by——
You, cousin Nevil, as I may remember——
[*To Warwick*] When Richard, with his eye brimful of tears,

Then checked and rated by Northumberland,
Did speak these words, now proved a prophecy?
"Northumberland, you ladder by the which
My cousin Bolingbroke ascends my throne"—
Though then, God knows, I had no such intent,
But that necessity so bowed the state
That I and greatness were compelled to kiss.
"The time shall come," thus did he follow it,
"The time will come, that foul sin, gathering head,
Shall break into corruption." so went on,
Foretelling this same time's condition
And the division of our amity.

Warwick. There is a history in all men's lives,
Figuring the natures of the times deceased;
The which observed, a man may prophesy,
With a near aim, of the main chance of things
As yet not come to life, who in their seeds
And weak beginning lie intreasured.
Such things become the hatch and brood of time;
And by the necessary form of this
King Richard might create a perfect guess
That great Northumberland, then false to him,
Would of that seed grow to a greater falseness;
Which should not find a ground to root upon,
Unless on you.

King. Are these things then necessities?
Then let us meet them like necessities.
And that same word even now cries out on us.
They say the Bishop and Northumberland
Are fifty thousand strong.

Warwick. It cannot be, my lord;
Rumor does double, like the voice and echo,
The numbers of the feared. Please it your grace
To go to bed. Upon my soul, my lord,
The powers that you already have sent forth
Shall bring this prize in very easily.
To comfort you the more, I have received
A certain instance that Glendower is dead.
Your majesty has been this fortnight ill,
And these unseasoned hours perforce must add
Unto your sickness.

King. I will take your counsel.

And were these inward wars once out of hand,
We would, dear lords, unto the Holy Land.

[*Exit All*]

[*Gloucestershire. Before Justice Shallow's house*]

[*Enter Shallow and Silence; filing in come Moldy,
Shadow, Wart, Feeble, Bullcalf, a Servant*]

Shallow. Come on, come on, come on, sir; give me your hand, sir,
give me your hand, sir. An early stirrer, by the rood! And how
does my good cousin Silence?

Silence. Good morrow, good cousin Shallow.

Shallow. And how does my cousin, your bedfellow? And your fairest
daughter and mine, my god-daughter Ellen?

Silence. Alas, a black ousel, cousin Shallow!

Shallow. By yea and nay, sir, I dare say my cousin William is become
a good scholar. He is at Oxford still, is he not?

Silence. Indeed, sir, to my cost.

Shallow. A' must, then, to the inns o' court shortly. I was once of
Clement's Inn, where I think they will talk of mad Shallow yet.

Silence. You were called "lusty Shallow" then, cousin.

Shallow. By the mass, I was called anything; and I would have
done anything indeed too, and roundly too. There was I, and
little John Doit of Staffordshire, and black George Barnes, and
Francis Pickbone, and Will Squele, a Cotswold man; you had
not four such swinge-bucklers in all the inns o' court again. And
I may say to you, we knew where the bona-robas were and had
the best of them all at commandment. Then was Jack Falstaff,
now Sir John, boy, and page to Thomas Mowbray, Duke of
Norfolk.

Silence. This Sir John, cousin, that comes here anon about soldiers?

Shallow. The same Sir John, the very same. I see him break Skogan's
head at the court-gate, when a' was a crack not thus high. and
the very same day did I fight with one Sampson Stockfish, a
fruiterer, behind Gray's Inn. Jesu, Jesu, the mad days that I have
spent! And to see how many of my old acquaintance are dead!

Silence. We shall all follow, cousin.

Shallow. Certain, 'tis certain; very sure, very sure. death, as the
Psalmist says, is certain to all; all shall die. How a good yoke of
bullocks at Stamford fair?

Silence. By my troth, I was not there.

Shallow. Death is certain. Is old Double of your town living yet?

Silence. Dead, sir.

Shallow. Jesu, Jesu, dead! A' drew a good bow; and dead! A' shot a fine shoot. John a Gaunt loved him well, and betted much money on his head. Dead! A' would have clapped in the clout at twelve score; and carried you a forehand shaft a fourteen and fourteen and a half, that it would have done a man's heart good to see. How a score of ewes now?

Silence. Thereafter as they be. a score of good ewes may be worth ten pounds.

Shallow. And is old Double dead?

Silence. Here come two of Sir John Falstaff's men, as I think.

[*Enter Bardolph, and another*]

Bardolph. Good morrow, honest gentlemen. I beseech you, which is Justice Shallow?

Shallow. I am Robert Shallow, sir; a poor esquire of this county, and one of the King's justices of the peace. what is your good pleasure with me?

Bardolph. My captain, sir, commends him to you; my captain, Sir John Falstaff, a tall gentleman, by heaven, and a most gallant leader.

Shallow. He greets me well, sir. I knew him a good backsword man. How does the good knight? May I ask how my lady his wife does?

Bardolph. Sir, pardon; a soldier is better accommodated than with a wife.

Shallow. It is well said, in faith, sir; and it is well said indeed too. Better accommodated! It is good; yea, indeed, is it. Good phrases are surely, and ever were, very commendable. Accommodated! it comes of "accommodo." Very good; a good phrase.

Bardolph. Pardon me, sir; I have heard the word. Phrase call you it? By this day, I know not the phrase; but I will maintain the word with my sword to be a soldier-like word, and a word of exceeding good command, by heaven. Accommodated; that is, when a man is, as they say, accommodated; or when a man is, being, whereby a' may be thought to be accommodated; which is an excellent thing.

Shallow. It is very just.

[*Enter Falstaff*]

Look, here comes good Sir John. Give me your good hand,
give me your worship's good hand. By my troth, you like well
and bear your years very well. Welcome, good Sir John.

Falstaff. I am glad to see you well, good Master Robert Shallow.
Master Surecard, as I think?

Shallow. No, Sir John; it is my cousin Silence, in commission with
me.

Falstaff. Good Master Silence, it well befits you should be of the
peace.

Silence. Your good worship is welcome.

Falstaff. Fie! this is hot weather, gentlemen. Have you provided me
here half a dozen sufficient men?

Shallow. Well, have we, sir. Will you sit?

Falstaff. Let me see them, I beseech you.

Shallow. Where's the roll? where's the roll? where's the roll? Let me
see, let me see, let me see. So, so, so, so, so, so, so. yea, well, sir.
Ralph Moldy! Let them appear as I call; let them do so, let them
do so. Let me see; where is Moldy?

Moldy. Here, if it please you.

Shallow. What think you, Sir John? a good-limbed fellow; young,
strong, and of good friends.

Falstaff. Is your name Moldy?

Moldy. Yea, if it please you.

Falstaff. 'Tis the more time you were used.

Shallow. Ha, ha, ha! most excellent, i' faith! things that are moldy
lack use. very singular good! Indeed, well said, Sir John, very
well said.

Falstaff. Prick him.

Moldy. I was pricked well enough before, if you could have let
me alone. My old dame will be undone now for one to do her
husbandry and her drudgery. You need not to have pricked me;
there are other men fitter to go out than I.

Falstaff. Go to. Peace, Moldy; you shall go. Moldy, it is time you
were spent.

Moldy. Spent!

Shallow. Peace, fellow, peace; stand aside. Know you where you are?
For the other, Sir John. Let me see. Simon Shadow!

Falstaff. Yea, indeed, let me have him to sit under. He's like to be a cold soldier.

Shallow. Where's Shadow?

Shadow. Here, sir.

Falstaff. Shadow, whose son are you?

Shadow. My mother's son, sir.

Falstaff. Your mother's son! Like enough; and your father's shadow. So the son of the female is the shadow of the male. It is often so indeed; but much of the father's substance!

Shallow. Do you like him, Sir John?

Falstaff. Shadow will serve for summer; prick him; for we have a number of shadows to fill up the muster-book.

Shallow. Thomas Wart!

Falstaff. Where's he?

Wart. Here, sir.

Falstaff. Is your name Wart?

Wart. Yea, sir.

Falstaff. You are a very ragged Wart.

Shallow. Shall I prick him down, Sir John?

Falstaff. It were superfluous; for his apparel is built upon his back and the whole frame stands upon pins. Prick him no more.

Shallow. Ha, ha, ha! You can do it, sir; you can do it. I commend you well. Francis Feeble!

Feeble. Here, sir.

Falstaff. What trade are you, Feeble?

Feeble. A woman's tailor, sir.

Shallow. Shall I prick him, sir?

Falstaff. You may. but if he had been a man's tailor, he'd ha' pricked you. Will you make as many holes in an enemy's battle as you have done in a woman's petticoat?

Feeble. I will do my good will, sir; you can have no more.

Falstaff. Well said, good woman's tailor! Well said, courageous Feeble! You will be as valiant as the wrathful dove or most magnanimous mouse. Prick the woman's tailor. Well, Master Shallow, deep, Master Shallow.

Feeble. I would Wart might have gone, sir.

Falstaff. I would you were a man's tailor, that you might mend him and make him fit to go. I cannot put him to a private soldier that is the leader of so many thousands; let that suffice, most forcible Feeble.

Feeble. It shall suffice, sir.

Falstaff. I am bound to you, reverend Feeble. Who is next?

Shallow. Peter Bullcalf on the green!

Falstaff. Yea, well, let's see Bullcalf.

Bullcalf. Here, sir.

Falstaff. Before God, a likely fellow! Come, prick me Bullcalf till he roar again.

Bullcalf. O Lord! Good my lord captain—

Falstaff. What, do you roar before you are pricked?

Bullcalf. O Lord, sir! I am a diseased man.

Falstaff. What disease have you?

Bullcalf. A whoreson cold, sir, a cough, sir, which I caught with ringing in the King's affairs upon his coronation-day, sir.

Falstaff. Come, you shall go to the wars in a gown; we will have away your cold; and I will take such order that your friends shall ring for you. Is here all?

Shallow. Here is two more called than your number; you must have but four here, sir; and so, I pray you, go in with me to dinner.

Falstaff. Come, I will go drink with you, but I cannot tarry dinner. I am glad to see you, by my troth, Master Shallow.

Shallow. O, Sir John, do you remember since we lay all night in the windmill in Saint George's field?

Falstaff. No more of that, Master Shallow, no more of that.

Shallow. Ha, 'twas a merry night. And is Jane Nightwork alive?

Falstaff. She lives, Master Shallow.

Shallow. She never could away with me.

Falstaff. Never, never; she would always say she could not abide Master Shallow.

Shallow. By the mass, I could anger her to the heart. She was then a bona-roba. Does she hold her own well?

Falstaff. Old, old, Master Shallow.

Shallow. Nay, she must be old; she cannot choose but be old; certain she's old; and had Robin Nightwork by old Nightwork before I came to Clement's Inn.

Silence. That's fifty-five year ago.

Shallow. Ha, cousin Silence, that you had seen that that this knight and I have seen! Ha, Sir John, said I well?

Falstaff. We have heard the chimes at midnight, Master Shallow.

Shallow. That we have, that we have, that we have; in faith, Sir John, we have. our watchword was "Hem boys!" Come, let's to dinner; come, let's to dinner. Jesus, the days that we have seen! Come, come.

[*Exit Falstaff and the Justices*]

Bullcalf. Good Master Corporate Bardolph, stand my friend; and here's four Harry ten shillings in French crowns for you. In very truth, sir, I had as lief be hanged, sir, as go. And yet, for my own part, sir, I do not care; but rather, because I am unwilling, and, for my own part, have a desire to stay with my friends; else, sir, I did not care, for my own part, so much.

Bardolph. Go to; stand aside.

Moldy. And, good master corporal captain, for my old dame's sake, stand my friend. She has nobody to do anything about her when I am gone; and she is old, and cannot help herself. You shall have forty, sir.

Bardolph. Go to; stand aside.

Feeble. By my troth, I care not; a man can die but once; we owe God a death. I'll never bear a base mind. if it be my destiny, so; if it be not, so. no man's too good to serve his Prince; and let it go which way it will, he that dies this year is quit for the next.

Bardolph. Well said; you're a good fellow.

Feeble. Faith, I'll bear no base mind.

[*Re-enter Falstaff and the Justices*]

Falstaff. Come, sir, which men shall I have?

Shallow. Four of which you please.

Bardolph. Sir, a word with you. I have three pound to free Moldy and Bullcalf.

Falstaff. Go to; well.

Shallow. Come, Sir John, which four will you have?

Falstaff. Do you choose for me.

Shallow. Well, then, Moldy, Bullcalf, Feeble, and Shadow.

Falstaff. Moldy and Bullcalf. For you, Moldy, stay at home till you are past service; and for your part, Bullcalf, grow till you come unto it. I will none of you.

Shallow. Sir John, Sir John, do not yourself wrong. they are your likeliest men, and I would have you served with the best.

Falstaff. Will you tell me, Master Shallow, how to choose a man? Care I for the limb, the thews, the stature, bulk, and big assemblance of a man! Give me the spirit, Master Shallow. Here's Wart; you see what a ragged appearance it is. A' shall charge you and discharge you with the motion of a pewterer's hammer, come off and on swifter than he that gibbets on the brewer's bucket. And this same half-faced fellow, Shadow; give me this man. He presents no mark to the enemy; the foeman may with as great aim level at the edge of a penknife. And for a retreat; how swiftly will this Feeble the woman's tailor run off! O, give me the spare men, and spare me the great ones. Put me a caliver into Wart's hand, Bardolph.

Bardolph. Hold, Wart, traverse; thus, thus, thus.

Falstaff. Come, manage me your caliver. So. Very well. go to. Very good, exceeding good. O, give me always a little, lean, old, chapped, bald shot. Well said, indeed, Wart; you're a good scab. Hold, there's a tester for you.

Shallow. He is not his craft's master; he does not do it right. I remember at Mile-end Green, when I lay at Clement's Inn—I was then Sir Dagonet in Arthur's show—there was a little quiver fellow, and a' would manage you his piece thus; and a' would about and about, and come you in and come you in. "Rah, tah, tah," would a' say; "bounce" would a' say; and away again would a' go, and again would 'a come. I shall never see such a fellow.

Falstaff. These fellows will do well. Master Shallow, God keep you, Master Silence. I will not use many words with you. Fare you well, gentlemen both. I thank you. I must a dozen mile tonight. Bardolph, give the soldiers coats.

Shallow. Sir John, the Lord bless you! God prosper your affairs! God send us peace! At your return visit our house; let our old acquaintance be renewed. peradventure I will with you to the court.

Falstaff. Before God, I would you would.

Shallow. Go to; I have spoke at a word. God keep you.

Falstaff. Fare you well, gentle gentlemen.

[Exit Justices]

On, Bardolph; lead the men away.

[Exit Bardolph and Recruits]

As I return, I will fetch off these justices. I do see the bottom of Justice Shallow. Lord, Lord, how subject we old men are to this vice of lying! This same starved justice has done nothing but prate to me of the wildness of his youth, and the feats he has done about Turnbull Street; and every third word a lie, duly paid to the hearer than the Turk's tribute. I do remember him at Clement's Inn like a man made after supper of a cheese-paring. when a' was naked, he was, for all the world, like a forked radish, with a head fantastically carved upon it with a knife. A' was so forlorn, that his dimensions to any thick sight were invincible. A' was the very genius of famine; yet lecherous as a monkey, and the whores called him mandrake. A' came ever in the rearward of the fashion, and sung those tunes to the overscutched huswifes that he heard the carmen whistle, and swear they were his fancies or his good-nights. And now is this vice's dagger become a squire, and talks as familiarly of John a Gaunt as if he had been sworn brother to him; and I'll be sworn a' never saw him but once in the Tilt-yard; and then he burst his head for crowding among the marshal's men. I saw it, and told John a Gaunt he beat his own name; for you might have thrust him and all his apparel into an eel-skin; the case of a treble oboe was a mansion for him, a court. and now has he land and beefs. Well, I'll be acquainted with him, if I return; and it shall go hard but I'll make him a philosopher's two stones to me. If the young dace be a bait for the old pike, I see no reason in the law of nature but I may snap at him. Let time shape, and there an end.

[Exit Falstaff]

Act Four

1

[*Yorkshire. Gaultree Forest*]

[*Enter the Archbishop of York, Mowbray, Hastings, and others*]

Archbishop. What is this forest called?

Hastings. 'Tis Gaultree Forest, if it shall please your grace.

Archbishop. Here stand, my lords; and send discoverers forth
To know the numbers of our enemies.

Hastings. We have sent forth already.

Archbishop. 'Tis well done.
My friends and brethren in these great affairs,
I must acquaint you that I have received
New-dated letters from Northumberland;
Their cold intent, tenor and substance, thus.
Here does he wish his person, with such powers
As might hold sortance with his quality,
The which he could not levy; whereupon
He is retired, to ripe his growing fortunes,
To Scotland. And concludes in hearty prayers
That your attempts may overlive the hazard
And fearful meeting of their opposite.

Mowbray. Thus do the hopes we have in him touch ground
And dash themselves to pieces.

[*Enter a Messenger*]

Hastings. Now, what news?

Messenger. West of this forest, scarcely off a mile,
In goodly form comes on the enemy;
And, by the ground they hide, I judge their number
Upon or near the rate of thirty thousand.

Mowbray. The just proportion that we gave them out.
Let us sway on and face them in the field.

152

Archbishop. What well-appointed leader fronts us here?

[*Enter Westmoreland*]

Mowbray. I think it is my Lord of Westmoreland.

Westmoreland. Health and fair greeting from our general,
  The Prince, Lord John and Duke of Lancaster.

Archbishop. Say on, my Lord of Westmoreland, in peace.
  What does concern your coming?

Westmoreland. Then, my lord,
  Unto your grace do I in chief address
  The substance of my speech. If that rebellion
  Came like itself, in base and abject routs,
  Led on by bloody youth, guarded with rags,
  And countenanced by boys and beggary,
  I say, if damned commotion so appeared,
  In his true, native, and most proper shape,
  You, reverend father, and these noble lords
  Had not been here, to dress the ugly form
  Of base and bloody insurrection
  With your fair honors. You, Lord Archbishop,
  Whose see is by a civil peace maintained,
  Whose beard the silver hand of peace has touched,
  Whose learning and good letters peace has tutored,
  Whose white investments figure innocence,
  The dove and very blessed spirit of peace,
  Wherefore you do so ill translate yourself
  Out of the speech of peace that bears such grace,
  Into the harsh and boisterous tongue of war;
  Turning your books to graves, your ink to blood,
  Your pens to lances and your tongue divine
  To a loud trumpet and a point of war?

Archbishop. Wherefore do I this? So the question stands.
  Briefly to this end. We are all diseased,
  And with our surfeiting and wanton hours
  Have brought ourselves into a burning fever,
  And we must bleed for it; of which disease
  Our late King, Richard, being infected, died.
  But, my most noble Lord of Westmoreland,
  I take not on me here as a physician,
  Nor do I as an enemy to peace
  Troop in the throngs of military men;
  But rather show awhile like fearful war,

To diet rank minds sick of happiness,
And purge the obstructions which begin to stop
Our very veins of life. Hear me more plainly.
I have in equal balance justly weighed
What wrongs our arms may do, what wrongs we suffer,
And find our griefs heavier than our offenses.
We see which way the stream of time does run,
And are enforced from our most quiet there
By the rough torrent of occasion;
And have the summary of all our griefs,
When time shall serve, to show in articles;
Which long before this we offered to the King,
And might by no suit gain our audience.
When we are wronged and would unfold our griefs,
We are denied access unto his person
Even by those men that most have done us wrong.
The dangers of the days but newly gone,
Whose memory is written on the earth
With yet appearing blood, and the examples
Of every minute's instance, present now,
Has put us in these ill-beseeming arms,
Not to break peace or any branch of it,
But to establish here a peace indeed,
Concurring, both in name and quality.

Westmoreland. When ever yet was your appeal denied?
Wherein have you been galled by the King?
What peer has been suborned to grate on you,
That you should seal this lawless bloody book
Of forged rebellion with a seal divine
And consecrate commotion's bitter edge?

Archbishop. My brother general, the commonwealth,
To brother born an household cruelty,
I make my quarrel in particular.

Westmoreland. There is no need of any such redress;
Or if there were, it not belongs to you.

Mowbray. Why not to him in part, and to us all
That feel the bruises of the days before,
And suffer the condition of these times
To lay a heavy and unequal hand
Upon our honors?

Westmoreland. O, my good Lord Mowbray,

Construe the times to their necessities,
And you shall say indeed, it is the time,
And not the King, that does you injuries.
Yet for your part, it not appears to me
Either from the King or in the present time
That you should have an inch of any ground
To build a grief on. Were you not restored
To all the Duke of Norfolk's signories,
Your noble and right well remembered father's?

Mowbray. What thing, in honor, had my father lost,
That need to be revived and breathed in me?
The King that loved him, as the state stood then,
Was force perforce compelled to banish him.
And then that Henry Bolingbroke and he,
Being mounted and both roused in their seats,
Their neighing coursers daring of the spur,
Their armed staves in charge, their beavers down,
Their eyes of fire sparkling through sights of steel,
And the loud trumpet blowing them together,
Then, then, when there was nothing could have stayed
My father from the breast of Bolingbroke,
O, when the King did throw his warder down,
His own life hung upon the staff he threw;
Then threw he down himself and all their lives
That by indictment and by dint of sword
Have since miscarried under Bolingbroke.

Westmoreland. You speak, Lord Mowbray, now you know not what.
The Earl of Hereford was reputed then
In England the most valiant gentleman.
Who knows on whom fortune would then have smiled?
But if your father had been victor there,
He never had borne it out of Coventry.
For all the country in a general voice
Cried hate upon him; and all their prayers and love
Were set on Hereford, whom they doted on
And blessed and graced indeed, more than the King.
But this is mere digression from my purpose.
Here come I from our princely general
To know your griefs; to tell you from his grace
That he will give you audience; and wherein
It shall appear that your demands are just,
You shall enjoy them, everything set off

That might so much as think you enemies.

Mowbray. But he has forced us to compel this offer;
And it proceeds from policy, not love.

Westmoreland. Mowbray, you overween to take it so;
This offer comes from mercy, not from fear.
For, lo! within a ken our army lies,
Upon my honor, all too confident
To give admittance to a thought of fear.
Our battle is more full of names than yours,
Our men more perfect in the use of arms,
Our armor all as strong, our cause the best;
Then reason will our hearts should be as good.
Say you not then our offer is compelled.

Mowbray. Well, by my will we shall admit no parley.

Westmoreland. That argues but the shame of your offense.
A rotten case abides no handling.

Hastings. Has the Prince John a full commission,
In very ample virtue of his father,
To hear and absolutely to determine
Of what conditions we shall stand upon?

Westmoreland. That is intended in the general's name.
I muse you make so slight a question.

Archbishop. Then take, my Lord of Westmoreland, this schedule,
For this contains our general grievances.
Each several article herein redressed,
All members of our cause, both here and hence,
That are insinewed to this action,
Acquitted by a true substantial form
And present execution of our wills
To us and to our purposes confined,
We come within our awful banks again
And knit our powers to the arm of peace.

Westmoreland. This will I show the general. Please you, lords,
In sight of both our battles we may meet;
And either end in peace, which God so frame!
Or to the place of difference call the swords
Which must decide it.

Archbishop. My lord, we will do so.

[*Exit Westmoreland*]

Mowbray. There is a thing within my bosom tells me

That no conditions of our peace can stand.

Hastings. Fear you not that. if we can make our peace
    Upon such large terms and so absolute
    As our conditions shall consist upon,
    Our peace shall stand as firm as rocky mountains.

Mowbray. Yea, but our valuation shall be such
    That every slight and false-derived cause,
    Yea, every idle, nice and wanton reason
    Shall to the King taste of this action;
    That, were our royal faiths martyrs in love,
    We shall be winnowed with so rough a wind
    That even our corn shall seem as light as chaff
    And good from bad find no partition.

Archbishop. No, no, my lord. Note this; the King is weary
    Of dainty and such picking grievances.
    For he has found to end one doubt by death
    Revives two greater in the heirs of life,
    And therefore will he wipe his tables clean
    And keep no tell-tale to his memory
    That may repeat and history his loss
    To new remembrance; for full well he knows
    He cannot so precisely weed this land
    As his misdoubts present occasion.
    His foes are so enrooted with his friends
    That, plucking to unfix an enemy,
    He does unfasten so and shake a friend.
    So that this land, like an offensive wife
    That has enraged him on to offer strokes,
    As he is striking, holds his infant up
    And hangs resolved correction in the arm
    That was upreared to execution.

Hastings. Besides, the King has wasted all his rods
    On late offenders, that he now does lack
    The very instruments of chastisement.
    So that his power, like to a fangless lion,
    May offer, but not hold.

Archbishop. 'Tis very true.
    And therefore be assured, my good Lord Marshal,
    If we do now make our atonement well,
    Our peace will, like a broken limb united,
    Grow stronger for the breaking.

Mowbray. Be it so.
Here is returned my Lord of Westmoreland.

[*Re-enter Westmoreland*]

Westmoreland. The Prince is here at hand. pleases your lordship
To meet his grace just distance between our armies.

Mowbray. Your grace of York, in God's name then, set forward.

Archbishop. Before, and greet his grace. My lord, we come.

[*Exit All*]

[*Another part of the forest*]

[*Enter on one side, Mowbray with attendants; a bit later
the Archbishop, Hastings, and others*]

[*On the other side, enter Prince John of Lancaster,
Westmoreland,Officers, and others*]

Lancaster. You are well encountered here, my cousin Mowbray.
Good day to you, gentle lord Archbishop;
And so to you, Lord Hastings, and to all.
My Lord of York, it better showed with you
When that your flock, assembled by the bell,
Encircled you to hear with reverence
Your exposition on the holy text
Than now to see you here an iron man,
Cheering a rout of rebels with your drum,
Turning the word to sword and life to death.
That man that sits within a monarch's heart,
And ripens in the sunshine of his favor,
Would he abuse the countenance of the King,
Alack, what mischiefs might he set abroach
In shadow of such greatness! With you, Lord Bishop,
It is even so. Who has not heard it spoken
How deep you were within the books of God?
To us the speaker in his parliament;
To us the imagined voice of God himself;
The very opener and intelligencer
Between the grace, the sanctities of heaven
And our dull workings. O, who shall believe
But you misuse the reverence of your place,
Employ the countenance and grace of heaven,
As a false favorite does his Prince's name,
In deeds dishonorable? You have taken up,
Under the counterfeited zeal of God,
The subjects of his substitute, my father,
And both against the peace of heaven and him
Have here up-swarmed them.
Archbishop. Good my Lord of Lancaster,
I am not here against your father's peace;
But, as I told my Lord of Westmoreland,

The time misordered does, in common sense,
Crowd us and crush us to this monstrous form
To hold our safety up. I sent your grace
The parcels and particulars of our grief,
The which has been with scorn shoved from the court,
Whereon this Hydra son of war is born;
Whose dangerous eyes may well be charmed asleep
With grant of our most just and right desires,
And true obedience, of this madness cured,
Stoop tamely to the foot of majesty.

Mowbray. If not, we ready are to try our fortunes
To the last man.

Hastings. And though we here fall down,
We have supplies to second our attempt.
If they miscarry, theirs shall second them;
And so success of mischief shall be born
And heir from heir shall hold this quarrel up
While England shall have generation.

Lancaster. You are too shallow, Hastings, much to shallow,
To sound the bottom of the after-times.

Westmoreland. Please your grace to answer them directly
How far forth you do like their articles.

Lancaster. I like them all, and do allow them well,
And swear here, by the honor of my blood,
My father's purposes have been mistook,
And some about him have too lavishly
Wrested his meaning and authority.
My lord, these griefs shall be with speed redressed;
Upon my soul, they shall. If this may please you,
Discharge your powers unto their several counties,
As we will ours; and here between the armies
Let's drink together friendly and embrace,
That all their eyes may bear those tokens home
Of our restored love and amity.

Archbishop. I take your Princely word for these redresses.

Lancaster. I give it you, and will maintain my word.
And thereupon I drink unto your grace.

Hastings. Go, captain, and deliver to the army
This news of peace. let them have pay, and part.
I know it will please them. Hie you, captain.

[Exit Officer]

Archbishop. To you, my noble Lord of Westmoreland.

Westmoreland. I pledge your grace; and, if you knew what pains
I have bestowed to breed this present peace,
You would drink freely. but my love to you
Shall show itself more openly hereafter.

Archbishop. I do not doubt you.

Westmoreland. I am glad of it.
Health to my lord and gentle cousin, Mowbray.

Mowbray. You wish me health in very happy season,
For I am, on the sudden, something ill.

Archbishop. Against ill chances men are ever merry;
But heaviness foreruns the good event.

Westmoreland. Therefore be merry, coz; since sudden sorrow
Serves to say thus, "Some good thing comes tomorrow."

Archbishop. Believe me, I am passing light in spirit.

Mowbray. So much the worse, if your own rule be true.

[Shouts within]

Lancaster. The word of peace is rendered. hark, how they shout!

Mowbray. This had been cheerful after victory.

Archbishop. A peace is of the nature of a conquest;
For then both parties nobly are subdued,
And neither party loser.

Lancaster. Go, my lord.
And let our army be discharged too.

[Exit Westmoreland]

And, good my lord, so please you, let our trains
March by us, that we may peruse the men
We should have coped withal.

Archbishop. Go, good Lord Hastings,
And, before they be dismissed, let them march by.

[Exit Hastings]

Lancaster. I trust, lords, we shall lie tonight together.

[Re-enter Westmoreland]

Now, cousin, wherefore stands our army still?

Westmoreland. The leaders, having charge from you to stand,

Will not go off until they hear you speak.

Lancaster. They know their duties.

[*Re-enter Hastings*]

Hastings. My lord, our army is dispersed already.
Like youthful steers unyoked, they take their courses
East, west, north, south; or, like a school broke up,
Each hurries toward his home and sporting-place.

Westmoreland. Good tidings, my Lord Hastings; for the which
I do arrest you, traitor, of high treason.
And you, lord archbishop, and you, Lord Mowbray,
Of capital treason I attach you both.

Mowbray. Is this proceeding just and honorable?

Westmoreland. Is your assembly so?

Archbishop. Will you thus break your faith?

Lancaster. I pawned you none.
I promised you redress of these same grievances
Whereof you did complain; which, by my honor,
I will perform with a most Christian care.
But for you, rebels, look to taste the due
Meet for rebellion and such acts as yours.
Most shallowly did you these arms commence,
Fondly brought here and foolishly sent hence.
Strike up our drums, pursue the scattered stray.
God, and not we, has safely fought today.
Some guard these traitors to the block of death,
Treason's true bed and yielder up of breath.

[*Exit All*]

[*Another part of the forest*]

[*Alarum. Excursions*]

[*Enter Falstaff and Colevile, meeting*]

Falstaff. What's your name, sir? Of what condition are you, and of
what place, I pray?

Colevile. I am a knight sir; and my name is Colevile of the Dale.

Falstaff. Well, then, Colevile is your name, a knight is your degree,
and your place the dale. Colevile shall be still your name, a
traitor your degree, and the dungeon your place, a place deep
enough; so shall you be still Colevile of the dale.

Colevile. Are not you Sir John Falstaff?

Falstaff. As good a man as he, sir, whoever I am. Do you yield, sir?
or shall I sweat for you? If I do sweat, they are the drops of your
lovers, and they weep for your death. Therefore rouse up fear
and trembling, and do observance to my mercy.

Colevile. I think you are Sir John Falstaff, and in that thought yield
me.

Falstaff. I have a whole school of tongues in this belly of mine,
and not a tongue of them all speaks any other word but my
name. If I had but a belly of any indifferency, I were simply the
most active fellow in Europe. My womb, my womb, my womb
undoes me. Here comes our general.

[*Enter Prince John of Lancaster, Westmoreland, Blunt,
and others*]

Lancaster. The heat is past; follow no further now.
Call in the powers, good cousin Westmoreland.

[*Exit Westmoreland*]

Now, Falstaff, where have you been all this while?
When everything is ended, then you come.
These tardy tricks of yours will, on my life,
One time or other break some gallows' back.

Falstaff. I would be sorry, my lord, but it should be thus. I never
knew yet but rebuke and check was the reward of valor. Do you
think me a swallow, an arrow, or a bullet? Have I, in my poor
and old motion, the expedition of thought? I have speeded here

with the very extremest inch of possibility; I have foundered nine score and odd posts. And here, travel-tainted as I am, have, in my pure and immaculate valor, taken Sir John Colevile of the dale, a most furious knight and valorous enemy. But what of that? He saw me, and yielded; that I may justly say, with the hook-nosed fellow of Rome, "I came, saw, and overcame."

Lancaster. It was more of his courtesy than your deserving.

Falstaff. I know not. here he is, and here I yield him. And I beseech your grace, let it be booked with the rest of this day's deeds; or, by the Lord, I will have it in a particular ballad else, with my own picture on the top on it, Colevile kissing my foot. to the which course if I be enforced, if you do not all show like gilt twopences to me, and I in the clear sky of fame overshine you as much as the full moon does the cinders of the element, which show like pins' heads to her, believe not the word of the noble. Therefore let me have right, and let desert mount.

Lancaster. Yours is too heavy to mount.

Falstaff. Let it shine, then.

Lancaster. Yours is too thick to shine.

Falstaff. Let it do something, my good lord, that may do me good, and call it what you will.

Lancaster. Is your name Colevile?

Colevile. It is, my lord.

Lancaster. A famous rebel are you, Colevile.

Falstaff. And a famous true subject took him.

Colevile. I am, my lord, but as my betters are
That led me here. Had they been ruled by me,
You should have won them dearer than you have.

Falstaff. I know not how they sold themselves. but you, like a kind fellow, gave yourself away gratis; and I thank you for you.

[*Re-enter Westmoreland*]

Lancaster. Now, have you left pursuit?

Westmoreland. Retreat is made and execution stayed.

Lancaster. Send Colevile with his confederates
To York, to present execution.
Blunt, lead him hence; and see you guard him sure.

[*Exit Blunt and others with Colevile*]

And now dispatch we toward the court, my lords.

I hear the King my father is sore sick.
Our news shall go before us to his majesty,
Which, cousin, you shall bear to comfort him,
And we with sober speed will follow you.

Falstaff. My lord, I beseech you, give me leave to go through
Gloucestershire. and, when you come to court, stand my good
lord, pray, in your good report.

Lancaster. Fare you well, Falstaff. I, in my condition,
Shall better speak of you than you deserve.

[Exit all but Falstaff]

Falstaff. I would you had but the wit. 'twere better than your
dukedom. Good faith, this same young sober-blooded boy does
not love me; nor a man cannot make him laugh; but that's no
marvel, he drinks no wine. There's never none of these demure
boys come to any proof; for thin drink does so over-cool their
blood, and making many fish-meals, that they fall into a kind
of male green-sickness; and then, when they marry, they get
wenches. They are generally fools and cowards; which some of
us should be too, but for inflammation. A good sherry-sack has
a two-fold operation in it. It ascends me into the brain; dries me
there all the foolish and dull and crudy vapors which environ
it; makes it apprehensive, quick, forgetive, full of nimble fiery
and delectable shapes; which, delivered over to the voice, the
tongue, which is the birth, becomes excellent wit. The second
property of your excellent sherry is, the warming of the blood;
which, before cold and settled, left the liver white and pale,
which is the badge of pusillanimity and cowardice; but the
sherry warms it and makes it course from the inwards to the
parts extremes. it illumines the face, which as a beacon gives
warning to all the rest of this little kingdom, man, to arm; and
then the vital commoners and inland petty spirits muster me
all to their captain, the heart, who, great and puffed up with
this retinue, does any deed of courage; and this valor comes of
sherry. So that skill in the weapon is nothing without sack, for
that sets it a-work; and learning a mere hoard of gold kept by
a devil, till sack commences it and sets it in act and use. Hereof
comes it that Prince Harry is valiant; for the cold blood he did
naturally inherit of his father, he has, like lean, sterile and bare
land, manured, husbanded and tilled with excellent endeavor
of drinking good and good store of fertile sherry, that he is
become very hot and valiant. If I had a thousand sons, the first

humane principle I would teach them should be, to forswear thin potations and to addict themselves to sack.

[*Enter Bardolph*]

How now, Bardolph!

Bardolph. The army is discharged all and gone.

Falstaff. Let them go. I'll through Gloucestershire; and there will I visit Master Robert Shallow, Esquire. I have him already tempering between my finger and my thumb, and shortly will I seal with him. Come away.

[*Exit All*]

[*Westminster. The Jerusalem Chamber*]

[*Enter the King (carried), Princes Thomas of Clarence,
Prince Humphrey of Gloucester, Warwick, and others*]

King. Now, lords, if God does give successful end
  To this debate that bleeds at our doors,
  We will our youth lead on to higher fields
  And draw no swords but what are sanctified.
  Our navy is addressed, our power collected,
  Our substitutes in absence well invested,
  And everything lies level to our wish.
  Only, we want a little personal strength;
  And pause us, till these rebels, now afoot,
  Come underneath the yoke of government.

Warwick. Both which we doubt not but your majesty
  Shall soon enjoy.

King. Humphrey, my son of Gloucester,
  Where is the Prince your brother?

Gloucester. I think he's gone to hunt, my lord, at Windsor.

King. And how accompanied?

Gloucester. I do not know, my lord.

King. Is not his brother, Thomas of Clarence, with him?

Gloucester. No, my good lord; he is in presence here.

Clarence. What would my lord and father?

King. Nothing but well to you, Thomas of Clarence.
  How chance you are not with the Prince your brother?
  He loves you, and you do neglect him, Thomas;
  You have a better place in his affection
  Than all your brothers. Cherish it, my boy,
  And noble offices you may effect
  Of mediation, after I am dead,
  Between his greatness and your other brethren.
  Therefore omit him not; blunt not his love,
  Nor lose the good advantage of his grace
  By seeming cold or careless of his will;
  For he is gracious, if he be observed.
  He has a tear for pity and a hand
  Open as day for melting charity.

Yet notwithstanding, being incensed, he's flint;
As humorous as winter and as sudden
As flaws congealed in the spring of day.
His temper, therefore, must be well observed.
Chide him for faults, and do it reverently,
When you perceive his blood inclined to mirth;
But, being moody, give him line and scope,
Till that his passions, like a whale on ground,
Confound themselves with working. Learn this, Thomas,
And you shall prove a shelter to your friends,
A hoop of gold to bind your brothers in,
That the united vessel of their blood,
Mingled with venom of suggestion—
As, force perforce, the age will pour it in—
Shall never leak, though it do work as strong
As aconitum or rash gunpowder.

Clarence. I shall observe him with all care and love.

King. Why are you not at Windsor with him, Thomas?

Clarence. He is not there today; he dines in London.

King. And how accompanied? can you tell that?

Clarence. With Poins, and other his continual followers.

King. Most subject is the fattest soil to weeds;
And he, the noble image of my youth,
Is overspread with them. therefore my grief
Stretches itself beyond the hour of death.
The blood weeps from my heart when I do shape
In forms imaginary the unguided days
And rotten times that you shall look upon
When I am sleeping with my ancestors.
For when his headstrong riot has no curb,
When rage and hot blood are his counsellors,
When means and lavish manners meet together,
O, with what wings shall his affections fly
Towards fronting peril and opposed decay!

Warwick. My gracious lord, you look beyond him quite.
The Prince but studies his companions
Like a strange tongue, wherein, to gain the language,
'Tis needful that the most immodest word
Be looked upon and learned; which once attained,
Your highness knows, comes to no further use
But to be known and hated. So, like gross terms,

The Prince will in the perfectness of time
Cast off his followers; and their memory
Shall as a pattern or a measure live,
By which his grace must mete the lives of other,
Turning past evils to advantages.

King. 'Tis seldom when the be does leave her comb
In the dead carrion.

[*Enter Westmoreland*]

Who's here? Westmoreland?

Westmoreland. Health to my sovereign, and new happiness
Added to that that I am to deliver!
Prince John your son does kiss your grace's hand.
Mowbray, the Bishop Scroop, Hastings and all
Are brought to the correction of your law;
There is not now a rebel's sword unsheathed,
But Peace puts forth her olive every where.
The manner how this action has been borne
Here at more leisure may your highness read,
With every course in his particular.

King. O Westmoreland, you are a summer bird,
Which ever in the haunch of winter sings
The lifting up of day.

[*Enter Harcourt*]

Look, here's more news.

Harcourt. From enemies heaven keep your majesty;
And, when they stand against you, may they fall
As those that I am come to tell you of!
The Earl Northumberland and the Lord Bardolph,
With a great power of English and of Scots,
Are by the sheriff of Yorkshire overthrown.
The manner and true order of the fight
This packet, please it you, contains at large.

King. And wherefore should these good news make me sick?
Will Fortune never come with both hands full,
But write her fair words still in foulest letters?
She either gives a stomach and no food;
Such are the poor, in health; or else a feast
And takes away the stomach; such are the rich,
That have abundance and enjoy it not.
I should rejoice now at this happy news;

And now my sight fails, and my brain is giddy.
O me! come near me; now I am much ill.

Gloucester. Comfort, your majesty!

Clarence. O my royal father!

Westmoreland. My sovereign lord, cheer up yourself, look up.

Warwick. Be patient, Princes; you do know, these fits
Are with his highness very ordinary.
Stand from him, give him air; he'll straight be well.

Clarence. No, no, he cannot long hold out these pangs.
The incessant care and labor of his mind
Has wrought the mure that should confine it in
So thin that life looks through and will break out.

Gloucester. The people fear me; for they do observe
Unfathered heirs and loathly births of nature.
The seasons change their manners, as the year
Had found some months asleep, and leaped them over.

Clarence. The river has thrice flowed, no ebb between;
And the old folk, time's doting chronicles,
Say it did so a little time before
That our great-grandsire, Edward, sicked and died.

Warwick. Speak lower, Princes, for the King recovers.

Gloucester. This apoplexy will certain be his end.

King. I pray you, take me up, and bear me hence
Into some other chamber. softly, pray.

[*Exit All*]

[*Another chamber*]

[*The King on a bed. Clarence, Gloucester, Warwick, and others*]

King. Let there be no noise made, my gentle friends;
Unless some dull and favorable hand
Will whisper music to my weary spirit.

Warwick. Call for the music in the other room.

King. Set me the crown upon my pillow here.

Clarence. His eye is hollow, and he changes much.

Warwick. Less noise! less noise!

[*Enter Prince Henry*]

Prince. Who saw the Duke of Clarence?

Clarence. I am here, brother, full of heaviness.

Prince. How now! rain within doors, and none abroad!
How does the King?

Gloucester. Exceeding ill.

Prince. Heard he the good news yet? Tell it him.

Gloucester. He altered much upon the hearing it.

Prince. If he be sick with joy, he'll recover without physic.

Warwick. Not so much noise, my lords. sweet Prince, speak low;
The King your father is disposed to sleep.

Clarence. Let us withdraw into the other room.

Warwick. Will it please your grace to go along with us?

Prince. No; I will sit and watch here by the *King.*

[*Exit All but the Prince*]

Why does the crown lie there upon his pillow,
Being so troublesome a bedfellow?
O polished perturbation! golden care!
That keep the ports of slumber open wide
To many a watchful night! sleep with it now!
Yet not so sound and half so deeply sweet
As he whose brow with homely biggen bound
Snores out the watch of night. O majesty!
When you do pinch your bearer, you do sit

Like a rich armor worn in heat of day,
That scalds with safety. By his gates of breath
There lies a downy feather which stirs not.
Did he suspire, that light and weightless down
Perforce must move. My gracious lord! my father!
This sleep is sound indeed; this is a sleep
That from this golden rigol has divorced
So many English kings. Your due from me
Is tears and heavy sorrows of the blood,
Which nature, love, and filial tenderness,
Shall, O dear father, pay you plenteously.
My due from you is this imperial crown,
Which, as immediate from your place and blood,
Derives itself to me. Lo, here it sits,
Which God shall guard.
And put the world's whole strength
Into one giant arm, it shall not force
This lineal honor from me. this from you
Will I to my leave, as 'tis left to me.

[*Exit Prince Hal*]

King. Warwick! Gloucester! Clarence!

[*Re-enter Warwick, Gloucester, Clarence, and the rest*]

Clarence. Does the King call?

Warwick. What would your majesty? How fares your grace?

King. Why did you leave me here alone, my lords?

Clarence. We left the Prince my brother here, my liege,
    Who undertook to sit and watch by you.

King. The Prince of Wales! Where is he? let me see him.
    He is not here.

Warwick. This door is open; he is gone this way.

Gloucester. He came not through the chamber where we stayed.

King. Where is the crown? who took it from my pillow?

Warwick. When we withdrew, my liege, we left it here.

King. The Prince has taken it hence. go, seek him out.
    Is he so hasty that he does suppose
    My sleep my death?
    Find him, my lord of Warwick; chide him here.

[*Exit Warwick*]

This part of his conjoins with my disease,
And helps to end me. See, sons, what things you are!
How quickly nature falls into revolt
When gold becomes her object!
For this the foolish over-careful fathers
Have broke their sleep with thoughts, their brains with care,
Their bones with industry;
For this they have engrossed and piled up
The cankered heaps of strange-achieved gold;
For this they have been thoughtful to invest
Their sons with arts and martial exercises;
When, like the bee, tolling from every flower
The virtuous sweets,
Our thighs packed with wax, our mouths with honey,
We bring it to the hive, and, like the bees,
Are murdered for our pains. This bitter taste
Yields his engrossments to the ending father.

[*Re-enter Warwick*]

Now where is he that will not stay so long
Till his friend sickness has determined me?

Warwick. My lord, I found the Prince in the next room,
    Washing with kindly tears his gentle cheeks,
    With such a deep demeanour in great sorrow
    That tyranny, which never quaffed but blood,
    Would, by beholding him, have washed his knife
    With gentle eye-drops. He is coming here.

King. But wherefore did he take away the crown?

[*Re-Enter Prince Henry*]

Lo, where he comes. Come here to me, Harry.
Depart the chamber, leave us here alone.

[*Exit All Warwick and the rest*]

Prince. I never thought to hear you speak again.

King. Your wish was father, Harry, to that thought.
    I stay too long by you, I weary you.
    Do you so hunger for my empty chair
    That you will needs invest you with my honors
    Before your hour be ripe? O foolish youth!
    You seek the greatness that will overwhelm you.
    Stay but a little; for my cloud of dignity
    Is held from falling with so weak a wind

That it will quickly drop. my day is dim.
You have stolen that which after some few hours
Were yours without offense; and at my death
You have sealed up my expectation.
Your life did manifest you loved me not,
And you will have me die assured of it.
You hide a thousand daggers in your thoughts
Which you have whetted on your stony heart,
To stab at half an hour of my life.
What! can you not forbear me half an hour?
Then get you gone and dig my grave yourself,
And bid the merry bells ring to your ear
That you are crowned, not that I am dead.
Let all the tears that should bedew my hearse
Be drops of balm to sanctify your head.
Only compound me with forgotten dust;
Give that which gave you life unto the worms.
Pluck down my officers, break my decrees;
For now a time is come to mock at form.
Harry the Fifth is crowned. up, vanity!
Down, royal state! all you sage counsellors, hence!
And to the English court assemble now,
From every region, apes of idleness!
Now, neighbor confines, purge you of your scum.
Have you a ruffian that will swear, drink, dance,
Revel the night, rob, murder, and commit
The oldest sins the newest kind of ways?
Be happy, he will trouble you no more;
England shall double gild his treble guilt,
England shall give him office, honor, might;
For the fifth Harry from curbed license plucks
The muzzle of restraint, and the wild dog
Shall flesh his tooth on every innocent.
O my poor kingdom, sick with civil blows!
When that my care could not withhold your riots,
What will you do when riot is your care?
O, you will be a wilderness again,
Peopled with wolves, your old inhabitants!

Prince. O, pardon me, my liege! but for my tears,
The moist impediments unto my speech,
I had forestalled this dear and deep rebuke
Before you with grief had spoke and I had heard

The course of it so far. There is your crown.
And He that wears the crown immortally
Long guard it yours! If I affect it more
Than as your honor and as your renown,
Let me no more from this obedience rise,
Which my most inward true and duteous spirit
Teacheth, this prostrate and exterior bending.
God witness with me, when I here came in,
And found no course of breath within your majesty,
How cold it struck my heart! If I do feign,
O, let me in my present wildness die
And never live to show the incredulous world
The noble change that I have purposed!
Coming to look on you, thinking you dead,
And dead almost, my liege, to think you were,
I spake unto this crown as having sense,
And thus upbraided it. "The care on you depending
Has fed upon the body of my father;
Therefore, you best of gold are worst of gold.
Other, less fine in carat, is more precious,
Preserving life in medicine potable;
But you, most fine, most honored, most renowned,
Have eaten your bearer up." Thus, my most royal liege,
Accusing it, I put it on my head,
To try with it, as with an enemy
That had before my face murdered my father,
The quarrel of a true inheritor.
But if it did infect my blood with joy,
Or swell my thoughts to any strain of pride;
If any rebel or vain spirit of mine
Did with the least affection of a welcome
Give entertainment to the might of it,
Let God forever keep it from my head
And make me as the poorest vassal is
That does with awe and terror kneel to it!

King. O my son,
God put it in your mind to take it hence,
That you might win the more your father's love,
Pleading so wisely in excuse of it!
Come here, Harry, sit you by my bed;
And hear, I think, the very latest counsel
That ever I shall breathe. God knows, my son,

By what by-paths and indirect crooked ways
I met this crown; and I myself know well
How troublesome it sat upon my head.
To you it shall descend with better quiet,
Better opinion, better confirmation;
For all the soil of the achievement goes
With me into the earth. It seemed in me
But as an honor snatched with boisterous hand,
And I had many living to upbraid
My gain of it by their assistances;
Which daily grew to quarrel and to bloodshed,
Wounding supposed peace. All these bold fears
You see with peril I have answered;
For all my reign has been but as a scene
Acting that argument. and now my death
Changes the mode; for what in me was purchased,
Falls upon you in a more fairer sort;
So you the garland wear successively.
Yet, though you stand more sure than I could do,
You are not firm enough, since griefs are green;
And all my friends, which you must make your friends,
Have but their stings and teeth newly taken out;
By whose fell working I was first advanced
And by whose power I well might lodge a fear
To be again displaced. Which to avoid,
I cut them off; and had a purpose now
To lead out many to the Holy Land,
Lest rest and lying still might make them look
Too near unto my state. Therefore, my Harry,
Be it your course to busy giddy minds
With foreign quarrels; that action, hence borne out,
May waste the memory of the former days.
More would I, but my lungs are wasted so
That strength of speech is utterly denied me.
How I came by the crown, O God, forgive;
And grant it may with you in true peace live!

Prince. My gracious liege,
  You won it, wore it, kept it, gave it me;
  Then plain and right must my possession be.
  Which I with more than with a common pain
  Against all the world will rightfully maintain.

  [*Enter Lord John of Lancaster*]

King. Look, look, here comes my John of Lancaster.

Lancaster. Health, peace, and happiness to my royal father!

King. You bring me happiness and peace, son John;
    But health, alack, with youthful wings is flown
    From this bare withered trunk. Upon your sight
    My worldly business makes a period.
    Where is my Lord of Warwick?

Prince. My Lord of Warwick!

        [Re-enter Warwick, and others]

King. Does any name particular belong
    Unto the lodging where I first did swoon?

Warwick. 'Tis called Jerusalem, my noble lord.

King. Laud be to God! even there my life must end.
    It has been prophesied to me many years,
    I should not die but in Jerusalem;
    Which vainly I supposed the Holy Land.
    But bear me to that chamber; there I'll lie;
    In that Jerusalem shall Harry die.

        [Exit All]

Act Five

[*Gloucestershire. Shallow's house*]

[*Enter Shallow, Falstaff, Bardolph, and Page*]

Shallow. By cock and pie, sir, you shall not away tonight. What, Davy, I say!

Falstaff. You must excuse me, Master Robert Shallow.

Shallow. I will not excuse you; you shall not be excused; excuses shall not be admitted; there is no excuse shall serve; you shall not be excused. Why, Davy!

[*Enter Davy*]

Davy. Here, sir.

Shallow. Davy, Davy, Davy, Davy, let me see, Davy; let me see, Davy; let me see. yea, well, William cook, bid him come here. Sir John, you shall not be excused.

Davy. Well, sir, thus; those precepts cannot be served; and, again, sir, shall we sow the headland with wheat?

Shallow. With red wheat, Davy. But for William cook. are there no young pigeons?

Davy. Yes, sir. Here is now the smith's note for shoeing and plough-irons.

Shallow. Let it be cast and paid. Sir John, you shall not be excused.

Davy. Now, sir, a new link to the bucket must needs be had. and, sir, do you mean to stop any of William's wages, about the sack he lost the other day at Hinckley fair?

Shallow. A' shall answer it. Some pigeons, Davy, a couple of short-legged hens, a joint of mutton, and any pretty little tiny kickshaws, tell William cook.

Davy. Does the man of war stay all night, sir?

Shallow. Yea, Davy. I will use him well. a friend in the court is better than a penny in purse. Use his men well, Davy; for they are arrant knaves, and will backbite.

Davy. No worse than they are backbitten, sir; for they have marvellous foul linen.

Shallow. Well conceited, Davy. About your business, Davy.

Davy. I beseech you, sir, to countenance William Visor of Woncot against Clement Perkes of the hill.

Shallow. There is many complaints, Davy, against that Visor. that Visor is an arrant knave, on my knowledge.

Davy. I grant your worship that he is a knave, sir; but yet, God forbid, sir, but a knave should have some countenance at his friend's request. An honest man, sir, is able to speak for himself, when a knave is not. I have served your worship truly, sir, this eight years; and if I cannot once or twice in a quarter bear out a knave against an honest man, I have but a very little credit with your worship. The knave is my honest friend, sir; therefore, I beseech your worship, let him be countenanced.

Shallow. Go to; I say he shall have no wrong. Look about, Davy.

[*Exit Davy*]

Where are you, Sir John? Come, come, come, off with your boots. Give me your hand, Master Bardolph.

Bardolph. I am glad to see your worship.

Shallow. I thank you with all my heart, kind Master Bardolph. And welcome, my tall fellow.

[*to the Page*] Come, Sir John.

Falstaff. I'll follow you, good Master Robert Shallow.

[*Exit Shallow*]

Bardolph, look to our horses.

[*Exit Bardolph and Page*]

If I were sawed into quantities, I should make four dozen of such bearded hermits' staves as Master Shallow. It is a wonderful thing to see the semblable coherence of his men's spirits and his. they, by observing of him, do bear themselves like foolish justices. He, by conversing with them, is turned into a justice-like serving-man. Their spirits are so married in conjunction with the participation of society that they flock together in consent, like so many wild geese. If I had a suit to Master Shallow, I would humor his men with the imputation of being near their master. If to his men, I would curry with Master Shallow that no man could better command his servants. It is certain that either wise bearing or ignorant carriage is caught, as men take diseases, one of another. therefore let men take heed of their company. I will devise matter enough out of this Shallow to keep Prince Harry in continual laughter the wearing out of six fashions, which is four terms, or two actions; and a' shall laugh without intervallums. O, it is much that a lie with a slight oath and a jest with a sad brow will do with a fellow that never had the ache in his shoulders! O, you shall see him laugh till his face be like a wet cloak ill laid up!

Shallow. [*Within*] Sir John!

Falstaff. I come, Master Shallow; I come, Master Shallow.

[*Exit Falstaff*]

Westminster. The palace.

[*Enter Warwick and the Lord Chief Justice, meeting*]

Warwick. How now, my Lord Chief Justice! Where away?

Chief Justice. How does the King?

Warwick. Exceeding well; his cares are now all ended.

Chief Justice. I hope, not dead.

Warwick. He's walked the way of nature;
    And to our purposes he lives no more.

Chief Justice. I would his Majesty had called me with him.
    The service that I truly did his life
    Has left me open to all injuries.

Warwick. Indeed I think the young King loves you not.

Chief Justice. I know he does not, and do arm myself
    To welcome the condition of the time,
    Which cannot look more hideously upon me
    Than I have drawn it in my fantasy.

[*Enter Lancaster, Clarence, Gloucester, Westmoreland,
        and others*]

Warwick. Here comes the heavy issue of dead Harry.
    O that the living Harry had the temper
    Of him, the worst of these three gentlemen!
    How many nobles then should hold their places,
    That must strike sail to spirits of vile sort!

Chief Justice. O God, I fear all will be overturned!

Lancaster. Good morrow, cousin Warwick, good morrow.

Gloucester and Clarence. Good morrow, cousin.

Lancaster. We meet like men that had forgot to speak.

Warwick. We do remember; but our argument
    Is all too heavy to admit much talk.

Lancaster. Well, peace be with him that has made us heavy!

Chief Justice. Peace be with us, lest we be heavier!

Gloucester. O, good my lord, you have lost a friend indeed;
    And I dare swear you borrow not that face
    Of seeming sorrow, it is sure your own.

Lancaster. Though no man be assured what grace to find,
You stand in coldest expectation.
I am the sorrier; would 'twere otherwise.

Clarence. Well, you must now speak Sir John Falstaff fair;
Which swims against your stream of quality.

Chief Justice. Sweet Princes, what I did, I did in honor,
Led by the impartial conduct of my soul;
And never shall you see that I will beg
A ragged and forestalled remission.
If truth and upright innocency fail me,
I'll to the King my master that is dead,
And tell him who has sent me after him.

Warwick. Here comes the Prince.

[*Enter King Henry the Fifth with attendants*]

Chief Justice. Good morrow; and God save your majesty!

King Harry. This new and gorgeous garment, majesty,
Sits not so easy on me as you think.
Brothers, you mix your sadness with some fear.
This is the English, not the Turkish court;
Not Amurath if Amurath succeeds,
But Harry Harry. Yet be sad, good brothers,
For, by my faith, it very well becomes you.
Sorrow so royally in you appears
That I will deeply put the fashion on
And wear it in my heart. Why then, be sad;
But entertain no more of it, good brothers,
Than a joint burden laid upon us all.
For me, by heaven, I bid you be assured,
I'll be your father and your brother too;
Let me but bear your love, I'll bear your cares.
Yet weep that Harry's dead, and so will I;
But Harry lives, that shall convert those tears
By number into hours of happiness.

Princes. We hope no otherwise from your majesty.

King Harry. You all look strangely on me. and you most;
You are, I think, assured I love you not.

Chief Justice. I am assured, if I be measured rightly,
Your majesty has no just cause to hate me.

King Harry. No!
How might a Prince of my great hopes forget

So great indignities you laid upon me?
What! Rate, rebuke, and roughly send to prison
The immediate heir of England! Was this easy?
May this be washed in Lethe, and forgotten?

Chief Justice. I then did use the person of your father;
The image of his power lay then in me;
And, in the administration of his law,
While I was busy for the commonwealth,
Your highness pleased to forget my place,
The majesty and power of law and justice,
The image of the King whom I presented,
And struck me in my very seat of judgment;
Whereon, as an offender to your father,
I gave bold way to my authority
And did commit you. If the deed were ill,
Be you contented, wearing now the garland,
To have a son set your decrees at nought,
To pluck down justice from your awful bench,
To trip the course of law and blunt the sword
That guards the peace and safety of your person;
Nay, more, to spurn at your most royal image,
And mock your workings in a second body.
Question your royal thoughts, make the case yours;
Be now the father and propose a son,
Hear your own dignity so much profaned,
See your most dreadful laws so loosely slighted,
Behold yourself so by a son disdained;
And then imagine me taking your part
And in your power soft silencing your son.
After this cold considerance, sentence me;
And, as you are a King, speak in your state
What I have done that misbecame my place,
My person, or my liege's sovereignty.

King Harry. You are right, justice, and you weigh this well;
Therefore still bear the balance and the sword.
And I do wish your honors may increase,
Till you do live to see a son of mine
Offend you and obey you, as I did.
So shall I live to speak my father's words.
"Happy am I, that have a man so bold,
That dares do justice on my proper son;
And not less happy, having such a son,

That would deliver up his greatness so
Into the hands of justice." You did commit me.
For which I do commit into your hand
The unstained sword that you have used to bear;
With this remembrance, that you use the same
With the like bold, just and impartial spirit
As you have done against me. There is my hand.
You shall be as a father to my youth.
My voice shall sound as you do prompt my ear,
And I will stoop and humble my intents
To your well-practiced wise directions.
And, princes all, believe me, I beseech you;
My father is gone wild into his grave,
For in his tomb lie my affections;
And with his spirit sadly I survive,
To mock the expectation of the world,
To frustrate prophecies and to raze out
Rotten opinion, who has writ me down
After my seeming. The tide of blood in me
Has proudly flowed in vanity till now.
Now does it turn and ebb back to the sea,
Where it shall mingle with the state of floods,
And flow henceforth in formal majesty.
Now call we our high court of parliament.
And let us choose such limbs of noble counsel,
That the great body of our state may go
In equal rank with the best governed nation;
That war, or peace, or both at once, may be
As things acquainted and familiar to us;
In which you, father, shall have foremost hand.
Our coronation done, we will accite,
As I before remembered, all our state.
And, God consigning to my good intents,
No Prince nor peer shall have just cause to say,
God shorten Harry's happy life one day!

[*Exit All*]

184

[*Gloucestershire. Shallow's orchard*]

[*Enter Falstaff, Shallow, Silence, Davy, Bardolph, and the Page*]

Shallow. Nay, you shall see my orchard, where, in an arbor, we will eat a last year's pippin of my own graffing, with a dish of caraways, and so forth. Come, cousin Silence. and then to bed.

Falstaff. Before God, you have here a goodly dwelling and a rich.

Shallow. Barren, barren, barren; beggars all, beggars all, Sir John. Well, good air. Spread, Davy; spread, Davy. Well said, Davy.

Falstaff. This Davy serves you for good uses; he is your serving-man and your husband.

Shallow. A good varlet, a good varlet, a very good varlet, Sir John. By the mass, I have drunk too much sack at supper. A good varlet. Now sit down, now sit down. Come, cousin.

Silence. Ah, sirrah! quoth I, we shall do nothing but eat, and make good cheer,
[*Singing*]
> And praise God for the merry year;
> When flesh is cheap and females dear,
> And lusty lads roam here and there
> So merrily,
> And ever among so merrily.

Falstaff. There's a merry heart! Good Master Silence, I'll give you a health for that anon.

Shallow. Give Master Bardolph some wine, Davy.

Davy. Sweet sir, sit; I'll be with you anon; most sweet sir, sit. Master page, good master page, sit. Proface! What you want in meat, we'll have in drink. But you must bear; the heart's all.

[*Exit Davy*]

Shallow. Be merry, Master Bardolph; and, my little soldier there, be merry.

Silence. Be merry, be merry, my wife has all.
[*Singing*]
> For women are shrews, both short and tall;
> 'Tis merry in hall when beards wag all;
> And welcome merry Shrove-tide.

Be merry, be merry.

Falstaff. I did not think Master Silence had been a man of this
mettle.

Silence. Who, I? I have been merry twice and once before now.

[*Re-enter Davy*]

Davy. [*To Bardolph*] There's a dish of leather-coats for you.

Shallow. Davy!

Davy. Your worship! I'll be with you straight
[*To Bardolph*] A cup of wine, sir?

Silence. A cup of wine that's brisk and fine,
[*Singing*]
> And drink unto the leman mine;
> And a merry heart lives long-a.

Falstaff. Well said, Master Silence.

Silence. If we shall be merry, now comes in the sweet of the night.

Falstaff. Health and long life to you, Master Silence!

Silence. Fill the cup, and let it come,
[*Singing*]
> I'll pledge you a mile to the bottom.

Shallow. Honest Bardolph, welcome. if you want anything and will
not call, beshrew your heart.

[*to the Page*] Welcome, my little tiny thief and welcome indeed
too. I'll drink to Master Bardolph, and to all the cavaleros about
London.

Davy. I hope to see London once before I die.

Bardolph. If I might see you there, Davy—

Shallow. By the mass, you'll crack a quart together, ha! Will you
not, Master Bardolph?

Bardolph. Yea, sir, in a pottle-pot.

Shallow. By God's liggens, I thank you. the knave will stick by you, I
can assure you that. A' will not out; he is true bred.

Bardolph. And I'll stick by him, sir.

Shallow. Why, there spoke a King. Lack nothing. be merry.

[*Knocking within*]

Look who's at door there, ho! Who knocks?

[*Exit Davy*]

Falstaff. [*To Silence, seeing him drinking*] Why, now you have done
me right.

Silence. Do me right,
[*Singing*]
                    And dub me knight.
                    Samingo.
Is it not so?

Falstaff. 'Tis so.

Silence. Is it so? Why then, say an old man can do somewhat.

[*Re-enter Davy*]

Davy. If it please your worship, there's one Pistol come from the
court with news.

Falstaff. From the court? Let him come in.

[*Enter Pistol*]

How now, Pistol!

Pistol. Sir John, God save you!

Falstaff. What wind blew you here, Pistol?

Pistol. Not the ill wind which blows no man to good. Sweet knight,
you are now one of the greatest men in this realm.

Silence. By'r lady, I think a' be, but goodman Puff of Barson.

Pistol. Puff!
Puff in your teeth, most recreant coward base!
Sir John, I am your Pistol and your friend,
And helter-skelter have I rode to you,
And tidings do I bring and lucky joys
And golden times and happy news of price.

Falstaff. I pray you now, deliver them like a man of this world.

Pistol. A foutre for the world and worldlings base!
I speak of Africa and golden joys.

Falstaff. O base Assyrian knight, what is your news?
Let King Cophetua know the truth thereof.

Silence. [*Singing*] And Robin Hood, Scarlet, and John.

Pistol. Shall dunghill curs confront the Helicons?
And shall good news be baffled?
Then, Pistol, lay your head in Furies' lap.

Shallow. Honest gentleman, I know not your breeding.

Pistol. Why then, lament therefore.

Shallow. Give me pardon, sir. if, sir, you come with news from the court, I take it there's but two ways, either to utter them, or conceal them. I am, sir, under the King, in some authority.

Pistol. Under which King, Besonian? speak, or die.

Shallow. Under King Harry.

Pistol. Harry the Fourth? or Fifth?

Shallow. Harry the Fourth.

Pistol. A foutre for your office!
Sir John, your tender lambkin now is King;
Harry the Fifth's the man. I speak the truth.
When Pistol lies, do this; and fig me, like
The bragging Spaniard.

Falstaff. What, is the old King dead?

Pistol. As nail in door. the things I speak are just.

Falstaff. Away, Bardolph! Saddle my horse. Master Robert Shallow, choose what office you will in the land, 'tis yours. Pistol, I will double-charge you with dignities.

Bardolph. O joyful day! I would not take a knighthood for my fortune.

Pistol. What! I do bring good news.

Falstaff. Carry Master Silence to bed. Master Shallow, my Lord Shallow—be what you will; I am fortune's steward—get on your boots. We'll ride all night. O sweet Pistol! Away, Bardolph!

[*Exit Bardolph*]

Come, Pistol, utter more to me; and withal devise something to do yourself good. Boot, boot, Master Shallow. I know the young King is sick for me. Let us take any man's horses; the laws of England are at my commandment. Blessed are they that have been my friends; and woe to my Lord Chief Justice!

Pistol. Let vultures vile seize on his lungs also!
"Where is the life that late I led?" say they.
Why, here it is; welcome these pleasant days!

[*Exit All*]

London. A street.

[*Enter Beadles, dragging in Hostess Quickly and Doll Tearsheet*]

Hostess. No, you arrant knave; I would to God that I might die, that I might have you hanged. you have drawn my shoulder out of joint.

First Beadle. The constables have delivered her over to me; and she shall have whipping-cheer enough, I warrant her. there has been a man or two lately killed about her.

Doll Tearsheet. Nut-hook, nut-hook, you lie. Come on; I'll tell you what, you damned tripe-visaged rascal, if the child I now go with do miscarry, you were better you had struck your mother, you paper-faced villain.

Hostess. O the Lord, that Sir John were come! He would make this a bloody day to somebody. But I pray God the fruit of her womb miscarry!

First Beadle. If it do, you shall have a dozen of cushions again; you have but eleven now. Come, I charge you both go with me; for the man is dead that you and Pistol beat among you.

Doll Tearsheet. I'll tell you what, you thin man in a censer, I will have you as soundly swinged for this—you blue-bottle rogue, you filthy famished correctioner, if you be not swinged, I'll forswear half-kirtles.

First Beadle. Come, come, you she knight-errant, come.

Hostess. O God, that right should thus overcome might! Well, of sufferance comes ease.

Doll Tearsheet. Come, you rogue, come; bring me to a justice.

Hostess. Ay, come, you starved blood-hound.

Doll Tearsheet. Goodman death, goodman bones!

Hostess. You atomy, you!

Doll Tearsheet. Come, you thin thing; come, you rascal!

First Beadle. Very well.

[*Exit All*]

[*A public street near Westminster Abbey*]

[*Enter two Grooms, strewing rushes*]

First Groom. More rushes, more rushes.

Second Groom. The trumpets have sounded twice.

First Groom. 'Twill be two o'clock before they come from the coronation. dispatch, dispatch.

[*Exit Grooms*]

[*Enter Falstaff, Shallow, Pistol, Bardolph, and Page*]

Falstaff. Stand here by me, Master Robert Shallow; I will make the King do you grace. I will leer upon him as a' comes by; and do but mark the countenance that he will give me.

Pistol. God bless your lungs, good knight!

Falstaff. Come here, Pistol; stand behind me. O, if I had had to have made new liveries, I would have bestowed the thousand pound I borrowed of you. But 'tis no matter; this poor show does better. This does infer the zeal I had to see him.

Shallow. It does so.

Falstaff. It shows my earnestness of affection—

Shallow. It does so.

Falstaff. My devotion—

Shallow. It does, it does, it does.

Falstaff. As it were, to ride day and night; and not to deliberate, not to remember, not to have patience to shift me—

Shallow. It is best, certain.

Falstaff. But to stand stained with travel, and sweating with desire to see him; thinking of nothing else, putting all affairs else in oblivion, as if there were nothing else to be done but to see him.

Pistol. 'Tis "semper idem," for "obsque hoc nihil est." 'Tis all in every part.

Shallow. 'Tis so, indeed.

Pistol. My knight, I will inflame your noble liver,
And make you rage.
Your Doll, and Helen of your noble thoughts,
Is in base durance and contagious prison;

Haled there
By most mechanical and dirty hand.
Rouse up revenge from ebon den with fell Alecto's snake,
For Doll is in. Pistol speaks nought but truth.

Falstaff. I will deliver her.

[*Shouts, within, and the trumpets sound*]

Pistol. There roared the sea, and trumpet-clangor sounds.

[*Enter King Harry, his retinue, and the Lord Chief Justice*]

Falstaff. God save your grace, King Hal; my royal Hal!

Pistol. The heavens you guard and keep, most royal imp of fame!

Falstaff. God save you, my sweet boy!

King. My Lord Chief Justice, speak to that vain man.

Chief Justice. Have you your wits? Know you what 'tis you speak?

Falstaff. My King! my Jove! I speak to you, my heart!

King. I know you not, old man. fall to your prayers;
How ill white hairs become a fool and jester!
I have long dreamed of such a kind of man,
So surfeit-swelled, so old, and so profane;
But, being awaked, I do despise my dream.
Make less your body hence, and more your grace;
Leave gormandizing; know the grave does gape
For you thrice wider than for other men.
Reply not to me with a fool-born jest.
Presume not that I am the thing I was;
For God does know, so shall the world perceive,
That I have turned away my former self;
So will I those that kept me company.
When you do hear I am as I have been,
Approach me, and you shall be as you were,
The tutor and the feeder of my riots.
Till then, I banish you, on pain of death,
As I have done the rest of my misleaders,
Not to come near our person by ten mile.
For competence of life I will allow you,
That lack of means enforce you not to evils.
And, as we hear you do reform yourselves,
We will, according to your strengths and qualities,
Give you advancement. Be it your charge, my lord,
To see performed the tenor of our word.

Set on.

[*Exit King and his court*]

Falstaff. Master Shallow, I owe you a thousand pounds.

Shallow. Yea, indeed, Sir John; which I beseech you to let me have home with me.

Falstaff. That can hardly be, Master Shallow. Do not you grieve at this; I shall be sent for in private to him. Look you, he must seem thus to the world. Fear not your advancements; I will be the man yet that shall make you great.

Shallow. I cannot perceive how, unless you give me your doublet and stuff me out with straw. I beseech you, good Sir John, let me have five hundred of my thousand.

Falstaff. Sir, I will be as good as my word. This that you heard was but a color.

Shallow. A color that I fear you will die in, Sir John.

Falstaff. Fear no colors. go with me to dinner. Come, Lieutenant Pistol; come, Bardolph. I shall be sent for soon at night.

[Re-enter Prince John, the Lord Chief Justice and Officers]

Chief Justice. Go, carry Sir John Falstaff to the Fleet.
    Take all his company along with him.

Falstaff. My lord, my lord—

Chief Justice. I cannot now speak. I will hear you soon.
    Take them away.

Pistol. Si fortuna me tormenta, spero me contenta.

[Exit all except Prince John and the Lord Chief Justice]

Lancaster. I like this fair proceeding of the King's.
    He has intent his wonted followers
    Shall all be very well provided for;
    But all are banished till their conversations
    Appear more wise and modest to the world.

Chief Justice. And so they are.

Lancaster. The King has called his parliament, my lord.

Chief Justice. He has.

Lancaster. I will lay odds that, before this year expire,
    We bear our civil swords and native fire
    As far as France. I heard a bird so sing,

Whose music, to my thinking, pleased the King.
Come, will you hence?

[*Exit All*]

Spoken by a Dancer.

First my fear; then my courtesy; last my speech. My fear is, your displeasure; my courtesy, my duty; and my speech, to beg your pardons. If you look for a good speech now, you undo me. For what I have to say is of my own making; and what indeed I should say will, I doubt, prove my own marring. But to the purpose, and so to the venture. Be it known to you, as it is very well, I was lately here in the end of a displeasing play, to pray your patience for it and to promise you a better. I meant indeed to pay you with this; which, if like an ill venture it come unluckily home, I break, and you, my gentle creditors, lose. Here I promised you I would be and here I commit my body to your mercies. Bate me some and I will pay you some and, as most debtors do, promise you infinitely. If my tongue cannot entreat you to acquit me, will you command me to use my legs? And yet that were but light payment, to dance out of your debt. But a good conscience will make any possible satisfaction, and so would I. All the gentlewomen here have forgiven me. if the gentlemen will not, then the gentlemen do not agree with the gentlewomen, which was never seen before in such an assembly. One word more, I beseech you. If you be not too much cloyed with fat meat, our humble author will continue the story, with Sir John in it, and make you merry with fair Katharine of France. where, for anything I know, Falstaff shall die of a sweat, unless already a' be killed with your hard opinions; for Oldcastle died a martyr, and this is not the man. My tongue is weary; when my legs are too, I will bid you good night. And so kneel down before you; but, indeed, to pray for the queen.

The End

Henry IV, Part One

Henry IV, Part Two

The Merry Wives of Windsor

Henry V

Act One

1

[*Windsor. In front of Page's house*]

[*Enter Justice Shallow, Slender, and Sir Hugh Evans*]

Shallow. Sir Hugh, persuade me not; I will make a Star Chamber matter of it; if he were twenty Sir John Falstaffs, he shall not abuse Robert Shallow, Esquire.

Slender. In the county of Gloucester, Justice of Peace, and Coram.

Shallow. Aye, cousin Slender, and Custalorum.

Slender. Aye, and Ratolorum too; and a gentleman born, Master Parson, who writes himself "Armigero" in any bill, warrant, quittance, or obligation— "Armigero."

Shallow. Aye, that I do; and have done any time these three hundred years.

Slender. All his successors, gone before him, has done it; and all his ancestors, that come after him, may: they may give the dozen white luces in their coat.

Shallow. It is an old coat.

Evans. The dozen white louses do become an old coat well; it agrees well, passant; it is a familiar beast to man, and signifies love.

Shallow. The luce is the fresh fish; the salt fish is an old coat.

Slender. I may quarter, coz.

Shallow. You may, by marrying.

Evans. It is marring indeed, if he quarter it.

Shallow. Not a whit.

Evans. Yes, py'r lady! If he has a quarter of your coat, there is but three skirts for yourself, in my simple conjectures; but that is all one. If Sir John Falstaff have committed disparagements unto you, I am of the church, and will be glad to do my benevolence, to make atonements and compremises between you.

Shallow. The Council shall hear it; it is a riot.

Evans. It is not meet the Council hear a riot; there is no fear of Got in a riot; the Council, look you, shall desire to hear the fear of Got, and not to hear a riot; take your vizaments in that.

Shallow. Ha! of my life, if I were young again, the sword should end it.

Evans. It is petter that friends is the sword and end it; and there is also another device in my prain, which peradventure prings goot discretions with it. There is Anne Page, which is daughter to Master George Page, which is pretty virginity.

Slender. Mistress Anne Page? She has brown hair, and speaks small like a woman.

Evans. It is that fery person for all the orld, as just as you will desire; and seven hundred pounds of moneys, and gold, and silver, is her grandsire upon his death's-bed—Got deliver to a joyful resurrections!—give, when she is able to overtake seventeen years old. It were a goot motion if we leave our pribbles and prabbles, and desire a marriage between Master Abraham and Mistress Anne Page.

Shallow. Did her grandsire leave her seven hundred pound?

Evans. Aye, and her father is make her a petter penny.

Shallow. I know the young gentlewoman; she has good gifts.

Evans. Seven hundred pounds, and possibilities, is goot gifts.

Shallow. Well, let us see honest Master Page. Is Falstaff there?

Evans. Shall I tell you a lie? I do despise a liar as I do despise one that is false; or as I despise one that is not true. The knight Sir John is there; and, I beseech you, be ruled by your well-willers. I will peat the door for Master Page.

[*Knocks*]

What, hoa! Got pless your house here!

Page. [*Within*] Who's there?

[*Enter Page*]

Evans. Here is Got's plessing, and your friend, and Justice
Shallow; and here young Master Slender, that peradventures shall tell you another tale, if matters grow to your likings.

Page. I am glad to see your worships well. I thank you for my venison, Master Shallow.

Shallow. Master Page, I am glad to see you; much good do it your good heart! I wished your venison better; it was ill killed. How does good Mistress Page?—and I thank you always with my heart, la! with my heart.

Page. Sir, I thank you.

Shallow. Sir, I thank you; by yea and no, I do.

Page. I am glad to see you, good Master Slender.

Slender. How does your fallow greyhound, sir? I heard say he was outrun on Cotsall.

Page. It could not be judged, sir.

Slender. You'll not confess, you'll not confess.

Shallow. That he will not. 'Tis your fault; 'tis your fault; 'tis a good dog.

Page. A cur, sir.

Shallow. Sir, he's a good dog, and a fair dog. Can there be more said? He is good, and fair. Is Sir John Falstaff here?

Page. Sir, he is within; and I would I could do a good office between you.

Evans. It is spoke as a Christians ought to speak.

Shallow. He has wronged me, Master Page.

Page. Sir, he does in some sort confess it.

Shallow. If it be confessed, it is not redressed; is not that so, Master Page? He has wronged me; indeed he has; at a word, he has, believe me; Robert Shallow, Esquire, says he is wronged.

Page. Here comes Sir John.

[*Enter Sir John Falstaff, Bardolph, Nym, and Pistol*]

Falstaff. Now, Master Shallow, you'll complain of me to the King?

Shallow. Knight, you have beaten my men, killed my deer, and broke open my lodge.

Falstaff. But not kissed your keeper's daughter.

Shallow. Tut, a pin! this shall be answered.

Falstaff. I will answer it straight: I have done all this. That is now answered.

Shallow. The Council shall know this.

Falstaff. 'Twere better for you if it were known in counsel: you'll be laughed at.

Evans. *Pauca verba*, Sir John; goot worts.

200

Falstaff. Good worts! good cabbage! Slender, I broke your head; what matter have you against me?

Slender. Marry, sir, I have matter in my head against you; and against your cony-catching rascals, Bardolph, Nym, and Pistol. They carried me to the tavern, and made me drunk, and afterwards picked my pocket.

Bardolph. You Banbury cheese!

Slender. Aye, it is no matter.

Pistol. How now, Mephostophilus!

Slender. Aye, it is no matter.

Nym. Slice, I say! *pauca, pauca;* slice! That's my humor.

Slender. Where's Simple, my man? Can you tell, cousin?

Evans. Peace, I pray you. Now let us understand. There is three umpires in this matter, as I understand: that is, Master Page, *fidelicet* Master Page; and there is myself, *fidelicet* myself; and the three party is, lastly and finally, my host of the Garter.

Page. We three to hear it and end it between them.

Evans. Fery goot. I will make a prief of it in my note-book; and we will afterwards ork upon the cause with as great discreetly as we can.

Falstaff. Pistol!

Pistol. He hears with ears.

Evans. The tevil and his tam! What phrase is this, "He hears with ear"? Why, it is affectations.

Falstaff. Pistol, did you pick Master Slender's purse?

Slender. Aye, by these gloves, did he—or I would I might never come in my own great chamber again else!—of seven groats in mill-sixpences, and two Edward shovel-boards that cost me two shilling and two pence apiece of Yead Miller, by these gloves.

Falstaff. Is this true, Pistol?

Evans. No, it is false, if it is a pick-purse.

Pistol. Ha, you mountain-foreigner! Sir John and master mine, I combat challenge of this latten bilbo. Word of denial in your labras here! Word of denial! Froth and scum, you lie.

Slender. By these gloves, then, 'twas he.

Nym. Be avised, sir, and pass good humors; I will say "marry trap" with you, if you run the nuthook's humor on me; that is the very note of it.

Slender. By this hat, then, he in the red face had it; for though I cannot remember what I did when you made me drunk, yet I am not altogether an ass.

Falstaff. What say you, Scarlet and John?

Bardolph. Why, sir, for my part, I say the gentleman had drunk himself out of his five sentences.

Evans. It is his five senses; fie, what the ignorance is!

Bardolph. And being fap, sir, was, as they say, cashiered; and so conclusions passed the careers.

Slender. Aye, you spake in Latin then too; but 'tis no matter; I'll never be drunk while I live again, but in honest, civil, godly company, for this trick. If I be drunk, I'll be drunk with those that have the fear of God, and not with drunken knaves.

Evans. So Got udge me, that is a virtuous mind.

Falstaff. You hear all these matters denied, gentlemen; you hear it.

[*Enter Mistress Anne Page, Mistress Ford and Mistress Page*]

Page. Nay, daughter, carry the wine in; we'll drink within.

[*Exit Anne Page*]

Slender. O heaven! this is Mistress Anne Page.

Page. How now, Mistress Ford!

Falstaff. Mistress Ford, by my troth, you are very well met; by your leave, good mistress. [*Kisses her*]

Page. Wife, bid these gentlemen welcome. Come, we have a hot venison pasty to dinner; come, gentlemen, I hope we shall drink down all unkindness.

[*Exit all but Shallow, Slender, and Evans*]

Slender. I had rather than forty shillings I had my *Book of Songs and Sonnets* here.

[*Enter Simple*]

How, Simple! Where have you been? I must wait on myself, must I? You have not the *Book of Riddles* about you, have you?

Simple. Book of Riddles! Why, did you not lend it to Alice Shortcake upon Allhallowmas last, a fortnight afore Michaelmas?

Shallow. Come, coz; come, coz; we stay for you. A word with you, coz; marry, this, coz: there is, as 'twere, a tender, a kind of tender, made afar off by Sir Hugh here. Do you understand me?

Slender. Aye, sir, you shall find me reasonable; if it be so, I shall do that that is reason.

Shallow. Nay, but understand me.

Slender. So I do, sir.

Evans. Give ear to his motions: Master Slender, I will description the matter to you, if you be capacity of it.

Slender. Nay, I will do as my cousin Shallow says; I pray you pardon me; he's a justice of peace in his country, simple though I stand here.

Evans. But that is not the question. The question is concerning your marriage.

Shallow. Aye, there's the point, sir.

Evans. Marry is it; the very point of it; to Mistress Anne Page.

Slender. Why, if it be so, I will marry her upon any reasonable demands.

Evans. But can you affection the oman? Let us command to know that of your mouth or of your lips; for divers philosophers hold that the lips is parcel of the mouth. Therefore, precisely, can you carry your good will to the maid?

Shallow. Cousin Abraham Slender, can you love her?

Slender. I hope, sir, I will do as it shall become one that would do reason.

Evans. Nay, Got's lords and his ladies! you must speak possitable, if you can carry her your desires towards her.

Shallow. That you must. Will you, upon good dowry, marry her?

Slender. I will do a greater thing than that upon your request, cousin, in any reason.

Shallow. Nay, conceive me, conceive me, sweet coz; what I do is to pleasure you, coz. Can you love the maid?

Slender. I will marry her, sir, at your request; but if there be no great love in the beginning, yet heaven may decrease it upon better acquaintance, when we are married and have more occasion to know one another. I hope upon familiarity will grow more contempt. But if you say "marry her," I will marry her; that I am freely dissolved, and dissolutely.

Evans. It is a fery discretion answer, save the fall is in the ord "dissolutely": the ort is, according to our meaning, "resolutely";

his meaning is good.

Shallow. Aye, I think my cousin meant well.

Slender. Aye, or else I would I might be hanged, la!

[*Enter Anne Page*]

Shallow. Here comes fair Mistress Anne. Would I were young for your sake, Mistress Anne!

Anne. The dinner is on the table; my father desires your worships' company.

Shallow. I will wait on him, fair Mistress Anne!

Evans. Od's plessed will! I will not be absence at the grace.

[*Exit Shallow and Evans*]

Anne. Will it please your worship to come in, sir?

Slender. No, I thank you, forsooth, heartily; I am very well.

Anne. The dinner attends you, sir.

Slender. I am not a-hungry, I thank you, forsooth. Go, sirrah, for all you are my man, go wait upon my cousin Shallow.

[*Exit Simple*]

A justice of peace sometime may be beholding to his friend for a man. I keep but three men and a boy yet, till my mother be dead. But what though? Yet I live like a poor gentleman born.

Anne. I may not go in without your worship; they will not sit till you come.

Slender. In faith, I'll eat nothing; I thank you as much as though I did.

Anne. I pray you, sir, walk in.

Slender. I had rather walk here, I thank you. I bruised my shin the other day with playing at sword and dagger with a master of fence—three veneys for a dish of stewed prunes —and, I with my ward defending my head, he hot my shin, and, by my troth, I cannot abide the smell of hot meat since. Why do your dogs bark so? Be there bears in the town?

Anne. I think there are, sir; I heard them talked of.

Slender. I love the sport well; but I shall as soon quarrel at it as any man in England. You are afraid, if you see the bear loose, are you not?

Anne. Aye, indeed, sir.

Slender. That's meat and drink to me now. I have seen Sackerson loose twenty times, and have taken him by the chain; but I warrant you, the women have so cried and shrieked at it that it passed; but women, indeed, cannot abide 'em; they are very ill-favored rough things.

[Enter Page]

Page. Come, gentle Master Slender, come; we stay for you.

Slender. I'll eat nothing, I thank you, sir.

Page. By cock and pie, you shall not choose, sir! Come, come.

Slender. Nay, pray you lead the way.

Page. Come on, sir.

Slender. Mistress Anne, yourself shall go first.

Anne. Not I, sir; pray you keep on.

Slender. Truly, I will not go first; truly, la! I will not do you that wrong.

Anne. I pray you, sir.

Slender. I'll rather be unmannerly than troublesome. You do yourself wrong indeed, la!

[Exit]

[*In front of Page's house*]

[*Enter Sir Hugh Evans and Simple*]

Evans. Go your ways, and ask of Doctor Caius' house which is the way; and there dwells one Mistress Quickly, which is in the manner of his nurse, or his dry nurse, or his cook, or his laundry, his washer, and his wringer.

Simple. Well, sir.

Evans. Nay, it is petter yet. Give her this letter; for it is a oman that altogether's acquaintance with Mistress Anne Page; and the letter is to desire and require her to solicit your master's desires to Mistress Anne Page. I pray you be gone. I will make an end of my dinner; there's pippins and cheese to come.

[*Exit*]

[*The Garter Inn*]

[*Enter Falstaff, Host, Bardolph, Nym, Pistol, and Robin*]

Falstaff. My host of the Garter!

Host. What says my bully rook? Speak scholarly and wisely.

Falstaff. Truly, my host, I must turn away some of my followers.

Host. Discard, bully Hercules; cashier; let them wag; trot, trot.

Falstaff. I sit at ten pounds a week.

Host. You are an emperor—Caesar, Keiser, and Pheazar. I will entertain Bardolph; he shall draw, he shall tap; said I well, bully Hector?

Falstaff. Do so, good my host.

Host. I have spoke; let him follow.

[*To Bardolph*] Let me see you froth and lime. I am at a word; follow.

[*Exit Host*]

Falstaff. Bardolph, follow him. A tapster is a good trade; an old cloak makes a new jerkin; a withered serving-man a fresh tapster. Go; adieu.

Bardolph. It is a life that I have desired; I will thrive.

Pistol. O base Hungarian wight! Will you the spigot wield?

[*Exit Bardolph*]

Nym. He was gotten in drink. Is not the humor conceited?

Falstaff. I am glad I am so acquit of this tinder-box: his thefts were too open; his filching was like an unskilful singer—he kept not time.

Nym. The good humor is to steal at a minute's rest.

Pistol. "Convey" the wise it call. "Steal" foh! A fico for the phrase!

Falstaff. Well, sirs, I am almost out at heels.

Pistol. Why, then, let kibes ensue.

Falstaff. There is no remedy; I must cony-catch; I must shift.

Pistol. Young ravens must have food.

Falstaff. Which of you know Ford of this town?

Pistol. I ken the wight; he is of substance good.

Falstaff. My honest lads, I will tell you what I am about.

Pistol. Two yards, and more.

Falstaff. No quips now, Pistol. Indeed, I am in the waist two yards about; but I am now about no waste; I am about thrift. Briefly, I do mean to make love to Ford's wife; I spy entertainment in her; she discourses, she carves, she gives the leer of invitation; I can construe the action of her familiar style; and the hardest voice of her behavior, to be Englished rightly, is "I am Sir John Falstaff's."

Pistol. He has studied her well, and translated her will out of honesty into English.

Nym. The anchor is deep; will that humor pass?

Falstaff. Now, the report goes she has all the rule of her husband's purse; he has a legion of angels.

Pistol. As many devils entertain; and "To her, boy," say I.

Nym. The humor rises; it is good; humor me the angels.

Falstaff. I have writ me here a letter to her; and here another to Page's wife, who even now gave me good eyes too, examined my parts with most judicious oeillades; sometimes the beam of her view gilded my foot, sometimes my portly belly.

Pistol. Then did the sun on dunghill shine.

Nym. I thank you for that humor.

Falstaff. O, she did so course over my exteriors with such a greedy intention that the appetite of her eye did seem to scorch me up like a burning-glass! Here's another letter to her. She bears the purse too; she is a region in Guiana, all gold and bounty. I will be cheaters to them both, and they shall be exchequers to me; they shall be my East and West Indies, and I will trade to them both. Go, bear you this letter to Mistress Page; and you this to Mistress Ford. We will thrive, lads, we will thrive.

Pistol. Shall I Sir Pandarus of Troy become, And by my side wear steel? Then Lucifer take all!

Nym. I will run no base humor. Here, take the humor-letter; I will keep the havior of reputation.

Falstaff. [*To Robin*] Hold, sirrah; bear you these letters tightly; Sail like my pinnace to these golden shores. Rogues, hence, avaunt! vanish like hailstones, go; Trudge, plod away in the hoof; seek shelter, pack! Falstaff will learn the humor of the age; French thrift, you rogues; myself, and skirted page.

[*Exit Falstaff and Robin*]

Pistol. Let vultures gripe your guts! for gourd and fullam holds,
   And high and low beguiles the rich and poor; Tester I'll have in
   pouch when you shall lack, Base Phrygian Turk!

Nym. I have operations in my head which be humors of revenge.

Pistol. Will you revenge?

Nym. By welkin and her star!

Pistol. With wit or steel?

Nym. With both the humors, I. I will discuss the humor of this love
   to Page.

Pistol. And I to Ford shall eke unfold How Falstaff, varlet vile, His
   dove will prove, his gold will hold, And his soft couch defile.

Nym. My humor shall not cool; I will incense Page to deal with
   poison; I will possess him with yellowness; for the revolt of mine is
   dangerous. That is my true humor.

Pistol. You are the Mars of malcontents; I second you; troop on

   .

[*Exit*]

[*Doctor Caius's house*]

[*Enter Mistress Quickly, Simple, and Rugby*]

Quickly. What, John Rugby! I pray you go to the casement and see if you can see my master, Master Doctor Caius, coming. If he do, in faith, and find anybody in the house, here will be an old abusing of God's patience and the King's English.

Rugby. I'll go watch.

Quickly. Go; and we'll have a posset for it soon at night, in faith, at the latter end of a sea-coal fire.

[*Exit Rugby*]

An honest, willing, kind fellow, as ever servant shall come in house withal; and, I warrant you, no tell-tale nor no breed-bate; his worst fault is that he is given to prayer; he is something peevish that way; but nobody but has his fault; but let that pass. Peter Simple you say your name is?

Simple. Aye, for fault of a better.

Quickly. And Master Slender's your master?

Simple. Aye, forsooth.

Quickly. Does he not wear a great round beard, like a glover's paring-knife?

Simple. No, forsooth; he has but a little whey face, with a little yellow beard, a Cain-coloured beard.

Quickly. A softly-sprighted man, is he not?

Simple. Aye, forsooth; but he is as tall a man of his hands as any is between this and his head; he has fought with a warrener.

Quickly. How say you? O, I should remember him. Does he not hold up his head, as it were, and strut in his gait?

Simple. Yes, indeed, does he.

Quickly. Well, heaven send Anne Page no worse fortune! Tell Master Parson Evans I will do what I can for your master. Anne is a good girl, and I wish—

[*Enter Rugby*]

Rugby. Out, alas! here comes my master.

Quickly. We shall all be shent. Run in here, good young man; go into this closet.

[*Shuts Simple in the closet*]

He will not stay long. What, John Rugby! John! what, John, I say! Go, John, go inquire for my master; I doubt he be not well that he comes not home.

[*Singing*] And down, down, adown-a, etc.

[*Enter Doctor Caius*]

Caius. Vat is you sing? I do not like des toys. Pray you, go and vetch me in my closet un boitier vert-a box, a green-a box. Do intend vat I speak? A green-a box.

Quickly. Aye, forsooth, I'll fetch it you. [*Aside*] I am glad he went not in himself; if he had found the young man, he would have been horn-mad.

Caius. Fe, fe, fe fe! ma foi, il fait fort chaud. Je m'en vais a la cour—la grande affaire.

Quickly. Is it this, sir?

Caius. Oui; mette le au mon pocket: depeche, quickly. Vere is dat knave, Rugby?

Quickly. What, John Rugby? John!

Rugby. Here, sir.

Caius. You are John Rugby, and you are Jack Rugby. Come, take-a your rapier, and come after my heel to the court.

Rugby. 'Tis ready, sir, here in the porch.

Caius. By my trot, I tarry too long. Od's me! Qu'ai j'oublie? Dere is some simples in my closet dat I vill not for the varld I shall leave behind.

Quickly. Ay me, he'll find the young man there, and be mad!

Caius. O diable, diable! vat is in my closet? Villainy! larron! [*Pulling Simple out*] Rugby, my rapier!

Quickly. Good master, be content.

Caius. Wherefore shall I be content-a?

Quickly. The young man is an honest man.

Caius. What shall de honest man do in my closet? Dere is no honest man dat shall come in my closet.

Quickly. I beseech you, be not so phlegmatic; hear the truth of it. He came of an errand to me from Parson Hugh.

Caius. Vell?

Simple. Aye, forsooth, to desire her to—

Quickly. Peace, I pray you.

Caius. Peace-a your tongue. Speak-a your tale.

Simple. To desire this honest gentlewoman, your maid, to speak a good word to Mistress Anne Page for my master, in the way of marriage.

Quickly. This is all, indeed, la! but I'll never put my finger in the fire, and need not.

Caius. Sir Hugh send-a you? Rugby, baillez me some paper. Tarry you a little-a-while.

[Caius Writes]

Quickly. *[Aside to Simple]* I am glad he is so quiet; if he had been throughly moved, you should have heard him so loud and so melancholy. But notwithstanding, man, I'll do you your master what good I can; and the very yea and the no is, the French doctor, my master—I may call him my master, look you, for I keep his house; and I wash, wring, brew, bake, scour, dress meat and drink, make the beds, and do all myself—

Simple. *[Aside to Quickly]* 'Tis a great charge to come under one body's hand.

Quickly. *[Aside to Simple]* Are you avised of that? You shall find it a great charge; and to be up early and down late; but notwithstanding—to tell you in your ear, I would have no words of it—my master himself is in love with Mistress Anne Page; but notwithstanding that, I know Anne's mind—that's neither here nor there.

Caius. You jack'nape; give-a this letter to Sir Hugh; by gar, it is a shallenge; I will cut his troat in de park; and I will teach a scurvy jack-a-nape priest to meddle or make. You may be gone; it is not good you tarry here. By gar, I will cut all his two stones; by gar, he shall not have a stone to throw at his dog.

[Exit Simple]

Quickly. Alas, he speaks but for his friend.

Caius. It is no matter-a ver dat. Do not you tell-a me dat I shall have Anne Page for myself? By gar, I vill kill de Jack priest; and I have appointed my host of de Jarteer to measure our weapon. By gar, I will myself have Anne Page.

Quickly. Sir, the maid loves you, and all shall be well. We must give folks leave to prate. What the good year!

Caius. Rugby, come to the court with me. By gar, if I have not Anne Page, I shall turn your head out of my door. Follow my heels, Rugby.

[Exit Caius and Rugby]

Quickly. You shall have a fool's-head of your own. No, I know Anne's mind for that; never a woman in Windsor knows more of Anne's mind than I do; nor can do more than I do with her, I thank heaven.

Fenton. [*Within*] Who's within there? ho!

Quickly. Who's there, I trow? Come near the house, I pray you.

[Enter Fenton]

Fenton. How now, good woman, how do you?

Quickly. The better that it pleases your good worship to ask.

Fenton. What news? How does pretty Mistress Anne?

Quickly. In truth, sir, and she is pretty, and honest, and gentle; and one that is your friend, I can tell you that by the way; I praise heaven for it.

Fenton. Shall I do any good, think you? Shall I not lose my suit?

Quickly. Troth, sir, all is in His hands above; but notwithstanding, Master Fenton, I'll be sworn on a book she loves you. Have not your worship a wart above your eye?

Fenton. Yes, indeed, have I; what of that?

Quickly. Well, thereby hangs a tale; good faith, it is such another Nan; but, I detest, an honest maid as ever broke bread. We had an hour's talk of that wart; I shall never laugh but in that maid's company! But, indeed, she is given too much to allicholy and musing; but for you—well, go to.

Fenton. Well, I shall see her today. Hold, there's money for you; let me have your voice in my behalf. If you see her before me, commend me.

Quickly. Will I? In faith, that we will; and I will tell your worship more of the wart the next time we have confidence; and of other wooers.

Fenton. Well, farewell; I am in great haste now.

Quickly. Farewell to your worship.

[Exit Fenton]

Truly, an honest gentleman; but Anne loves him not; for I know Anne's mind as well as another does. Out upon it, what have I forgot?

[Exit]

Act Two

1

[*In front of Page's house*]

[*Enter Mistress Page, holding a letter*]

Mistress Page. What! have I scaped love-letters in the holiday-time
of my beauty, and am I now a subject for them? Let me see.
    [*Reads*]
    "Ask me no reason why I love you; for though Love
    use Reason for his precisian, he admits him not for
    his counsellor. You are not young, no more am I; go
    to, then, there's sympathy. You are merry, so am I; ha!
    ha! then there's more sympathy. You love sack, and so
    do I; would you desire better sympathy? Let it suffice
    you, Mistress Page at the least, if the love of soldier
    can suffice—that I love you. I will not say, Pity me:
    'tis not a soldier-like phrase; but I say, Love me. By
    me, Your own true knight, By day or night, Or any
    kind of light, With all his might, For you to fight,
    John Falstaff."

What a Herod of Jewry is this! O wicked, wicked world! One that
is well-nigh worn to pieces with age to show himself a young
gallant! What an unweighed behavior has this Flemish drunkard
picked—with the devil's name! —out of my conversation, that
he dares in this manner assay me? Why, he has not been thrice
in my company! What should I say to him? I was then frugal
of my mirth. Heaven forgive me! Why, I'll exhibit a bill in
the parliament for the putting down of men. How shall I be
revenged on him? for revenged I will be, as sure as his guts are
made of puddings.

[*Enter Mistress Ford*]

Mistress Ford. Mistress Page! trust me, I was going to your house.

Mistress Page. And, trust me, I was coming to you. You look very ill.

Mistress Ford. Nay, I'll never believe that; I have to show to the contrary.

Mistress Page. Faith, but you do, in my mind.

Mistress Ford. Well, I do, then; yet, I say, I could show you to the contrary. O Mistress Page, give me some counsel.

Mistress Page. What's the matter, woman?

Mistress Ford. O woman, if it were not for one trifling respect, I could come to such honor!

Mistress Page. Hang the trifle, woman; take the honor. What is it? Dispense with trifles; what is it?

Mistress Ford. If I would but go to hell for an eternal moment or so, I could be knighted.

Mistress Page. What? You lie. Sir Alice Ford! These knights will hack; and so you should not alter the article of your gentry.

Mistress Ford. We burn daylight. Here, read, read; perceive how I might be knighted. I shall think the worse of fat men as long as I have an eye to make difference of men's liking. And yet he would not swear; praised women's modesty, and gave such orderly and well-behaved reproof to all uncomeliness that I would have sworn his disposition would have gone to the truth of his words; but they do no more adhere and keep place together than the "Hundredth Psalm" to the tune of "Greensleeves." What tempest, I trow, threw this whale, with so many tuns of oil in his belly, ashore at Windsor? How shall I be revenged on him? I think the best way were to entertain him with hope, till the wicked fire of lust have melted him in his own grease. Did you ever hear the like?

Mistress Page. Letter for letter, but that the name of Page and Ford differs. To your great comfort in this mystery of ill opinions, here's the twin-brother of your letter; but let yours inherit first, for, I protest, mine never shall. I warrant he has a thousand of these letters, writ with blank space for different names—sure, more!—and these are of the second edition. He will print them, out of doubt; for he cares not what he puts into the press when he would put us two. I had rather be a giantess and lie under Mount Pelion. Well, I will find you twenty lascivious turtles ere one chaste man.

Mistress Ford. Why, this is the very same; the very hand, the very words. What does he think of us?

Mistress Page. Nay, I know not; it makes me almost ready to wrangle with my own honesty. I'll entertain myself like one that I am not acquainted withal; for, sure, unless he know some strain in me that I know not myself, he would never have boarded me in this fury.

Mistress Ford. "Boarding" call you it? I'll be sure to keep him above deck.

Mistress Page. So will I; if he come under my hatches, I'll never to sea again. Let's be revenged on him; let's appoint him a meeting, give him a show of comfort in his suit, and lead him on with a fine-baited delay, till he has pawned his horses to my host of the Garter.

Mistress Ford. Nay, I will consent to act any villainy against him that may not sully the chariness of our honesty. O that my husband saw this letter! It would give eternal food to his jealousy.

Mistress Page. Why, look where he comes; and my good man too; he's as far from jealousy as I am from giving him cause; and that, I hope, is an unmeasurable distance.

Mistress Ford. You are the happier woman.

Mistress Page. Let's consult together against this greasy knight. Come here.

[*They retire*]

[*Enter Ford with Pistol, and Page with Nym*]

Ford. Well, I hope it be not so.

Pistol. Hope is a curtal dog in some affairs. Sir John affects your wife.

Ford. Why, sir, my wife is not young.

Pistol. He woos both high and low, both rich and poor, Both young and old, one with another, Ford; He loves the gallimaufry. Ford, perpend.

Ford. Love my wife!

Pistol. With liver burning hot. Prevent, or go you, Like Sir Actaeon he, with Ringwood at your heels. O, odious is the name!

Ford. What name, sir?

Pistol. The horn, I say. Farewell. Take heed, have open eye, for thieves do foot by night; Take heed, ere summer comes, or cuckoo birds do sing. Away, Sir Corporal Nym. Believe it, Page; he speaks sense.

[*Exit Pistol*]

Ford. [*Aside*] I will be patient; I will find out this.

Nym. [*To Page*] And this is true; I like not the humor of lying. He has wronged me in some humors; I should have borne the humored letter to her; but I have a sword, and it shall bite upon my necessity. He loves your wife; there's the short and the long. My name is Corporal Nym; I speak, and I avouch; 'Tis true. My name is Nym, and Falstaff loves your wife. Adieu! I love not the humor of bread and cheese; and there's the humor of it. Adieu.

[*Exit Nym*]

Page. "The humor of it," quoth 'a! Here's a fellow frights English out of his wits.

Ford. I will seek out Falstaff.

Page. I never heard such a drawling, affecting rogue.

Ford. If I do find it—well.

Page. I will not believe such a Cataian though the priest of the town commended him for a true man.

Ford. 'Twas a good sensible fellow. Well.

[*Mistress Page and Mistress Ford come forward*]

Page. How now, Meg!

Mistress Page. Where go you, George? Hark you.

Mistress Ford. How now, sweet Frank, why are you melancholy?

Ford. I melancholy! I am not melancholy. Get you home; go.

Mistress Ford. Faith, you have some crotchets in your head now. Will you go, Mistress Page?

[*Enter Mistress Quickly*]

Mistress Page. Have with you. You'll come to dinner, George? [*Aside to Mistress Ford*] Look who comes yonder; she shall be our messenger to this paltry knight.

Mistress Ford. [*Aside to Mistress Page*] Trust me, I thought on her; she'll fit it.

Mistress Page. You are come to see my daughter Anne?

218

Quickly. Aye, forsooth; and, I pray, how does good Mistress Anne?

Mistress Page. Go in with us and see; we have an hour's talk with you.

[*Exit Mistress Page, Mistress Ford, and Mistress Quickly*]

Page. How now, Master Ford!

Ford. You heard what this knave told me, did you not?

Page. Yes; and you heard what the other told me?

Ford. Do you think there is truth in them?

Page. Hang 'em, slaves! I do not think the knight would offer it; but these that accuse him in his intent towards our wives are a yoke of his discarded men; very rogues, now they be out of service.

Ford. Were they his men?

Page. Truly, were they.

Ford. I like it never the better for that. Does he lie at the Garter?

Page. Aye, indeed, does he. If he should intend this voyage toward my wife, I would turn her loose to him; and what he gets more of her than sharp words, let it lie on my head.

Ford. I do not misdoubt my wife; but I would be loath to turn them together. A man may be too confident. I would have nothing lie on my head. I cannot be thus satisfied.

[*Enter Host*]

Page. Look where my ranting host of the Garter comes. There is either liquor in his pate or money in his purse when he looks so merrily. How now, my host!

Host. How now, bully rook! You are a gentleman. Cavaleiro Justice, I say.

[*Enter Shallow*]

Shallow. I follow, my host, I follow. Good even and twenty, good Master Page! Master Page, will you go with us? We have sport in hand.

Host. Tell him, Cavaleiro Justice; tell him, bully rook.

Shallow. Sir, there is a fray to be fought between Sir Hugh the Welsh priest and Caius the French doctor.

Ford. Good my host of the Garter, a word with you.

Host. What say you, my bully rook?

[*They go aside*]

Shallow. [*To Page*] Will you go with us to behold it? My merry host has had the measuring of their weapons; and, I think, has appointed them contrary places; for, believe me, I hear the parson is no jester. Hark, I will tell you what our sport shall be.

[*They converse apart*]

Host. Have you no suit against my knight, my guest-cavaleiro?

Ford. None, I protest; but I'll give you a pottle of burnt sack to give me recourse to him, and tell him my name is Brook—only for a jest.

Host. My hand, bully; you shall have egress and regress— said I well?—and your name shall be Brook. It is a merry knight. Will you go, Mynheers?

Shallow. Have with you, my host.

Page. I have heard the Frenchman has good skill in his rapier.

Shallow. Tut, sir, I could have told you more. In these times you stand on distance, your passes, stoccadoes, and I know not what. 'Tis the heart, Master Page; 'tis here, 'tis here. I have seen the time with my long sword I would have made you four tall fellows skip like rats.

Host. Here, boys, here, here! Shall we wag?

Page. Have with you. I had rather hear them scold than fight.

[*Exit all but Ford*]

Ford. Though Page be a secure fool, and stands so firmly on his wife's frailty, yet I cannot put off my opinion so easily. She was in his company at Page's house, and what they made there I know not. Well, I will look further into it, and I have a disguise to sound Falstaff. If I find her honest, I lose not my labor; if she be otherwise, 'tis labor well bestowed.

[*Exit*]

[A room in the Garter Inn]

[Enter Falstaff and Pistol]

Falstaff. I will not lend you a penny.

Pistol. I will retort the sum in equipage.

Falstaff. Not a penny.

Pistol. Why, then the world's my oyster. Which I with sword will open.

Falstaff. Not a penny. I have been content, sir, you should lay my countenance to pawn. I have grated upon my good friends for three reprieves for you and your coach-fellow, Nym; or else you had looked through the grate, like a geminy of baboons. I am damned in hell for swearing to gentlemen my friends you were good soldiers and tall fellows; and when Mistress Bridget lost the handle of her fan, I took it upon my honor you had it not.

Pistol. Did not you share? Had you not fifteen pence?

Falstaff. Reason, you rogue, reason. Think you I'll endanger my soul gratis? At a word, hang no more about me, I am no gibbet for you. Go—a short knife and a throng!— to your manor of Pickt-hatch; go. You'll not bear a letter for me, you rogue! You stand upon your honor! Why, you unconfinable baseness, it is as much as I can do to keep the terms of my honor precise. I, I, I myself sometimes, leaving the fear of God on the left hand, and hiding my honor in my necessity, am fain to shuffle, to hedge, and to lurch; and yet you, rogue, will ensconce your rags, your cat-a-mountain looks, your red-lattice phrases, and your bold-beating oaths, under the shelter of your honor! You will not do it, you!

Pistol. I do relent; what would you more of man?

[Enter Robin]

Robin. Sir, here's a woman would speak with you.

Falstaff. Let her approach.

[Enter Mistress Quickly]

Quickly. Give your worship good morrow.

Falstaff. Good morrow, good wife.

Quickly. Not so, if it please your worship.

Falstaff. Good maid, then.

Quickly. I'll be sworn; As my mother was, the first hour I was born.

Falstaff. I do believe the swearer. What with me?

Quickly. Shall I vouchsafe your worship a word or two?

Falstaff. Two thousand, fair woman; and I'll vouchsafe you the hearing.

Quickly. There is one Mistress Ford, sir—I pray, come a little nearer this ways. I myself dwell with Master Doctor Caius.

Falstaff. Well, on: Mistress Ford, you say—

Quickly. Your worship says very true. I pray your worship come a little nearer this ways.

Falstaff. I warrant you nobody hears—my own people, my own people.

Quickly. Are they so? God bless them, and make them his servants!

Falstaff. Well; Mistress Ford, what of her?

Quickly. Why, sir, she's a good creature. Lord, Lord, your worship's a wanton! Well, heaven forgive you, and all of us, I pray.

Falstaff. Mistress Ford; come, Mistress Ford—

Quickly. Well, this is the short and the long of it: you have brought her into such a canaries as 'tis wonderful. The best courtier of them all, when the court lay at Windsor, could never have brought her to such a canary. Yet there have been knights, and lords, and gentlemen, with their coaches; I warrant you, coach after coach, letter after letter, gift after gift; smelling so sweetly, all musk, and so rushling, I warrant you, in silk and gold; and in such alligant terms; and in such wine and sugar of the best and the fairest, that would have won any woman's heart; and I warrant you, they could never get an eye-wink of her. I had myself twenty angels given me this morning; but I defy all angels, in any such sort, as they say, but in the way of honesty; and, I warrant you, they could never get her so much as sip on a cup with the proudest of them all; and yet there have been earls, nay, which is more, pensioners; but, I warrant you, all is one with her.

Falstaff. But what says she to me? Be brief, my good she— Mercury.

Quickly. Well, she has received your letter; for which she thanks you a thousand times; and she gives you to notify that her husband will be absence from his house between ten and eleven.

Falstaff. Ten and eleven?

Quickly. Aye, forsooth; and then you may come and see the picture, she says, that you wot of. Master Ford, her husband, will be from home. Alas, the sweet woman leads an ill life with him! He's a very jealousy man; she leads a very frampold life with him, good heart.

Falstaff. Ten and eleven. Woman, commend me to her; I will not fail her.

Quickly. Why, you say well. But I have another messenger to your worship. Mistress Page has her hearty commendations to you too; and let me tell you in your ear, she's as fartuous a civil modest wife, and one, I tell you, that will not miss your morning nor evening prayer, as any is in Windsor, whoever be the other; and she bade me tell your worship that her husband is seldom from home, but she hopes there will come a time. I never knew a woman so dote upon a man: surely I think you have charms, la! Yes, in truth.

Falstaff. Not I, I assure you; setting the attraction of my good parts aside, I have no other charms.

Quickly. Blessing on your heart for it!

Falstaff. But, I pray you, tell me this: has Ford's wife and Page's wife acquainted each other how they love me?

Quickly. That were a jest indeed! They have not so little grace, I hope—that were a trick indeed! But Mistress Page would desire you to send her your little page of all loves. Her husband has a marvellous infection to the little page; and truly Master Page is an honest man. Never a wife in Windsor leads a better life than she does; do what she will, say what she will, take all, pay all, go to bed when she list, rise when she list, all is as she will; and truly she deserves it; for if there be a kind woman in Windsor, she is one. You must send her your page; no remedy.

Falstaff. Why, I will.

Quickly. Nay, but do so then; and, look you, he may come and go between you both; and in any case have a nay-word, that you may know one another's mind, and the boy never need to understand any thing; for 'tis not good that children should know any wickedness. Old folks, you know, have discretion, as they say, and know the world.

Falstaff. Fare you well; commend me to them both. There's my purse; I am yet your debtor. Boy, go along with this woman.

[*Exit Quickly and Robin*]

This news distracts me.

Pistol. [*Aside*] This punk is one of Cupid's carriers; Clap on more sails; pursue; up with your fights; Give fire; she is my prize, or ocean whelm them all!

[*Exit*]

Falstaff. Say you so, old Jack; go your ways; I'll make more of your old body than I have done. Will they yet look after you? Will you, after the expense of so much money, be now a gainer? Good body, I thank you. Let them say 'tis grossly done; so it be fairly done, no matter.

[*Enter Bardolph*]

Bardolph. Sir John, there's one Master Brook below would fain speak with you, and be acquainted with you; and has sent your worship a moming's draught of sack.

Falstaff. Brook is his name?

Bardolph. Aye, sir.

Falstaff. Call him in.

[*Exit Bardolph*]

Such Brooks are welcome to me, that o'erflows such liquor. Ah, ha! Mistress Ford and Mistress Page, have I encompassed you? Go to; via!

[*Enter Bardolph, with Ford disguised*]

Ford/Brook. Bless you, sir!

Falstaff. And you, sir! Would you speak with me?

Ford/Brook. I make bold to press with so little preparation upon you.

Falstaff. You're welcome. What's your will? Give us leave, drawer
  .

[*Exit Bardolph*]

Ford/Brook. Sir, I am a gentleman that has spent much; my name is Brook.

Falstaff. Good Master Brook, I desire more acquaintance of you.

Ford/Brook. Good Sir John, I sue for you—not to charge you; for I must let you understand I think myself in better plight for a lender than you are;which has something emboldened me to this unseasoned intrusion; for they say, if money go before, all ways do lie open.

Falstaff. Money is a good soldier, sir, and will on.

Ford/Brook. Truly, and I have a bag of money here troubles me; if you will help to bear it, Sir John, take all, or half, for easing me of the carriage.

Falstaff. Sir, I know not how I may deserve to be your porter.

Ford/Brook. I will tell you, sir, if you will give me the hearing.

Falstaff. Speak, good Master Brook; I shall be glad to be your servant.

Ford/Brook. Sir, I hear you are a scholar—I will be brief with you —and you have been a man long known to me, though I had never so good means as desire to make myself acquainted with you. I shall discover a thing to you, wherein I must very much lay open my own imperfection; but, good Sir John, as you have one eye upon my follies, as you hear them unfolded, turn another into the register of your own, that I may pass with a reproof the easier, since you yourself know how easy is it to be such an offender.

Falstaff. Very well, sir; proceed.

Ford/Brook. There is a gentlewoman in this town, her husband's name is Ford.

Falstaff. Well, sir.

Ford/Brook. I have long loved her, and, I protest to you, bestowed much on her; followed her with a doting observance; engrossed opportunities to meet her; feed every slight occasion that could but niggardly give me sight of her; not only bought many presents to give her, but have given largely to many to know what she would have given; briefly, I have pursued her as love has pursued me; which has been on the wing of all occasions. But whatsoever I have merited, either in my mind or in my means, meed, I am sure, I have received none, unless experience be a jewel; that I have purchased at an infinite rate, and that has taught me to say this: "Love like a shadow flies when substance love pursues; Pursuing that that flies, and flying what pursues.'

Falstaff. Have you received no promise of satisfaction at her hands?

Ford/Brook. Never.

Falstaff. Have you importuned her to such a purpose?

Ford/Brook. Never.

Falstaff. Of what quality was your love, then?

Ford/Brook. Like a fair house built on another man's ground; so that I have lost my edifice by mistaking the place where erected it.

Falstaff. To what purpose have you unfolded this to me?

Ford/Brook. When I have told you that, I have told you all. Some say that though she appear honest to me, yet in other places she enlarges her mirth so far that there is shrewd construction made of her. Now, Sir John, here is the heart of my purpose: you are a gentleman of excellent breeding, admirable discourse, of great admittance, authentic in your place and person, generally allowed for your many war-like, courtlike, and learned preparations.

Falstaff. O, sir!

Ford/Brook. Believe it, for you know it. There is money; spend it, spend it; spend more; spend all I have; only give me so much of your time in exchange of it as to lay an amiable siege to the honesty of this Ford's wife; use your art of wooing, win her to consent to you; if any man may, you may as soon as any.

Falstaff. Would it apply well to the vehemency of your affection, that I should win what you would enjoy? I think you prescribe to yourself very preposterously.

Ford/Brook. O, understand my drift. She dwells so securely on the excellency of her honor that the folly of my soul dares not present itself; she is too bright to be looked against. Now, could I come to her with any detection in my hand, my desires had instance and argument to commend themselves; I could drive her then from the ward of her purity, her reputation, her marriage vow, and a thousand other her defenses, which now are too too strongly embattled against me. What say you to it, Sir John?

Falstaff. Master Brook, I will first make bold with your money; next, give me your hand; and last, as I am a gentleman, you shall, if you will, enjoy Ford's wife.

Ford/Brook. O good sir!

Falstaff. I say you shall.

Ford/Brook. Want no money, Sir John; you shall want none.

Falstaff. Want no Mistress Ford, Master Brook; you shall want none. I shall be with her, I may tell you, by her own appointment; even as you came in to me her assistant, or go-between, parted from me; I say I shall be with her between ten and eleven; for at that time the jealous rascally knave, her husband, will be forth. Come you to me at night; you shall know how I speed.

Ford/Brook. I am blest in your acquaintance. Do you know Ford, Sir?

Falstaff. Hang him, poor cuckoldly knave! I know him not; yet I wrong him to call him poor; they say the jealous wittolly knave has masses of money; for which his wife seems to me well-favored. I will use her as the key of the cuckoldly rogue's coffer; and there's my harvest-home.

Ford/Brook. I would you knew Ford, sir, that you might avoid him if you saw him.

Falstaff. Hang him, mechanical salt-butter rogue! I will stare him out of his wits; I will awe him with my cudgel; it shall hang like a meteor over the cuckold's horns. Master Brook, you shall know I will predominate over the peasant, and you shall lie with his wife. Come to me soon at night. Ford's a knave, and I will aggravate his style; you, Master Brook, shall know him for knave and cuckold. Come to me soon at night.

[*Exit*]

Ford. What a damned Epicurean rascal is this! My heart is ready to crack with impatience. Who says this is improvident jealousy? My wife has sent to him; the hour is fixed; the match is made. Would any man have thought this? See the hell of having a false woman! My bed shall be abused, my coffers ransacked, my reputation gnawn at; and I shall not only receive this villainous wrong, but stand under the adoption of abominable terms, and by him that does me this wrong. Terms! names! Amaimon sounds well; Lucifer, well; Barbason, well; yet they are devils' additions, the names of fiends. But cuckold! Wittol! Cuckold! the devil himself has not such a name. Page is an ass, a secure ass; he will trust his wife; he will not be jealous; I will rather trust a Fleming with my butter, Parson Hugh the Welshman with my cheese, an Irishman with my aqua-vitae bottle, or a thief to walk my ambling gelding, than my wife with herself. Then she plots, then she ruminates, then she devises; and what they think in their hearts they may effect, they will break their hearts but they will effect. God be praised for my jealousy! Eleven o'clock the hour. I will prevent this, detect my wife, be revenged on Falstaff, and laugh at Page. I will about it; better three hours too soon than a minute too late. Fie, fie, fie! cuckold! cuckold! cuckold!

[*Exit*]

[A field near Windsor]

[Enter Caius and Rugby]

Caius. Jack Rugby!

Rugby. Sir?

Caius. Vat is de clock, Jack?

Rugby. 'Tis past the hour, sir, that Sir Hugh promised to meet.

Caius. By gar, he has save his soul dat he is no come; he has pray
   his Pible well dat he is no come; by gar, Jack Rugby, he is dead
   already, if he be come.

Rugby. He is wise, sir; he knew your worship would kill him if he
   came.

Caius. By gar, de herring is no dead so as I vill kill him.
   Take your rapier, Jack; I vill tell you how I vill kill him.

Rugby. Alas, sir, I cannot fence!

Caius. Villainy, take your rapier.

Rugby. Forbear; here's company.

[Enter Host, Shallow, Slender, and Page]

Host. Bless you, bully doctor!

Shallow. Save you, Master Doctor Caius!

Page. Now, good Master Doctor!

Slender. Give you good morrow, sir.

Caius. Vat be all you, one, two, tree, four, come for?

Host. To see you fight, to see you foin, to see you traverse; to see
   you here, to see you there; to see you pass your punto, your
   stock, your reverse, your distance, your montant. Is he dead, my
   Ethiopian? Is he dead, my Francisco? Ha, bully! What says my
   Aesculapius? my Galen? my heart of elder? Ha! is he dead, bully
   stale? Is he dead?

Caius. By gar, he is de coward Jack priest of de world; he is not
   show his face.

Host. You are a Castalion-King-Urinal. Hector of Greece, my boy!

Caius. I pray you, bear witness that me have stay six or seven, two
   tree hours for him, and he is no come.

Shallow. He is the wiser man, Master Doctor: he is a curer of souls, and you a curer of bodies; if you should fight, you go against the hair of your professions. Is it not true, Master Page?

Page. Master Shallow, you have yourself been a great fighter, though now a man of peace.

Shallow. Bodykins, Master Page, though I now be old, and of the peace, if I see a sword out, my finger itches to make one. Though we are justices, and doctors, and churchmen, Master Page, we have some salt of our youth in us; we are the sons of women, Master Page.

Page. 'Tis true, Master Shallow.

Shallow. It will be found so, Master Page. Master Doctor Caius, I come to fetch you home. I am sworn of the peace; you have showed yourself a wise physician, and Sir Hugh has shown himself a wise and patient churchman. You must go with me, Master Doctor.

Host. Pardon, Guest Justice. A word, Mounseur Mockwater.

Caius. Mock-vater! Vat is dat?

Host. Mockwater, in our English tongue, is valour, bully.

Caius. By gar, then I have as much mockvater as de Englishman. Scurvy jack-dog priest! By gar, me vill cut his ears.

Host. He will clapper-claw you tightly, bully.

Caius. Clapper-de-claw! Vat is dat?

Host. That is, he will make you amends.

Caius. By gar, me do look he shall clapper-de-claw me; for, by gar, me vill have it.

Host. And I will provoke him to it, or let him wag.

Caius. Me tank you for dat.

Host. And, moreover, bully—but first: [*Aside to the others*] Master Guest, and Master Page, and eke Cavaleiro Slender, go you through the town to Frogmore.

Page. [*Aside*] Sir Hugh is there, is he?

Host. [*Aside*] He is there. See what humor he is in; and I will bring the doctor about by the fields. Will it do well?

Shallow. [*Aside*] We will do it. Page, Shallow, and Slender. Adieu, good Master Doctor.

[*Exit Page, Shallow, and Slender*]

Caius. By gar, me vill kill de priest; for he speak for a jack-an-ape to Anne Page.

Host. Let him die. Sheathe your impatience; throw cold water on your choler; go about the fields with me through Frogmore; I will bring you where Mistress Anne Page is, at a farmhouse, a-feasting; and you shall woo her. Cried game! Said I well?

Caius. By gar, me dank you vor dat; by gar, I love you; and I shall procure-a you de good guest, de earl, de knight, de lords, de gentlemen, my patients.

Host. For which I will be your adversary toward Anne Page. Said I well?

Caius. By gar, 'tis good; vell said.

Host. Let us wag, then.

Caius. Come at my heels, Jack Rugby.

[*Exit*]

Act Three

1

[A field near Frogmore]

[Enter Sir Hugh Evans and Simple]

Evans. I pray you now, good Master Slender's serving-man, and friend Simple by your name, which way have you looked for Master Caius, that calls himself Doctor of Physic?

Simple. Well, sir, the pittie-ward, the park-ward; every way; old Windsor way, and every way but the town way.

Evans. I most fehemently desire you, you will also look that way.

Simple. I will, Sir.

[Exit]

Evans. Pless my soul, how full of chollors I am, and trempling of mind! I shall be glad if he have deceived me. How melancholies I am! I will knog his urinals about his knave's costard when I have goot opportunities for the ork. Pless my soul!

[Sings]

> To shallow rivers, to whose falls
> Melodious birds sings madrigals;
> There will we make our peds of roses,
> And a thousand fragrant posies.
> To shallow—

Mercy on me! I have a great dispositions to cry.

[Sings]

> Melodious birds sing madrigals—
> Whenas I sat in Pabylon—
> And a thousand vagram posies.
> To shallow, etc.

[*Enter Simple*]

Simple. Yonder he is, coming this way, Sir Hugh.

Evans. He's welcome.

[*Sings*]

To shallow rivers, to whose falls—
Heaven prosper the right!

What weapons is he?

Simple. No weapons, sir. There comes my master, Master Shallow, and another gentleman, from Frogmore, over the stile, this way.

Evans. Pray you give me my gown; or else keep it in your arms.

[*Takes out a book*]

[*Enter Page, Shallow, and Slender*]

Shallow. How now, Master Parson! Good morrow, good Sir Hugh. Keep a gamester from the dice, and a good student from his book, and it is wonderful.

Slender. [*Aside*] Ah, sweet Anne Page!

Page. Save you, good Sir Hugh!

Evans. Pless you from his mercy sake, all of you!

Shallow. What, the sword and the word! Do you study them both, Master Parson?

Page. And youthful still, in your doublet and hose, this raw rheumatic day!

Evans. There is reasons and causes for it.

Page. We are come to you to do a good office, Master Parson.

Evans. Fery well; what is it?

Page. Yonder is a most reverend gentleman, who, belike having received wrong by some person, is at most odds with his own gravity and patience that ever you saw.

Shallow. I have lived fourscore years and upward; I never heard a man of his place, gravity, and learning, so wide of his own respect.

Evans. What is he?

Page. I think you know him: Master Doctor Caius, the renowned French physician.

Evans. Got's will and his passion of my heart! I had as lief you would tell me of a mess of porridge.

Page. Why?

Evans. He has no more knowledge in Hibocrates and Galen, and he is a knave besides—a cowardly knave as you would desires to be acquainted withal.

Page. I warrant you, he's the man should fight with him.

Slender. [*Aside*] O sweet Anne Page!

Shallow. It appears so, by his weapons. Keep them asunder; here comes Doctor Caius.

[*Enter Host, Caius, and Rugby*]

Page. Nay, good Master Parson, keep in your weapon.

Shallow. So do you, good Master Doctor.

Host. Disarm them, and let them question; let them keep their limbs whole and hack our English.

Caius. I pray you, let-a me speak a word with your ear. Verefore will you not meet-a me?

Evans. [*Aside to Caius*] Pray you use your patience; in good time.

Caius. By gar, you are de coward, de Jack dog, John ape.

Evans. [*Aside to Caius*] Pray you, let us not be laughing-stocks to other men's humors; I desire you in friendship, and I will one way or other make you amends.

[*Aloud*] I will knog your urinals about your knave's cogscomb for missing your meetings and appointments.

Caius. Diable! Jack Rugby—mine Host de Jarteer—have I not stay for him to kill him? Have I not, at de place I did appoint?

Evans. As I am a Christians soul, now, look you, this is the place appointed. I'll be judgment by my host of the Garter.

Host. Peace, I say, Gallia and Gaul, French and Welsh, soul-curer and body-curer.

Caius. Aye, dat is very good! excellent!

Host. Peace, I say. Hear my host of the Garter. Am I politic? am I subtle? am I a Machiavel? Shall I lose my doctor? No; he gives me the potions and the motions. Shall I lose my parson, my priest, my Sir Hugh? No; he gives me the proverbs and the noverbs. Give me your hand, terrestrial; so. Give me your hand, celestial; so. Boys of art, I have deceived you both; I have directed you to wrong places; your hearts are mighty, your skins are whole, and let burnt sack be the issue. Come, lay their swords to pawn. Follow me, lads of peace; follow, follow, follow.

Shallow. Trust me, a mad host. Follow, gentlemen, follow.

Slender. [Aside] O sweet Anne Page!

[*Exit all but Caius and Evans*]

Caius. Ha, do I perceive dat? Have you make-a de sot of us, ha, ha?

Evans. This is well; he has made us his vlouting-stog. I desire you that we may be friends; and let us knog our prains together to be revenge on this same scall, scurvy, cogging companion, the host of the Garter.

Caius. By gar, with all my heart. He promise to bring me where is Anne Page; by gar, he deceive me too.

Evans. Well, I will smite his noddles. Pray you follow.

[*Exit*]

[*A street in Windsor*]

[*Enter Mistress Page and Robin*]

Mistress Page. Nay, keep your way, little gallant; you were wont to be a follower, but now you are a leader. Whether had you rather lead my eyes, or eye your master's heels?

Robin. I had rather, forsooth, go before you like a man than follow him like a dwarf.

Mistress Page. O, you are a flattering boy; now I see you'll be a courtier.

[*Enter Ford*]

Ford. Well met, Mistress Page. Where go you?

Mistress Page. Truly, sir, to see your wife. Is she at home?

Ford. Ay; and as idle as she may hang together, for want of company. I think, if your husbands were dead, you two would marry.

Mistress Page. Be sure of that—two other husbands.

Ford. Where had you this pretty weathercock?

Mistress Page. I cannot tell what the dickens his name is my husband had him of. What do you call your knight's name, sirrah?

Robin. Sir John Falstaff.

Ford. Sir John Falstaff!

Mistress Page. He, he; I can never hit on his name. There is such a league between my good man and he! Is your wife at home indeed?

Ford. Indeed she is.

Mistress Page. By your leave, sir. I am sick till I see her.

[*Exit Mistress Page and Robin*]

Ford. Has Page any brains? Has he any eyes? Has he any thinking? Sure, they sleep; he has no use of them. Why, this boy will carry a letter twenty mile as easy as a cannon will shoot pointblank twelve score. He pieces out his wife's inclination; he gives her folly motion and advantage; and now she's going to my wife, and Falstaff's boy with her. A man may hear this shower sing in the wind. And Falstaff's boy with her! Good plots! They are laid; and our revolted wives share damnation together. Well; I will take him, then torture my wife, pluck the borrowed veil of modesty from the so seeming Mistress Page, divulge Page himself for a secure and wilful Actaeon; and to these violent proceedings all my neighbours shall cry aim. [*Clock strikes*] The clock gives me my cue, and my assurance bids me search; there I shall find Falstaff. I shall be rather praised for this than mocked; for it is as positive as the earth is firm that Falstaff is there. I will go.

[*Enter Page, Shallow, Slender, Host, Evans, Caius, and Rugby*]

Shallow, Page, etc. Well met, Master Ford.

Ford. Trust me, a good knot; I have good cheer at home, and I pray you all go with me.

Shallow. I must excuse myself, Master Ford.

Slender. And so must I, sir; we have appointed to dine with Mistress Anne, and I would not break with her for more money than I'll speak of.

Shallow. We have lingered about a match between Anne Page and my cousin Slender, and this day we shall have our answer.

Slender. I hope I have your good will, father Page.

Page. You have, Master Slender; I stand wholly for you. But my wife, Master Doctor, is for you altogether.

Caius. Aye, be-gar; and de maid is love-a me; my nursh-a Quickly tell me so mush.

Host. What say you to young Master Fenton? He capers, he dances, he has eyes of youth, he writes verses, he speaks holiday, he smells April and May; he will carry it, he will carry it; 'tis in his buttons; he will carry it.

Page. Not by my consent, I promise you. The gentleman is of no having: he kept company with the wild Prince and Poins; he is of too high a region, he knows too much. No, he shall not knit a knot in his fortunes with the finger of my substance; if he take her, let him take her simply; the wealth I have waits on my consent, and my consent goes not that way.

Ford. I beseech you, heartily, some of you go home with me to dinner: besides your cheer, you shall have sport; I will show you a monster. Master Doctor, you shall go; so shall you, Master Page; and you, Sir Hugh.

Shallow. Well, fare you well; we shall have the freer wooing at Master Page's.

[*Exit Shallow and Slender*]

Caius. Go home, John Rugby; I come anon.

[*Exit Rugby*]

Host. Farewell, my hearts; I will to my honest knight Falstaff, and drink canary with him.

[*Exit Host*]

Ford. [*Aside*] I think I shall drink in pipe-wine first with him. I'll make him dance. Will you go, gentles?

All. Have with you to see this monster.

[*Exit*]

[Ford's house]

[Enter Mistress Ford and Mistress Page]

Mistress Ford. What, John! what, Robert!

Mistress Page. Quickly, quickly! Is the buck-basket—

Mistress Ford. I warrant. What, Robin, I say!

[Enter Servants with a basket]

Mistress Page. Come, come, come.

Mistress Ford. Here, set it down.

Mistress Page. Give your men the charge; we must be brief.

Mistress Ford. Well, as I told you before, John and Robert, be ready here hard by in the brew-house; and when I suddenly call you, come forth, and, without any pause or staggering, take this basket on your shoulders. That done, trudge with it in all haste, and carry it among the whitsters in Datchet Mead, and there empty it in the muddy ditch close by the Thames side.

Mrs. Page. You will do it?

Mistress Ford. I have told them over and over; they lack no direction. Be gone, and come when you are called.

[Exit Servants]

Mistress Page. Here comes little Robin.

[Enter Robin]

Mistress Ford. How now, my eyas-musket, what news with you?

Robin. My Master Sir John is come in at your back door, Mistress Ford, and requests your company.

Mistress Page. You little Jack-a-Lent, have you been true to us?

Robin. Aye, I'll be sworn. My master knows not of your being here, and has threatened to put me into everlasting liberty, if I tell you of it; for he swears he'll turn me away.

Mistress Page. You are a good boy; this secrecy of yours shall be a tailor to you, and shall make you a new doublet and hose. I'll go hide me.

Mistress Ford. Do so. Go tell your master I am alone.

[Exit Robin]

Mistress Page, remember you your cue.

Mistress Page. I warrant you; if I do not act it, hiss me.

[Exit Mistress Page]

Mistress Ford. Go to, then; we'll use this unwholesome humidity, this gross watery pumpion; we'll teach him to know turtles from jays.

[Enter Falstaff]

Falstaff. Have I caught you, my heavenly jewel? Why, now let me die, for I have lived long enough; this is the period of my ambition. O this blessed hour!

Mistress Ford. O sweet Sir John!

Falstaff. Mistress Ford, I cannot cog, I cannot prate, Mistress Ford. Now shall I sin in my wish; I would your husband were dead; I'll speak it before the best lord, I would make you my lady.

Mistress Ford. I your lady, Sir John? Alas, I should be a pitiful lady.

Falstaff. Let the court of France show me such another. I see how your eye would emulate the diamond; you have the right arched beauty of the brow that becomes the ship-tire, the tire-valiant, or any tire of Venetian admittance.

Mistress Ford. A plain kerchief, Sir John; my brows become nothing else, nor that well neither.

Falstaff. By the Lord, you art a tyrant to say so; you would make an absolute courtier, and the firm fixture of your foot would give an excellent motion to your gait in a semi-circled farthingale. I see what you were, if Fortune your foe were, not Nature, your friend. Come, you cannot hide it.

Mistress Ford. Believe me, there's no such thing in me.

Falstaff. What made me love you? Let that persuade you there's something extraordinary in you. Come, I cannot cog, and say you are this and that, like a many of these lisping hawthorn-buds that come like women in men's apparel, and smell like Bucklersbury in simple time; I cannot; but I love you, none but you; and you deserve it.

Mistress Ford. Do not betray me, sir; I fear you love Mistress Page.

Falstaff. You might as well say I love to walk by the Counter-gate, which is as hateful to me as the reek of a lime-kiln.

Mistress Ford. Well, heaven knows how I love you; and you shall one day find it.

Falstaff. Keep in that mind; I'll deserve it.

Mistress Ford. Nay, I must tell you, so you do; or else I could not be in that mind.

Robin. [*Within*] Mistress Ford, Mistress Ford! here's Mistress Page at the door, sweating and blowing and looking wildly, and would needs speak with you presently.

Falstaff. She shall not see me; I will ensconce me behind the arras.

Mistress Ford. Pray you, do so; she's a very tattling woman.

[*Falstaff hides himself*]

[*Enter Mistress Page and Robin*]

What's the matter? How now!

Mistress Page. O Mistress Ford, what have you done? You're shamed, you're overthrown, you're undone for ever.

Mistress Ford. What's the matter, good Mistress Page?

Mistress Page. O well-a-day, Mistress Ford, having an honest man to your husband, to give him such cause of suspicion!

Mistress Ford. What cause of suspicion?

Mistress Page. What cause of suspicion? Out upon you, how am I mistook in you!

Mistress Ford. Why, alas, what's the matter?

Mistress Page. Your husband's coming here, woman, with all the officers in Windsor, to search for a gentleman that he says is here now in the house, by your consent, to take an ill advantage of his absence. You are undone.

Mistress Ford. 'Tis not so, I hope.

Mistress Page. Pray heaven it be not so that you have such a man here; but 'tis most certain your husband's coming, with half Windsor at his heels, to search for such a one. I come before to tell you. If you know yourself clear, why, I am glad of it; but if you have a friend here, convey, convey him out. Be not amazed; call all your senses to you; defend your reputation, or bid farewell to your good life forever.

Mistress Ford. What shall I do? There is a gentleman, my dear friend; and I fear not my own shame as much as his peril. I had rather than a thousand pound he were out of the house.

Mistress Page. For shame, never stand "you had rather" and "you had rather"! Your husband's here at hand; bethink you of some conveyance; in the house you cannot hide him. O, how have you deceived me! Look, here is a basket; if he be of any reasonable stature, he may creep in here; and throw foul linen upon him, as if it were going to bucking, or—it is whiting-time—send him by your two men to Datchet Mead.

Mistress Ford. He's too big to go in there. What shall I do?

Falstaff. [*Coming forward*] Let me see it, let me see it. O, let me see it! I'll in, I'll in; follow your friend's counsel; I'll in.

Mistress Page. What, Sir John Falstaff! [*Aside to Falstaff*] Are these your letters, knight?

Falstaff. [*Aside to Mistress Page*] I love you and none but you; help me away.—Let me creep in here; I'll never— [*Gets into the basket; they cover him with foul linen*]

Mistress Page. Help to cover your master, boy. Call your men, Mistress Ford. You dissembling knight!

Mistress Ford. What, John! Robert! John!

[*Exit Robin*]

[*Enter Servants*]

Go, take up these clothes here, quickly; where's the cowl-staff? Look how you drumble. Carry them to the laundress in Datchet Mead; quickly, come.

[*Enter Ford, Page, Caius, and Sir Hugh Evans*]

Ford. Pray you come near. If I suspect without cause, why then make sport at me, then let me be your jest; I deserve it. How now, where bear you this?

Servant. To the laundress, forsooth.

Mistress Ford. Why, what have you to do where they bear it? You were best meddle with buck-washing.

Ford. Buck? I would I could wash myself of the buck! Buck, buck, buck! ay, buck! I warrant you, buck; and of the season too, it shall appear.

[*Exit Servants with basket*]

Gentlemen, I have dreamed tonight; I'll tell you my dream. Here, here, here be my keys; ascend my chambers, search, seek, find out. I'll warrant we'll unkennel the fox. Let me stop this way first.

[*Locking the door*]

So, now uncape.

Page. Good Master Ford, be contented; you wrong yourself too much.

Ford. True, Master Page. Up, gentlemen, you shall see sport anon; follow me, gentlemen.

[*Exit*]

Evans. This is fery fantastical humors and jealousies.

Caius. By gar, 'tis no the fashion of France; it is not jealous in France.

Page. Nay, follow him, gentlemen; see the issue of his search.

[*Exit Evans, Page, and Caius*]

Mistress Page. Is there not a double excellency in this?

Mistress Ford. I know not which pleases me better, that my husband is deceived, or Sir John.

Mistress Page. What a taking was he in when your husband asked who was in the basket!

Mistress Ford. I am half afraid he will have need of washing; so throwing him into the water will do him a benefit.

Mistress Page. Hang him, dishonest rascal! I would all of the same strain were in the same distress.

Mistress Ford. I think my husband has some special suspicion of Falstaff's being here, for I never saw him so gross in his jealousy till now.

Mistress Page. I will lay a plot to try that, and we will yet have more tricks with Falstaff. His dissolute disease will scarce obey this medicine.

Mistress Ford. Shall we send that foolish carrion, Mistress Quickly, to him, and excuse his throwing into the water, and give him another hope, to betray him to another punishment?

Mistress Page. We will do it; let him be sent for tomorrow eight o'clock, to have amends.

[*Enter Ford, Page, Caius, and Sir Hugh Evans*]

Ford. I cannot find him; may be the knave bragged of that he could not compass.

Mistress Page. [*Aside to Mistress Ford*] Heard you that?

Mistress Ford. You use me well, Master Ford, do you?

Ford. Aye, I do so.

Mistress Ford. Heaven make you better than your thoughts!

Ford. Amen.

Mistress Page. You do yourself mighty wrong, Master Ford.

Ford. Aye, aye; I must bear it.

Evans. If there be any pody in the house, and in the chambers, and in the coffers, and in the presses, heaven forgive my sins at the day of judgment!

Caius. Be gar, nor I too; there is no bodies.

Page. Fie, fie, Master Ford, are you not ashamed? What spirit, what devil suggests this imagination? I would not have your distemper in this kind for the wealth of Windsor Castle.

Ford. 'Tis my fault, Master Page; I suffer for it.

Evans. You suffer for a pad conscience. Your wife is as honest a omans as I will desires among five thousand, and five hundred too.

Caius. By gar, I see 'tis an honest woman.

Ford. Well, I promised you a dinner. Come, come, walk in the Park. I pray you pardon me; I will hereafter make known to you why I have done this. Come, wife, come, Mistress Page; I pray you pardon me; pray heartily, pardon me.

Page. Let's go in, gentlemen; but, trust me, we'll mock him. I do invite you tomorrow morning to my house to breakfast; after, we'll a-birding together; I have a fine hawk for the bush. Shall it be so?

Ford. Any thing.

Evans. If there is one, I shall make two in the company.

Caius. If there be one or two, I shall make-a the turd.

Ford. Pray you go, Master Page.

Evans. I pray you now, remembrance tomorrow on the lousy knave, my host.

Caius. Dat is good; by gar, with all my heart.

Evans. A lousy knave, to have his gibes and his mockeries!

[*Exit All*]

[*In front of Page's house*]

[*Enter Fenton and Anne Page*]

Fenton. I see I cannot get your father's love; Therefore no more turn me to him, sweet Nan.

Anne. Alas, how then?

Fenton. Why, you must be yourself. He does object I am too great of birth; And that, my state being galled with my expense, I seek to heal it only by his wealth. Besides these, other bars he lays before me, My riots past, my wild societies; And tells me 'tis a thing impossible I should love you but as a property.

Anne. Maybe he tells you true.

Fenton. No, heaven so speed me in my time to come!
Albeit I will confess your father's wealth
Was the first motive that I wooed you, Anne;
Yet, wooing you, I found you of more value
Than stamps in gold, or sums in sealed bags;
And 'tis the very riches of yourself
That now I aim at.

Anne. Gentle Master Fenton, Yet seek my father's love; still seek it, sir. If opportunity and humblest suit Cannot attain it, why then—hark you here.

[*They converse apart*]

[*Enter Shallow, Slender, and Mistress Quickly*]

Shallow. Break their talk, Mistress Quickly; my kinsman shall speak for himself.

Slender. I'll make a shaft or a bolt on it; 'slid, 'tis but venturing.

Shallow. Be not dismayed.

Slender. No, she shall not dismay me. I care not for that, but that I am afeard.

Quickly. Hark ye, Master Slender would speak a word with you.

Anne. I come to him. [*Aside*] This is my father's choice.
O, what a world of vile ill-favored faults
Looks handsome in three hundred pounds a year!

Quickly. And how does good Master Fenton? Pray you, a word with you.

Shallow. She's coming; to her, coz. O boy, you had a father!

Slender. I had a father, Mistress Anne; my uncle can tell you good jests of him. Pray you, uncle, tell Mistress Anne the jest how my father stole two geese out of a pen, good uncle.

Shallow. Mistress Anne, my cousin loves you.

Slender. Aye, that I do; as well as I love any woman in Gloucestershire.

Shallow. He will maintain you like a gentlewoman.

Slender. Aye, that I will come cut and longtail, under the degree of a squire.

Shallow. He will make you a hundred and fifty pounds jointure.

Anne. Good Master Shallow, let him woo for himself.

Shallow. Well, I thank you for it; I thank you for that good comfort. She calls you, coz; I'll leave you.

Anne. Now, Master Slender—

Slender. Now, good Mistress Anne—

Anne. What is your will?

Slender. My Will! 'Od's heartlings, that's a pretty jest indeed! I never made my will yet, I thank heaven; I am not such a sickly creature, I give heaven praise.

Anne. I mean, Master Slender, what would you with me?

Slender. Truly, for my own part I would little or nothing with you. Your father and my uncle has made motions; if it be my luck, so; if not, happy man be his dole! They can tell you how things go better than I can. You may ask your father; here he comes.

[*Enter Page and Mistress Page*]

Page. Now, Master Slender! Love him, daughter Anne— Why, how now, what does Master Fenton here? You wrong me, sir, thus still to haunt my house. I told you, sir, my daughter is disposed of.

Fenton. Nay, Master Page, be not impatient.

Mistress Page. Good Master Fenton, come not to my child.

Page. She is no match for you.

Fenton. Sir, will you hear me?

Page. No, good Master Fenton. Come, Master Shallow; come, son Slender; in. Knowing my mind, you wrong me, Master Fenton.

[Exit Page, Shallow, and Slender]

Quickly. Speak to Mistress Page.

Fenton. Good Mistress Page, for that I love your daughter
In such a righteous fashion as I do,
Perforce, against all checks, rebukes, and manners,
I must advance the colors of my love,
And not retire. Let me have your good will.

Anne. Good mother, do not marry me to yond fool.

Mistress Page. I mean it not; I seek you a better husband.

Quickly. That's my master, Master Doctor.

Anne. Alas, I had rather be set quick in the earth. And bowled to
death with turnips.

Mistress Page. Come, trouble not yourself.
Good Master Fenton,
I will not be your friend, nor enemy;
My daughter will I question how she loves you,
And as I find her, so am I affected;
Till then, farewell, sir; she must needs go in;
Her father will be angry.

Fenton. Farewell, gentle mistress; farewell, Nan.

[Exit Mistress Page and Anne]

Quickly. This is my doing now: "Nay," said I "will you cast away
your child on a fool, and a physician? Look on Master Fenton."
This is my doing.

Fenton. I thank you; and I pray you, once tonight
Give my sweet Nan this ring.
There's for your pains.

Quickly. Now Heaven send you good fortune!

[Exit Fenton]

A kind heart he has; a woman would run through fire and
water for such a kind heart. But yet I would my master had
Mistress Anne; or I would Master Slender had her; or, in sooth,
I would Master Fenton had her; I will do what I can for them
all three, for so I have promised, and I'll be as good as my
word; but speciously for Master Fenton. Well, I must of another
errand to Sir John Falstaff from my two mistresses. What a
beast am I to slack it!

[Exit Mistress Quickly]

[The Garter Inn]

[Enter Falstaff and Bardolph]

Falstaff. Bardolph, I say!

Bardolph. Here, sir.

Falstaff. Go fetch me a quart of sack; put a toast in it.

[Exit Bardolph]

Have I lived to be carried in a basket, like a barrow of butcher's offal, and to be thrown in the Thames? Well, if I be served such another trick, I'll have my brains taken out and buttered, and give them to a dog for a new-year's gift. The rogues slighted me into the river with as little remorse as they would have drowned a blind bitch's puppies, fifteen in the litter; and you may know by my size that I have a kind of alacrity in sinking; if the bottom were as deep as hell I should down. I had been drowned but that the shore was shelvy and shallow—a death that I abhor; for the water swells a man; and what a thing should I have been when had been swelled! I should have been a mountain of mummy.

[Enter Bardolph, with sack]

Bardolph. Here's Mistress Quickly, sir, to speak with you

Falstaff. Come, let me pour in some sack to the Thames water; for my belly's as cold as if I had swallowed snowballs for pills to cool the reins. Call her in.

Bardolph. Come in, woman.

[Enter Mistress Quickly]

Quickly. By your leave; I cry you mercy. Give your worship good morrow.

Falstaff. Take away these chalices. Go, brew me a pottle of sack finely.

Bardolph. With eggs, sir?

Falstaff. Simple of itself; I'll no pullet-sperm in my brewage.

[Exit Bardolph]

How now!

Quickly. Marry, sir, I come to your worship from Mistress Ford.

Falstaff. Mistress Ford! I have had ford enough; I was thrown into the ford; I have my belly full of ford.

Quickly. Alas the day, good heart, that was not her fault! She does so take on with her men; they mistook their erection.

Falstaff. So did I mine, to build upon a foolish woman's promise.

Quickly. Well, she laments, sir, for it, that it would yearn your heart to see it. Her husband goes this morning a-birding; she desires you once more to come to her between eight and nine; I must carry her word quickly. She'll make you amends, I warrant you.

Falstaff. Well, I will visit her. Tell her so; and bid her think what a man is. Let her consider his frailty, and then judge of my merit.

Quickly. I will tell her.

Falstaff. Do so. Between nine and ten, say you?

Quickly. Eight and nine, sir.

Falstaff. Well, be gone; I will not miss her.

Quickly. Peace be with you, sir.

[*Exit*]

Falstaff. I marvel I hear not of Master Brook; he sent me word to stay within. I like his money well. O, here he comes.

[*Enter Ford disguised*]

Ford. Bless you, sir!

Falstaff. Now, Master Brook, you come to know what has passed between me and Ford's wife?

Ford. That, indeed, Sir John, is my business.

Falstaff. Master Brook, I will not lie to you; I was at her house the hour she appointed me.

Ford. And sped you, sir?

Falstaff. Very ill-favoredly, Master Brook.

Ford. How so, sir; did she change her determination?

Falstaff. No. Master Brook; but the peaking cornuto her husband, Master Brook, dwelling in a continual alarum of jealousy, comes me in the instant of our encounter, after we had embraced, kissed, protested, and, as it were, spoke the prologue of our comedy; and at his heels a rabble of his companions, there provoked and instigated by his distemper, and, forthwith, to search his house for his wife's love.

Ford. What, while you were there?

Falstaff. While I was there.

Ford. And did he search for you, and could not find you?

Falstaff. You shall hear. As good luck would have it, comes in one Mistress Page, gives intelligence of Ford's approach; and, in her invention and Ford's wife's distraction, they conveyed me into a buck-basket.

Ford. A buck-basket!

Falstaff. By the Lord, a buck-basket! Rammed me in with foul shirts and smocks, socks, foul stockings, greasy napkins, that, Master Brook, there was the rankest compound of villainous smell that ever offended nostril.

Ford. And how long lay you there?

Falstaff. Nay, you shall hear, Master Brook, what I have suffered to bring this woman to evil for your good. Being thus crammed in the basket, a couple of Ford's knaves, his hinds, were called forth by their mistress to carry me in the name of foul clothes to Datchet Lane; they took me on their shoulders; met the jealous knave their master in the door; who asked them once or twice what they had in their basket. I quaked for fear lest the lunatic knave would have searched it; but Fate, ordaining he should be a cuckold, held his hand. Well, on went he for a search, and away went I for foul clothes. But mark the sequel, Master Brook—I suffered the pangs of three several deaths: first, an intolerable fright to be detected with a jealous rotten bell-wether; next, to be compassed like a good bilbo in the circumference of a peck, hilt to point, heel to head; and then, to be stopped in, like a strong distillation, with stinking clothes that fretted in their own grease. Think of that —a man of my kidney. Think of that—that am as subject to heat as butter; a man of continual dissolution and thaw. It was a miracle to scape suffocation. And in the height of this bath, when I was more than half-stewed in grease, like a Dutch dish, to be thrown into the Thames, and cooled, glowing hot, in that surge, like a horse-shoe; think of that —hissing hot. Think of that, Master Brook.

Ford. In good sadness, sir, I am sorry that for my sake you have suffered all this. My suit, then, is desperate; you'll undertake her no more.

Falstaff. Master Brook, I will be thrown into Etna, as I have been into Thames, ere I will leave her thus. Her husband is this morning gone a-birding; I have received from her another embassy of meeting; between eight and nine is the hour, Master Brook.

Ford. 'Tis past eight already, sir.

Falstaff. Is it? I will then address me to my appointment. Come to me at your convenient leisure, and you shall know how I speed; and the conclusion shall be crowned with your enjoying her. Adieu. You shall have her, Master Brook; Master Brook, you shall cuckold Ford.

[*Exit*]

Ford. Hum! ha! Is this a vision? Is this a dream? Do I sleep? Master Ford, awake; awake, Master Ford. There's a hole made in your best coat, Master Ford. This 'tis to be married; this 'tis to have linen and buck-baskets! Well, I will proclaim myself what I am; I will now take the lecher; he is at my house. He cannot scape me; 'tis impossible he should; he cannot creep into a halfpenny purse nor into a pepper box. But, lest the devil that guides him should aid him, I will search impossible places. Though what I am I cannot avoid, yet to be what I would not shall not make me tame. If I have horns to make one mad, let the proverb go with me—I'll be horn mad.

[*Exit*]

Act Four

[*Windsor. A street*]

[*Enter Mistress Page, Mistress Quickly, and William*]

Mistress Page. Is he at Master Ford's already, think you?

Quickly. Sure he is by this; or will be presently; but truly he is very courageous mad about his throwing into the water. Mistress Ford desires you to come suddenly.

Mistress Page. I'll be with her by and by; I'll but bring my young man here to school. Look where his master comes; 'tis a playing day, I see.

[*Enter Sir Hugh Evans*]

How now, Sir Hugh, no school today?

Evans. No; Master Slender is let the boys leave to play.

Quickly. Blessing of his heart!

Mistress Page. Sir Hugh, my husband says my son profits nothing in the world at his book; I pray you ask him some questions in his accidence.

Evans. Come here, William; hold up your head; come.

Mistress Page. Come on, sirrah; hold up your head; answer your master; be not afraid.

Evans. William, how many numbers is in nouns?

William. Two.

Quickly. Truly, I thought there had been one number more, because they say "Od's nouns."

Evans. Peace your tattlings. What is "fair," William?

William. Pulcher.

Quickly. Polecats! There are fairer things than polecats, sure.

Evans. You are a very simplicity oman; I pray you, peace. What is "lapis," William?

William. A stone.

Evans. And what is "a stone," William?

William. A pebble.

Evans. No, it is "lapis'; I pray you remember in your prain.

William. Lapis.

Evans. That is a good William. What is he, William, that does lend articles?

William. Articles are borrowed of the pronoun, and be thus declined: *Singulariter, nominativo; hic, haec, hoc.*

Evans. Nominativo, hig, hag, hog; pray you, mark: *genitivo, hujus.* Well, what is your accusative case?

William. Accusativo, hinc.

Evans. I pray you, have your remembrance, child. *Accusativo, hung, hang, hog.*

Quickly. "Hang-hog" is Latin for bacon, I warrant you.

Evans. Leave your prabbles, oman. What is the focative case, William?

William. O-vocativo, O.

Evans. Remember, William: focative is caret.

Quickly. And that's a good root.

Evans. Oman, forbear.

Mistress Page. Peace.

Evans. What is your genitive case plural, William?

William. Genitive case?

Evans. Ay.

William. Genitive: *horum, harum, horum.*

Quickly. Vengeance of Jenny's case; fie on her! Never name her, child, if she be a whore.

Evans. For shame, oman.

Quickly. You do ill to teach the child such words. He teaches him to hick and to hack, which they'll do fast enough of themselves; and to call "horum"; fie upon you!

Evans. Oman, art you lunatics? Have you no understandings for your cases, and the numbers of the genders? You are as foolish Christian creatures as I would desires.

Mistress Page. Please hold your peace.

Evans. Show me now, William, some declensions of your pronouns.

William. Forsooth, I have forgot.

Evans. It is *qui, quae, quod*; if you forget your qui's, your quae's, and your quod's, you must be preeches. Go your ways and play; go.

Mistress Page. He is a better scholar than I thought he was.

Evans. He is a good sprag memory. Farewell, Mistress Page.

Mistress Page. Adieu, good Sir Hugh.

[*Exit Sir Hugh*]

Get you home, boy. Come, we stay too long.

[*Exit*]

[*Ford's house*]

[*Enter Falstaff and Mistress Ford*]

Falstaff. Mistress Ford, your sorrow has eaten up my sufferance. I
see you are obsequious in your love, and I profess requital to a
hair's breadth; not only, Mistress Ford, in the simple office of
love, but in all the accoutrement, complement, and ceremony of
it. But are you sure of your husband now?

Mistress Ford. He's a-birding, sweet Sir John.

Mistress Page. [*Within*] What hoa, gossip Ford, what hoa!

Mistress Ford. Step into the chamber, Sir John.

[*Exit Falstaff*]

[*Enter Mistress Page*]

Mistress Page. How now, sweetheart, who's at home besides
yourself?

Mistress Ford. Why, none but my own people.

Mistress Page. Indeed?

Mistress Ford. No, certainly. [*Aside to her*] Speak louder.

Mistress Page. Truly, I am so glad you have nobody here.

Mistress Ford. Why?

Mistress Page. Why, woman, your husband is in his old lunes
again. He so takes on yonder with my husband; so rails against
all married mankind; so curses all Eve's daughters, of what
complexion soever; and so buffets himself on the forehead,
crying "Peer-out, peer-out!" that any madness I ever yet beheld
seemed but tameness, civility, and patience, to this his distemper
he is in now. I am glad the fat knight is not here.

Mistress Ford. Why, does he talk of him?

Mistress Page. Of none but him; and swears he was carried out,
the last time he searched for him, in a basket; protests to my
husband he is now here; and has drawn him and the rest of their
company from their sport, to make another experiment of his
suspicion. But I am glad the knight is not here; now he shall see
his own foolery.

Mistress Ford. How near is he, Mistress Page?

Mistress Page. Hard by, at street end; he will be here anon.

Mistress Ford. I am undone: the knight is here.

Mistress Page. Why, then, you are utterly shamed, and he's but a dead man. What a woman are you! Away with him, away with him; better shame than murder.

Mistress Ford. Which way should he go? How should I bestow him? Shall I put him into the basket again?

[Enter Falstaff]

Falstaff. No, I'll come no more in the basket. May I not go out ere he come?

Mistress Page. Alas, three of Master Ford's brothers watch the door with pistols, that none shall issue out; otherwise you might slip away ere he came. But what make you here?

Falstaff. What shall I do? I'll creep up into the chimney.

Mistress Ford. There they always use to discharge their birding-pieces.

Mistress Page. Creep into the kiln-hole.

Falstaff. Where is it?

Mistress Ford. He will seek there, on my word. Neither press, coffer, chest, trunk, well, vault, but he has an abstract for the remembrance of such places, and goes to them by his note. There is no hiding you in the house.

Falstaff. I'll go out then.

Mistress Page. If you go out in your own semblance, you die, Sir John. Unless you go out disguised.

Mistress Ford. How might we disguise him?

Mistress Page. Alas the day, I know not! There is no woman's gown big enough for him; otherwise he might put on a hat, a muffler, and a kerchief, and so escape.

Falstaff. Good hearts, devise something; any extremity rather than a mischief.

Mistress Ford. My Maid's aunt, the fat woman of Brainford, has a gown above.

Mistress Page. On my word, it will serve him; she's as big as he is; and there's her thrummed hat, and her muffler too. Run up, Sir John.

Mistress Ford. Go, go, sweet Sir John. Mistress Page and I will look some linen for your head.

Mistress Page. Quick, quick; we'll come dress you straight. Put on the gown the while.

[*Exit Falstaff*]

Mistress Ford. I would my husband would meet him in this shape; he cannot abide the old woman of Brainford; he swears she's a witch, forbade her my house, and has threatened to beat her.

Mistress Page. Heaven guide him to your husband's cudgel; and the devil guide his cudgel afterwards!

Mistress Ford. But is my husband coming?

Mistress Page. Aye, in good sadness is he; and talks of the basket too, howsoever he has had intelligence.

Mistress Ford. We'll try that; for I'll appoint my men to carry the basket again, to meet him at the door with it as they did last time.

Mistress Page. Nay, but he'll be here presently; let's go dress him like the witch of Brainford.

Mistress Ford. I'll first direct my men what they shall do with the basket. Go up; I'll bring linen for him straight.

[*Exit*]

Mistress Page. Hang him, dishonest varlet! we cannot misuse him enough.
We'll leave a proof, by that which we will do,
Wives may be merry and yet honest too.
We do not act that often jest and laugh; 'Tis old but true:
Still swine eats all the draff.

[*Exit*]

[*Enter Mistress Ford, with two Servants*]

Mistress Ford. Go, sirs, take the basket again on your shoulders; your master is hard at door; if he bid you set it down, obey him; quickly, dispatch.

[*Exit*]

First Servant. Come, come, take it up.

Second Servant. Pray heaven it be not full of knight again.

First Servant. I hope not; I had lief as bear so much lead.

[*Enter Ford, Page, Shallow, Caius, and Sir Hugh Evans*]

Ford. Aye, but if it prove true, Master Page, have you any way then to unfool me again? Set down the basket, villain! Somebody call my wife. Youth in a basket! O you panderly rascals, there's a knot, a ging, a pack, a conspiracy against me. Now shall the devil be shamed. What, wife, I say! Come, come forth; behold what honest clothes you send forth to bleaching.

Page. Why, this passes, Master Ford; you are not to go loose any longer; you must be pinioned.

Evans. Why, this is lunatics. This is mad as a mad dog.

Shallow. Indeed, Master Ford, this is not well, indeed.

Ford. So say I too, sir.

[*Enter Mistress Ford*]

Come here, Mistress Ford; Mistress Ford, the honest woman, the modest wife, the virtuous creature, that has the jealous fool to her husband! I suspect without cause, Mistress, do I?

Mistress Ford. Heaven be my witness, you do, if you suspect me in any dishonesty.

Ford. Well said, brazen-face; hold it out. Come forth, sirrah.

[*Pulling clothes out of the basket*]

Page. This passes!

Mistress Ford. Are you not ashamed? Let the clothes alone.

Ford. I shall find you anon.

Evans. 'Tis unreasonable. Will you take up your wife's clothes? Come away.

Ford. Empty the basket, I say.

Mistress Ford. Why, man, why?

Ford. Master Page, as I am a man, there was one conveyed out of my house yesterday in this basket. Why may not he be there again? In my house I am sure he is; my intelligence is true; my jealousy is reasonable. Pluck me out all the linen.

Mistress Ford. If you find a man there, he shall die a flea's death.

Page. Here's no man.

Shallow. By my fidelity, this is not well, Master Ford; this wrongs you.

Evans. Master Ford, you must pray, and not follow the imaginations of your own heart; this is jealousies.

Ford. Well, he's not here I seek for.

Page. No, nor nowhere else but in your brain.

Ford. Help to search my house this one time. If I find not what
I seek, show no colour for my extremity; let me forever be
your table sport; let them say of me "As jealous as Ford, that
searched a hollow walnut for his wife's leman." Satisfy me once
more; once more search with me.

Mistress Ford. What, hoa, Mistress Page! Come you and the old
woman down; my husband will come into the chamber.

Ford. Old woman? what old woman's that?

Mistress Ford. Why, it is my maid's aunt of Brainford.

Ford. A witch, a quean, an old cozening quean! Have I not forbid
her my house? She comes of errands, does she? We are simple
men; we do not know what's brought to pass under the
profession of fortune-telling. She works by charms, by spells,
by the figure, and such daubery as this is, beyond our element.
We know nothing. Come down, you witch, you hag you; come
down, I say.

Mistress Ford. Nay, good sweet husband! Good gentlemen, let him
not strike the old woman.

[*Enter Falstaff disguised and Mistress Page*]

Mistress Page. Come, Mother Prat; come. give me your hand.

Ford. I'll prat her.

[*Beating him*]

Out of my door, you witch, you hag, you. baggage, you polecat,
you ronyon! Out, out! I'll conjure you, I'll fortune-tell you.

[*Exit Falstaff*]

Mistress Page. Are you not ashamed? I think you have killed the
poor woman.

Mistress Ford. Nay, he will do it. 'Tis a goodly credit for you.

Ford. Hang her, witch!

Evans. By yea and no, I think the oman is a witch indeed; I like not
when a oman has a great peard; I spy a great peard under his
muffler.

Ford. Will you follow, gentlemen? I beseech you follow; see but the
issue of my jealousy; if I cry out thus upon no trail, never trust
me when I open again.

Page. Let's obey his humor a little further. Come, gentlemen.

[*Exit all but Mistress Ford and Mistress Page*]

Mistress Page. Trust me, he beat him most pitifully.

Mistress Ford. Nay, by the mass, that he did not; he beat him most unpitifully I thought.

Mistress Page. I'll have the cudgel hallowed and hung over the altar; it has done meritorious service.

Mistress Ford. What think you? May we, with the warrant of womanhood and the witness of a good conscience, pursue him with any further revenge?

Mistress Page. The spirit of wantonness is sure scared out of him; if the devil have him not in fee-simple, with fine and recovery, he will never, I think, in the way of waste, attempt us again.

Mistress Ford. Shall we tell our husbands how we have served him?

Mistress Page. Yes, by all means; if it be but to scrape the figures out of your husband's brains. If they can find in their hearts the poor unvirtuous fat knight shall be any further afflicted, we two will still be the ministers.

Mistress Ford. I'll warrant they'll have him publicly shamed; and I think there would be no period to the jest, should he not be publicly shamed.

Mistress Page. Come, to the forge with it then; shape it. I would not have things cool.

[*Exit*]

[*The Garter Inn*]

[*Enter Host and Bardolph*]

Bardolph. Sir, the Germans desire to have three of your horses; the Duke himself will be tomorrow at court, and they are going to meet him.

Host. What duke should that be comes so secretly? I hear not of him in the court. Let me speak with the gentlemen; they speak English?

Bardolph. Aye, sir; I'll call them to you.

Host. They shall have my horses, but I'll make them pay; I'll sauce them; they have had my house a week at command; I have turned away my other guests. They must come off; I'll sauce them. Come.

[*Exit*]

[Ford's house]

[Enter Page, Ford, Mistress Page, Mistress Ford, and Sir Hugh Evans]

Evans. 'Tis one of the best discretions of a oman as ever did look upon.

Page. And did he send you both these letters at an instant?

Mistress Page. Within a quarter of an hour.

Ford. Pardon me, wife. Henceforth, do what you will;
I rather will suspect the sun with cold
Than you with wantonness.
Now does your honor stand,
In him that was of late an heretic,
As firm as faith.

Page. 'Tis well, 'tis well; no more.
Be not as extreme in submission as in offence;
But let our plot go forward. Let our wives
Yet once again, to make us public sport,
Appoint a meeting with this old fat fellow,
Where we may take him and disgrace him for it.

Ford. There is no better way than that they spoke of.

Page. How? To send him word they'll meet him in the
Park at midnight? Fie, fie! he'll never come!

Evans. You say he has been thrown in the rivers; and has been grievously peaten as an old oman; methinks there should be terrors in him, that he should not come; methinks his flesh is punished; he shall have no desires.

Page. So think I too.

Mistress Ford. Devise but how you'll use him when he comes, And let us two devise to bring him there.

Mistress Page. There is an old tale goes that Herne the Hunter,
Sometime a keeper here in Windsor Forest,
Does all the winter-time, at still midnight,
Walk round about an oak, with great ragged horns;
And there he blasts the tree, and takes the cattle,
And makes milch-kine yield blood, and shakes a chain
In a most hideous and dreadful manner.

You have heard of such a spirit, and well you know
The superstitious idle-headed eld
Received, and did deliver to our age,
This tale of Herne the Hunter for a truth.

Page. Why yet there want not many that do fear
In deep of night to walk by this Herne's oak.
But what of this?

Mistress Ford. Well, this is our device—
That Falstaff at that oak shall meet with us,
Disguised, like Herme, with huge horns on his head.

Page. Well, let it not be doubted but he'll come,
And in this shape. When you have brought him there,
What shall be done with him? What is your plot?

Mistress Page. That likewise have we thought upon, and thus:
Nan Page my daughter, and my little son,
And three or four more of their growth, we'll dress
Like urchins, ouphes, and fairies, green and white,
With rounds of waxen tapers on their heads,
And rattles in their hands; upon a sudden,
As Falstaff, she, and I, are newly met,
Let them from forth a sawpit rush at once
With some diffused song; upon their sight
We two in great amazedness will fly.
Then let them all encircle him about,
And fairy-like, to pinch the unclean knight;
And ask him why, that hour of fairy revel,
In their so sacred paths he dares to tread
In shape profane.

Mistress Ford. And till he tell the truth,
Let the supposed fairies pinch him sound,
And burn him with their tapers.

Mistress Page. The truth being known,
We'll all present ourselves; dis-horn the spirit,
And mock him home to Windsor.

Ford. The children must Be practised well to this or they'll never do it.

Evans. I will teach the children their behaviors; and I will be like a jack-an-apes also, to burn the knight with my taber.

Ford. That will be excellent. I'll go buy them vizards.

Mistress Page. My Nan shall be the Queen of all the Fairies,

Finely attired in a robe of white.

Page. That silk will I go buy.

[*Aside*] And in that time
Shall Master Slender steal my Nan away,
And marry her at Eton.—
Go, send to Falstaff straight.

Ford. Nay, I'll to him again, in name of Brook;
He'll tell me all his purpose. Sure, he'll come.

Mistress Page. Fear not you that. Go get us properties
And tricking for our fairies.

Evans. Let us about it. It is admirable pleasures, and fery honest
knaveries.

[Exit Page, Ford, and Evans]

Mistress Page. Go, Mistress Ford. Send Quickly to Sir John to know
his mind.

[Exit Mistress Ford]

I'll to the Doctor; he has my good will,
And none but he, to marry with Nan Page.
That Slender, though well landed, is an idiot;
And he my husband best of all affects.
The Doctor is well moneyed, and his friends
Potent at court; he, none but he, shall have her,
Though twenty thousand worthier come to crave her.

[Exit]

[The Garter Inn]

[Enter Host and Simple]

Host. What would you have, boor? What, thick-skin? Speak, breathe, discuss; brief, short, quick, snap.

Simple. Indeed, sir, I come to speak with Sir John Falstaff from Master Slender.

Host. There's his chamber, his house, his castle, his standing-bed and truckle-bed; 'tis painted about with the story of the Prodigal, fresh and new. Go, knock and call; he'll speak like an Anthropophaginian unto you. Knock, I say.

Simple. There's an old woman, a fat woman, gone up into his chamber; I'll be so bold as stay, sir, till she come down; I come to speak with her, indeed.

Host. Ha! a fat woman? The knight may be robbed. I'll call. Bully knight! Bully Sir John! Speak from your lungs military. Art you there? It is your host, your Ephesian, calls.

Falstaff. [*Above*] How now, my host?

Host. Here's a Bohemian-Tartar tarries the coming down of your fat woman. Let her descend, bully, let her descend; my chambers are honorible. Fie, privacy, fie!

[Enter Falstaff]

Falstaff. There was, my host, an old fat woman even now with, me; but she's gone.

Simple. Pray you, sir, was it not the wise woman of Brainford?

Falstaff. Aye, indeed was it, mussel-shell. What would you with her?

Simple. My master, sir, my Master Slender, sent to her, seeing her go through the streets, to know, sir, whether one Nym, sir, that beguiled him of a chain, had the chain or no.

Falstaff. I spake with the old woman about it.

Simple. And what says she, I pray, sir?

Falstaff. Well, she says that the very same man that beguiled Master Slender of his chain cozened him of it.

Simple. I would I could have spoken with the woman herself; I had other things to have spoken with her too, from him.

Falstaff. What are they? Let us know.

Host. Aye, come; quick.

Simple. I may not conceal them, sir.

Falstaff. Conceal them, or you die.

Simple.. Why, sir, they were nothing but about Mistress Anne Page: to know if it were my master's fortune to have her or no.

Falstaff. 'Tis, 'tis his fortune.

Simple. What sir?

Falstaff. To have her, or no. Go; say the woman told me so.

Simple. May I be bold to say so, sir?

Falstaff. Aye, sir, like who more bold?

Simple., I thank your worship; I shall make my master glad with these tidings.

[*Exit Simple*]

Host. You are clerkly, you are clerkly, Sir John. Was there a wise woman with you?

Falstaff. Aye, that there was, my host; one that has taught me more wit than ever I learned before in my life; and I paid nothing for it neither, but was paid for my learning.

[*Enter Bardolph*]

Bardolph. Out, alas, sir, cozenage, mere cozenage!

Host. Where be my horses? Speak well of them, varletto.

Bardolph. Run away with the cozeners; for so soon as I came beyond Eton, they threw me off from behind one of them, in a slough of mire; and set spurs and away, like three German devils, three Doctor Faustuses.

Host. They are gone but to meet the Duke, villain; do not say they be fled. Germans are honest men.

[*Enter Sir Hugh Evans*]

Evans. Where is my host?

Host. What is the matter, sir?

Evans. Have a care of your entertainments. There is a friend of mine come to town tells me there is three cozen-germans that has cozened all the hosts of Readins, of Maidenhead, of Colebrook, of horses and money. I tell you for good will, look you; you are wise, and full of gibes and vlouting-stogs, and 'tis not convenient you should be cozened. Fare you well.

[Exit]

[Enter Doctor Caius]

Caius. Vere is my host de Jarteer?

Host. Here, Master Doctor, in perplexity and doubtful dilemma.

Caius. I cannot tell vat is dat; but it is tell-a me dat you make grand preparation for a Duke de Jamany. By my trot, dere is no duke that the court is know to come; I tell you for good will. Adieu.

[Exit]

Host. Hue and cry, villain, go! Assist me, knight; I am undone. Fly, run, hue and cry, villain; I am undone.

[Exit Host and Bardolph]

Falstaff. I would all the world might be cozened, for I have been cozened and beaten too. If it should come to the ear of the court how I have been transformed, and how my transformation has been washed and cudgelled, they would melt me out of my fat, drop by drop, and liquor fishermen's boots with me; I warrant they would whip me with their fine wits till I were as crestfallen as a dried pear. I never prospered since I forswore myself at primero. Well, if my wind were but long enough to say my prayers, would repent.

[Enter Mistress Quickly]

Now! whence come you?

Quickly. From the two parties, forsooth.

Falstaff. The devil take one party and his dam the other! And so they shall be both bestowed. I have suffered more for their sakes, more than the villainous inconstancy of man's disposition is able to bear.

Quickly. And have not they suffered? Yes, I warrant; speciously one of them; Mistress Ford, good heart, is beaten black and blue, that you cannot see a white spot about her.

Falstaff. What tell you me of black and blue? I was beaten myself into all the colors of the rainbow; and was like to be apprehended for the witch of Brainford. But that my admirable dexterity of wit, my counterfeiting the action of an old woman, delivered me, the knave constable had set me in the stocks, in the common stocks, for a witch.

Quickly. Sir, let me speak with you in your chamber; you shall hear how
   things go, and, I warrant, to your content. Here is a letter will say
   somewhat. Good hearts, what ado here is to bring you together!
   Sure, one of you does not serve heaven well, that you are so crossed.

Falstaff. Come up into my chamber.

[Exit]

[*The Garter Inn*]

[*Enter Fenton and Host*]

Host. Master Fenton, talk not to me; my mind is heavy; I will give
over all.

Fenton. Yet hear me speak. Assist me in my purpose,
And, as I am a gentleman, I'll give you
A hundred pound in gold more than your loss.

Host. I will hear you, Master Fenton; and I will, at the least, keep
your counsel.

Fenton. From time to time I have acquainted you
With the dear love I bear to fair Anne Page;
Who, mutually, has answered my affection,
So far forth as herself might be her chooser,
Even to my wish. I have a letter from her
Of such contents as you will wonder at;
The mirth whereof so larded with my matter
That neither, singly, can be manifested
Without the show of both. Fat Falstaff
Has a great scene. The image of the jest
I'll show you here at large. Hark, good my host:
To-night at Herne's oak, just between twelve and one,
Must my sweet Nan present the Fairy Queen—
The purpose why is here-in which disguise,
While other jests are something rank on foot,
Her father has commanded her to slip
Away with Slender, and with him at Eton
Immediately to marry; she has consented. Now, sir,
Her mother, even strong against that match
And firm for Doctor Caius, has appointed
That he shall likewise shuffle her away
While other sports are tasking of their minds,
And at the deanery, where a priest attends,
Straight marry her. To this her mother's plot
She seemingly obedient likewise has
Made promise to the doctor. Now thus it rests:
Her father means she shall be all in white;
And in that habit, when Slender sees his time
To take her by the hand and bid her go,

She shall go with him; her mother has intended
The better to denote her to the doctor—
For they must all be masked and vizarded—
That quaint in green she shall be loose enrobed,
With ribands pendent, flaring about her head;
And when the doctor spies his vantage ripe,
To pinch her by the hand, and, on that token,
The maid has given consent to go with him.

Host. Which means she to deceive, father or mother?

Fenton. Both, my good host, to go along with me.
And here it rests—that you'll procure the vicar
To stay for me at church, between twelve and one,
And in the lawful name of marrying,
To give our hearts united ceremony.

Host. Well, husband your device; I'll to the vicar.
Bring you the maid, you shall not lack a priest.

Fenton. So shall I evermore be bound to you;
Besides, I'll make a present recompense.

[*Exit*]

Act Five

1

[*The Garter Inn*]

[*Enter Falstaff and Mistress Quickly*]

Falstaff. Please, no more prattling; go. I'll hold. This is the third time; I hope good luck lies in odd numbers. Away, go; they say there is divinity in odd numbers, either in nativity, chance, or death. Away.

Quickly. I'll provide you a chain, and I'll do what I can to get you a pair of horns.

Falstaff. Away, I say; time wears; hold up your head, and mince.

[*Exit Mistress Quickly*]

[*Enter Ford disguised*]

How now, Master Brook. Master Brook, the matter will be known tonight or never. Be you in the Park about midnight, at Herne's oak, and you shall see wonders.

Ford. Went you not to her yesterday, sir, as you told me you had appointed?

Falstaff. I went to her, Master Brook, as you see, like a poor old man; but I came from her, Master Brook, like a poor old woman. That same knave Ford, her husband, has the finest mad devil of jealousy in him, Master Brook, that ever governed frenzy. I will tell you—he beat me grievously in the shape of a woman; for in the shape of man, Master Brook, I fear not Goliath with a weaver's beam; because I know also life is a shuttle. I am in haste; go along with me; I'll. tell you all, Master Brook. Since I plucked geese, played truant, and whipped top, I knew not what 'twas to be beaten till lately. Follow me. I'll tell you strange things of this knave—Ford, on whom tonight I will be revenged, and I will deliver his wife into your hand. Follow. Strange things in hand, Master Brook! Follow.

[*Exit*]

[*Windsor Park*]

[*Enter Page, Shallow, and Slender*]

Page. Come, come; we'll couch in the Castle ditch till we see the light of our fairies. Remember, son Slender, my daughter.

Slender. Aye, forsooth; I have spoke with her, and we have a nay-word how to know one another. I come to her in white and cry "mum"; she cries "budget," and by that we know one another.

Shallow. That's good too; but what needs either your mum or her budget? The white will decipher her well enough. It has struck ten o'clock.

Page. The night is dark; light and spirits will become it well. Heaven prosper our sport! No man means evil but the devil, and we shall know him by his horns. Let's away; follow me.

[*Exit*]

[A street leading to the Park]

[Enter Mistress Page, Mistress Ford, and Doctor Caius]

Mistress Page. Master Doctor, my daughter is in green; when you see your time, take her by the hand, away with her to the deanery, and dispatch it quickly. Go before into the Park; we two must go together.

Caius. I know vat I have to do; adieu.

Mistress Page. Fare you well, sir.

[Exit Caius]

My husband will not rejoice so much at the abuse of Falstaff as he will chafe at the doctor's marrying my daughter; but 'tis no matter; better a little chiding than a great deal of heartbreak.

Mistress Ford. Where is Nan now, and her troop of fairies, and the Welsh devil, Hugh?

Mistress Page. They are all couched in a pit hard by Herne's oak, with obscured lights; which, at the very instant of Falstaff's and our meeting, they will at once display to the night.

Mistress Ford. That cannot choose but amaze him.

Mistress Page. If he be not amazed, he will be mocked; if he be amazed, he will every way be mocked.

Mistress Ford. We'll betray him finely.

Mistress Page. Against such lewdsters and their lechery, Those that betray them do no treachery.

Mistress Ford. The hour draws on. To the oak, to the oak!

[Exit]

4

[*Windsor Park*]

[*Enter Sir Hugh Evans like a satyr, with Others as fairies*]

Evans. Trib, trib, fairies; come; and remember your parts. Be pold, I pray you; follow me into the pit; and when I give the watchords, do as I pid you. Come, come; trib, trib.

[*Exit*]

[Deep in the Park]

[Enter Falstaff dressed as Herne]

Falstaff. The Windsor bell has struck twelve; the minute draws on. Now the hot-blooded gods assist me! Remember, Jove, you were a bull for your Europa; love set on your horns. O powerful love! that in some respects makes a beast a man; in some other a man a beast. You were also, Jupiter, a swan, for the love of Leda. O omnipotent love! how near the god drew to the complexion of a goose! A fault done first in the form of a beast—O Jove, a beastly fault!—and then another fault in the semblance of a fowl— think on it, Jove, a foul fault! When gods have hot backs what shall poor men do? For me, I am here a Windsor stag; and the fattest, I think, in the forest. Send me a cool rut-time, Jove, or who can blame me to piss my tallow? Who comes here? my doe?

[Enter Mistress Ford and Mistress Page]

Mistress Ford. Sir John! Are you there, my deer, my male deer.

Falstaff. My doe with the black scut! Let the sky rain potatoes; let it thunder to the tune of Greensleeves, hail kissing-comfits, and snow eringoes; let there come a tempest of provocation, I will shelter me here.

[Embracing her]

Mistress Ford. Mistress Page is come with me, sweetheart.

Falstaff. Divide me like a bribed buck, each a haunch; I will keep my sides to myself, my shoulders for the fellow of this walk, and my horns I bequeath your husbands. Am I a woodman, ha? Speak I like Herne the Hunter? Why, now is Cupid a child of conscience; he makes restitution. As I am a true spirit, welcome!

[A noise of horns]

Mistress Page. Alas, what noise?

Mistress Ford. Heaven forgive our sins!

Falstaff. What should this be?

Mistress Ford. } Away, away.
Mistress Page. }

[They run off]

Falstaff. I think the devil will not have me damned, lest the oil that's in me should set hell on fire; he would never else cross me thus.

[Enter Sir Hugh Evans as a satyr, Anne Page as a fairy, and others as the Fairy Queen, fairies, and Hobgoblin; all with tapers]

Fairy Queen. Fairies, black, grey, green, and white,
You moonshine revellers, and shades of night,
You orphan heirs of fixed destiny,
Attend your office and your quality.
Crier Hobgoblin, make the fairy oyes.

Puck. Elves, list your names; silence, you airy toys.
Cricket, to Windsor chimneys shall you leap;
Where fires you find unraked, and hearths unswept,
There pinch the maids as blue as bilberry;
Our radiant Queen hates sluts and sluttery.

Falstaff. They are fairies; he that speaks to them shall die. I'll wink and couch; no man their works must eye.

[Lies down upon his face]

Evans. Where's Pede? Go you, and where you find a maid
That, ere she sleep, has thrice her prayers said,
Raise up the organs of her fantasy
Sleep she as sound as careless infancy;
But those as sleep and think not on their sins,
Pinch them, arms, legs, backs, shoulders, sides, and shins.

Fairy Queen. About, about; Search Windsor castle, elves, within and out;
Strew good luck, ouphes, on every sacred room,
That it may stand till the perpetual doom
In state as wholesome as in state 'tis fit,
Worthy the owner and the owner it.
The several chairs of order look you scour
With juice of balm and every precious flower;
Each fair instalment, coat, and several crest,
With loyal blazon, evermore be blessed!
And nightly, meadow-fairies, look you sing,
Like to the Garter's compass, in a ring;
The expressure that it bears, green let it be,
More fertile-fresh than all the field to see;
And "Honi soit qui mal y pense" write
In emerald tufts, flowers purple, blue and white;

Like sapphire, pearl, and rich embroidery,
Buckled below fair knighthood's bending knee.
Fairies use flowers for their charactery.
Away, disperse; but till 'tis one o'clock,
Our dance of custom round about the oak
Of Herne the Hunter let us not forget.

Evans. Pray you, lock hand in hand; yourselves in order set;
And twenty glow-worms shall our lanterns be,
To guide our measure round about the tree.
But, stay. I smell a man of middle earth.

Falstaff. Heavens defend me from that Welsh fairy, lest he transform
me to a piece of cheese!

Puck. Vile worm, you were overlooked even in your birth.

Fairy Queen. With trial-fire touch me his finger-end;
If he be chaste, the flame will back descend,
And turn him to no pain; but if he start,
It is the flesh of a corrupted heart.

Puck. A trial, come.

Evans. Come, will this wood take fire?

[They put tapers to his fingers, he starts]

Falstaff. Oh, oh, oh!

Fairy Queen. Corrupt, corrupt, and tainted in desire!
About him, fairies; sing a scornful rhyme;
And, as you trip, still pinch him to your time.
   Fie on sinful fantasy!
   Fie on lust and luxury!
   Lust is but a bloody fire,
   Kindled with unchaste desire,
   Fed in heart, whose flames aspire,
   As thoughts do blow them, higher and higher.
   Pinch him, fairies, mutually;
   Pinch him for his villainy;
   Pinch him and burn him and turn him about,
   Till candles and star-light and moonshine be out.

[They pinch Falstaff. Doctor Caius steals away a fairy in green;
Slender takes a fairy in white; and Fenton steals away Anne
Page. A hunting horn sounds. All the fairies run away. Falstaff
removes his buck's head, and stands]

[Enter Page, Ford, Mistress Page, Mistress Ford, and Evans]

Page. Nay, do not fly; I think we have watched you now. Will none but Herne the Hunter serve your turn?

Mistress Page. I pray you, come, hold up the jest no higher.
Now, good Sir John, how like you Windsor wives?
See you these, husband? Do not these fair yokes
Become the forest better than the town?

Ford. Now, sir, who's a cuckold now? Master Brook, Falstaff's a knave, a cuckoldly knave; here are his horns, Master Brook; and, Master Brook, he has enjoyed nothing of Ford's but his buck-basket, his cudgel, and twenty pounds of money, which must be paid to Master Brook; his horses are arrested for it, Master Brook.

Mistress Ford. Sir John, we have had ill luck; we could never meet. I will never take you for my love again; but I will always count you my deer.

Falstaff. I do begin to perceive that I am made an ass.

Ford. Aye, and an ox too; both the proofs are extant.

Falstaff. And these are not fairies? I was three or four times in the thought they were not fairies; and yet the guiltiness of my mind, the sudden surprise of my powers, drove the grossness of the foppery into a received belief, in despite of the teeth of all rhyme and reason, that they were fairies. See now how wit may be made a Jack-a-Lent when 'tis upon ill employment.

Evans. Sir John Falstaff, serve Got, and leave your desires, and fairies will not pinse you.

Ford. Well said, fairy Hugh.

Evans. And leave you your jealousies too, I pray you.

Ford. I will never mistrust my wife again, till you are able to woo her in good English.

Falstaff. Have I laid my brain in the sun, and dried it, that it wants matter to prevent so gross, over-reaching as this? Am I ridden with a Welsh goat too? Shall I have a cox-comb of frieze? 'Tis time I were choked with a piece of toasted cheese.

Evans. Seese is not good to give putter; your belly is all putter.

Falstaff. "Seese" and "putter"! Have I lived to stand at the taunt of one that makes fritters of English? This is enough to be the decay of lust and late-walking through the realm.

Mistress Page. Why, Sir John, do you think, though we would have thrust virtue out of our hearts by the head and shoulders, and have given ourselves without scruple to hell, that ever the devil could have made you our delight?

Ford. What, a hodge-pudding? a bag of flax?

Mistress Page. A puffed man?

Page. Old, cold, withered, and of intolerable entrails?

Ford. And one that is as slanderous as Satan?

Page. And as poor as Job?

Ford. And as wicked as his wife?

Evans. And given to fornications, and to taverns, and sack, and wine, and metheglins, and to drinkings, and swearings, and starings, pribbles and prabbles?

Falstaff. Well, I am your theme; you have the start of me; I am dejected; I am not able to answer the Welsh flannel; ignorance itself is a plummet over me; use me as you will.

Ford. Indeed, sir, we'll bring you to Windsor, to one Master Brook, that you have cozened of money, to whom you should have been a pander. Over and above that you have suffered, I think to repay that money will be a biting affliction.

Page. Yet be cheerful, knight; you shall eat a posset tonight at my house, where I will desire you to laugh at my wife, that now laughs at you. Tell her Master Slender has married her daughter.

Mistress Page. [*Aside*] Doctors doubt that; if Anne Page be my daughter, she is, by this, Doctor Caius' wife.

[*Enter Slender*]

Slender. Whoa, ho, ho, father Page!

Page. Son, how now! how now, son! Have you dispatched'?

Slender. Dispatched! I'll make the best in Gloucestershire know on it; would I were hanged, la, else!

Page. Of what, son?

Slender. I came yonder at Eton to marry Mistress Anne Page, and she's a great lubberly boy. If it had not been in the church, I would have swinged him, or he should have swinged me. If I did not think it had been Anne Page, would I might never stir!—and 'tis a postmaster's boy.

Page. Upon my life, then, you took the wrong.

Slender. What need you tell me that? I think so, when I took a boy for a girl. If I had been married to him, for all he was in woman's apparel, I would not have had him.

Page. Why, this is your own folly. Did not I tell you how you should know my daughter by her garments?

Slender. I went to her in white and cried "mum" and she cried "budget" as Anne and I had appointed; and yet it was not Anne, but a postmaster's boy.

Mistress Page. Good George, be not angry. I knew of your purpose; turned my daughter into green; and, indeed, she is now with the Doctor at the deanery, and there married.

[*Enter Caius*]

Caius. Vere is Mistress Page? By gar, I am cozened; I have married un garcon, a boy; un paysan, by gar, a boy; it is not Anne Page; by gar, I am cozened.

Mistress Page. Why, did you take her in green?

Caius. Aye, be gar, and 'tis a boy; be gar, I'll raise all Windsor.

[*Exit Caius*]

Ford. This is strange. Who has got the right Anne?

Page. My heart misgives me; here comes Master Fenton.

[*Enter Fenton and Anne Page*]

How now, Master Fenton!

Anne. Pardon, good father. Good my mother, pardon.

Page. Now, Mistress, how chance you went not with Master Slender?

Mistress Page. Why went you not with Master Doctor, maid?

Fenton. You do amaze her. Hear the truth of it.
You would have married her most shamefully,
Where there was no proportion held in love.
The truth is, she and I, long since contracted,
Are now so sure that nothing can dissolve us.
The offense is holy that she has committed;
And this deceit loses the name of craft,
Of disobedience, or unduteous title,
Since therein she does evitate and shun
A thousand irreligious cursed hours,
Which forced marriage would have brought upon her.

Ford. Stand not amazed; here is no remedy.
In love, the heavens themselves do guide the state;
Money buys lands, and wives are sold by fate.

Falstaff. I am glad, though you have taken a special stand to strike
  at me, that your arrow has glanced.

Page. Well, what remedy? Fenton, heaven give you joy!
  What cannot be eschewed must be embraced.

Falstaff. When night-dogs run, all sorts of deer are chased.

Mistress Page. Well, I will muse no further. Master Fenton,
  Heaven give you many, many merry days!
  Good husband, let us every one go home,
  And laugh this sport over by a country fire;
  Sir John and all.

Ford. Let it be so. Sir John,
  To Master Brook you yet shall hold your word;
  For he, tonight, shall lie with Mistress Ford.

[*Exit*]

The End

Henry IV, Part One

Henry IV, Part Two

The Merry Wives of Windsor

Henry V

Prologue

Chorus. O, for a Muse of fire, that would ascend
    The brightest heaven of invention;
    A kingdom for a stage, princes to act,
    And monarchs to behold the swelling scene.
    Then should the warlike Harry, like himself,
    Assume the port of Mars, and at his heels,
    Leashed in, like hounds, should famine, sword, and fire
    Crouch for employment. But pardon, Gentles all;
    The flat unraised spirits, that has dared,
    On this unworthy scaffold, to bring forth
    So great an object. Can this cock-pit hold
    The vasty fields of France? Or may we cram
    Within this wooden O, the very casks
    That did affright the air at Agincourt?
    O, pardon; since a crooked figure may
    Attest in little place a million,
    And let us, ciphers to this great accompt,

On your imaginary forces work.
Suppose, within the girdle of these walls
Are now confined two mighty monarchies,
Whose high, up-reared, and abutting fronts,
The perilous narrow ocean parts asunder.
Piece out our imperfections with your thoughts;
Into a thousand parts divide one man,
And make imaginary puissance.
Think when we talk of horses, that you see them
Printing their proud hoofs in the receiving Earth;
For 'tis your thoughts that now must deck our Kings,
Carry them here and there; jumping over times;
Turning the accomplishment of many years
Into an hour-glass; for the which supply,
Admit me chorus to this history;
Who prologue-like, your humble patience pray,
Gently to hear, kindly to judge our play.

[*Exit*]

Act One

1

[*London. Antechamber in the King's Palace*]

[*Enter Archbishop of Canterbury and Bishop of Ely*]

Archbishop. My Lord, I'll tell you, that self bill is urged,
   Which in the eleventh year of the last King's reign
   Was like, and had indeed against us passed,
   But that the scambling and unquiet time
   Did push it out of farther question.

Bishop of Ely. But how, my Lord, shall we resist it now?

Archbishop. It must be thought on; if it pass against us,
   We lose the better half of our possession;
   For all the temporal lands, which men devout
   By testament have given to the Church,
   Would they strip from us; being valued thus,
   As much as would maintain, to the King's honor,
   Full fifteen Earls, and fifteen hundred Knights,
   Six thousand and two hundred good Esquires;
   And to relief of lazars, and weak age
   Of indigent faint souls, past corporal toil,
   A hundred alms-houses, right well supplied;
   And to the coffers of the King beside,
   A thousand pounds by the year. Thus runs the bill.

Bishop of Ely. This would drink deep.

Archbishop. 'Twould drink the cup and all.

Bishop of Ely. But what prevention?

Archbishop. The King is full of grace, and fair regard.

Bishop of Ely. And a true lover of the holy Church.

Archbishop. The courses of his youth promised it not.
   The breath no sooner left his father's body,
   But that his wildness, mortified in him,
   Seemed to die too; yea, at that very moment,

Consideration like an angel came,
And whipped the offending Adam out of him;
Leaving his body as a paradise,
To envelop and contain celestial spirits.
Never was such a sudden scholar made;
Never came reformation in a flood,
With such a heady currance scouring faults;
Nor never hydra-headed wilfulness
So soon did lose his Seat; and all at once;
As in this King.

Bishop of Ely. We are blessed in the change.

Archbishop. Hear him but reason in divinity;
And all-admiring, with an inward wish
You would desire the King were made a prelate;
Hear him debate of commonwealth affairs;
You would say, it has been all in all his study;
Listen his discourse of war; and you shall hear
A fearful battle rendered you in music.
Turn him to any cause of policy,
The Gordian Knot of it he will unloose,
Familiar as his garter; that when he speaks,
The air, a chartered libertine, is still,
And the mute wonder lurk in men's ears,
To steal his sweet and honeyed sentences;
So that the art and practical part of life,
Must be the Mistress to this theoric.
Which is a wonder how his Grace should glean it,
Since his addiction was to courses vain,
His companions unlettered, rude, and shallow,
His hours filled up with riots, banquets, sports;
And never noted in him any study,
Any retirement, any sequestration,
From open haunts and popularity.

Bishop of Ely. The strawberry grows underneath the nettle,
And wholesome berries thrive and ripen best,
Neighbored by fruit of baser quality;
And so the Prince obscured his contemplation
Under the veil of wildness, which, no doubt,
Grew like the summer grass, fastest by night,
Unseen, yet crescive in his faculty.

Archbishop. It must be so; for miracles are ceased;
And therefore we must needs admit the means,

How things are perfected.

Bishop of Ely. But my good Lord;
How now for mitigation of this bill,
Urged by the commons? Does his Majesty
Incline to it, or no?

Archbishop. He seems indifferent;
Or rather swaying more upon our part,
Than cherishing the exhibiters against us;
For I have made an offer to his Majesty,
Upon our spiritual convocation,
And in regard of causes now in hand,
Which I have opened to his Grace at large,
As touching France, to give a greater sum,
Than ever at one time the clergy yet
Did to his predecessors part withal.

Bishop of Ely. How did this offer seem received, my Lord?

Archbishop. With good acceptance of his Majesty;
Save that there was not time enough to hear,
As I perceived his Grace would fain have done,
The severals and unhidden passages
Of his true titles to some certain dukedoms,
And generally, to the Crown and Seat of France,
Derived from Edward, his great grandfather.

Bishop of Ely. What was the impediment that broke this off?

Archbishop. The French Ambassador upon that instant.
Craved audience; and the hour I think is come,
To give him hearing; Is it four o'clock?

Bishop of Ely. It is

Archbishop. Then go we in, to know his embassy;
Which I could with a ready guess declare,
Before the Frenchman speak a word of it

Bishop of Ely. I'll wait upon you, and I long to hear it.

[*Exit Both*]

[*Main Hall in the Palace*]

[*Enter the King, Humphrey, Bedford, Clarence, Warwick,
Westmoreland, and Exeter*]

King Henry. Where is my gracious Lord of Canterbury?

Exeter. Not here in presence.

King Henry. Send for him, good Uncle.

Westmerland. Shall we call in the Ambassador, my Liege?

King Henry. Not yet, my cousin; we would be resolved,
Before we hear him, of some things of weight,
That task our thoughts, concerning us and France.

[*Enter two Bishops*]

Archbishop. God and his angels guard your sacred Throne,
And make you long become it.

King Henry. Sure we thank you.
My learned Lord, we pray you to proceed,
And justly and religiously unfold,
Why the Law Salic, that they have in France,
Or should or should not bar us in our claim;
And God forbid, my dear and faithful Lord,
That you should fashion, wrest, or bow your reading,
Or nicely charge your understanding soul,
With opening titles miscreate, whose right
Suits not in native colors with the truth;
For God does know, how many now in health,
Shall drop their blood, in approbation
Of what your reverence shall incite us to.
Therefore take heed how you impawn our person,
How you awake our sleeping sword of war;
We charge you in the name of God take heed;
For never two such Kingdoms did contend,
Without much fall of blood, whose guiltless drops
Are every one, a woe, a sore complaint,
Against him, whose wrongs gives edge unto the swords,
That makes such waste in brief mortality.
Under this conjuration, speak my Lord;
For we will hear, note, and believe in heart,

That what you speak, is in your conscience washed,
As pure as sin with baptism.

Archbishop. Then hear me gracious Sovereign, and you Peers,
That owe yourselves, your lives, and services,
To this Imperial Throne. There is no bar
To make against your Highness' claim to France,
But this which they produce from Pharamond,
"In terram Salicam Mulieres ne succedant,"
No woman shall succeed in Salic land;
Which Salic land, the French unjustly gloze
To be the Realm of France, and Pharamond
The founder of this law, and female bar.
Yet their own authors faithfully affirm,
That the Land Salic is in Germany,
Between the floods of Sala and of Elbe;
Where Charles the Great, having subdued the Saxons,
There left behind and settled certain French;
Who, holding in disdain the German women
For some dishonest manners of their life,
Established then this law; to wit, no female
Should be inheritrix in Salic land;
Which Salic, as I said, between Elbe and Sala,
Is at this day in Germany, called Meissen.
Then does it well appear, the Salic Law
Was not devised for the Realm of France;
Nor did the French possess the Salic land,
Until four hundred one and twenty years
After defunction of King Pharamond,
Idly supposed the founder of this law,
Who died within the year of our redemption,
Four hundred twenty six; and Charlemagne
Subdued the Saxons, and did seat the French
Beyond the River Sala, in the year
Eight hundred five. Besides, their writers say,
King Pepin, which deposed Childrik,
Did as heir General, being descended
Of Blithild, which was daughter to King Clothair,
Make claim and title to the Crown of France.
Hugh Capet also, who usurped the Crown
Of Charles the Duke of Lorraine, sole heir male
Of the true line and stock of Charlemagne;
To find his title with some shows of truth,

Though in pure truth it was corrupt and naught,
Conveyed himself as the heir to the Lady Lingare,
Daughter to Charlemagne, who was the son
To Louis the Emperor, and Louis the son
Of Charles the Great; also King Louis the Tenth,
Who was sole heir to the Usurper Capet,
Could not keep quiet in his conscience,
Wearing the Crown of France, till satisfied,
That fair Queen Isabel, his grandmother,
Was lineal of the Lady Ermengare,
Daughter to Charles the foresaid Duke of Lorraine;
By the which marriage, the line of Charles the Great
Was re-united to the Crown of France.
So, that as clear as is the summer's sun,
King Pepin's title, and Hugh Capet's claim,
King Louis his satisfaction, all appear
To hold in right and title of the female;
So do the Kings of France unto this day.
Howbeit, they would hold up this Salic Law,
To bar your Highness claiming from the female,
And rather choose to hide them in a net,
Than amply to embar their crooked titles,
Usurped from you and your progenitors.

King Henry. May I with right and conscience make this claim?

Archbishop. The sin upon my head, dread Sovereign;
For in the Book of Numbers is it writ,
When the man dies, let the inheritance
Descend unto the daughter. Gracious Lord,
Stand for your own, unwind your bloody flag ,
Look back into your mighty ancestors;
Go, my dread Lord, to your great grandsire's tomb,
From whom you claim; invoke his warlike spirit,
And your great Uncles, Edward the Black Prince,
Who on the French ground played a tragedy,
Making defeat on the full power of France;
While his most mighty father on a hill
Stood smiling, to behold his lion's whelp
Forage in blood of French nobility.
O, noble English, that could entertain
With half their forces, the full pride of France,
And let another half stand laughing by,
All out of work, and cold for action.

Bishop of Ely. Awake remembrance of these valiant dead,
  And with your puissant arm renew their feats;
  You are their heir, you sit upon their throne;
  The blood and courage that renowned them,
  Runs in your veins; and my thrice-puissant Liege
  Is in the very May-morn of his youth,
  Ripe for exploits and mighty enterprises.

Exeter. Your brother Kings and Monarchs of the Earth
  Do all expect, that you should rouse yourself,
  As did the former lions of your blood.

Westmoreland. They know your Grace has cause, and means, and
    might;
  So has your Highness; never King of England
  Had nobles richer, and more loyal subjects,
  Whose hearts have left their bodies here in England,
  And lie pavillioned in the fields of France.

Archbishop. O, let their bodies follow, my dear Liege
  With blood, and sword and fire, to win your right;
  In aid whereof, we of the spiritualty
  Will raise your Highness such a mighty sum,
  As never did the clergy at one time
  Bring in to any of your ancestors.

King Henry. We must not only arm to invade the French,
  But lay down our proportions, to defend
  Against the Scot, who will make inroad upon us,
  With all advantages.

Archbishop. They of those marches, gracious Sovereign,
  Shall be a wall sufficient to defend
  Our inland from the pilfering borderers.

King Henry. We do not mean the coursing snatchers only,
  But fear the main intendment of the Scot,
  Who has been still a giddy neighbor to us;
  For you shall read, that my great grandfather
  Never went with his forces into France,
  But that the Scot, on his unfurnished kingdom,
  Came pouring like the tide into a breach,
  With ample and brim fullness of his force,
  Galling the gleaned land with hot assays,
  Girding with grievous siege, castles and towns;
  That England being empty of defense,
  Has shook and trembled at the ill neighborhood.

Archbishop. She has been the more feared than harmed, my Liege;
   For hear her but exampled by herself,
   When all her chivalry has been in France,
   And she a mourning widow of her nobles,
   Shee has herself not only well defended,
   But taken and impounded as a stray,
   The King of Scots; whom she did send to France,
   To fill King Edward's fame with prisoner Kings,
   And make their chronicle as rich with praise,
   As is the ooze and bottom of the sea
   With sunken wreck, and sum-less treasuries.

Bishop of Ely. But there's a saying very old and true,
   If that you will France win, then with Scotland first begin.
   For once the eagle, England, being in prey,
   To her unguarded nest, the weasel, Scot,
   Comes sneaking, and so sucks her Princely eggs,
   Playing the mouse in absense of the cat,
   To tame and havoc more than she can eat.

Exeter. It follows then, the cat must stay at home,
   Yet that is but a crushed necessity,
   Since we have locks to safeguard necessaries,
   And pretty traps to catch the petty theeves.
   While that the armed hand does fight abroad,
   The advised head defends itself at home;
   For government, though high, and low, and lower,
   Put into parts, does keep in one consent,
   Congreeing in a full and natural close,
   Like music.

Archbishop. Therefore does heaven divide
   The state of man in diverse functions,
   Setting endeavour in continual motion;
   To which is fixed as an aim or butt,
   Obedience; for so work the honey bees,
   Creatures that by a rule in nature teach
   The act of order to a peopled kingdom.
   They have a King, and officers of sorts,
   Where some like magistrates correct at home;
   Others, like merchants venture trade abroad;
   Others, like soldiers armed in their stings,
   Make boot upon the summer's velvet buds;
   Which pillage, they with merry march bring home
   To the tent-royal of their Emperor;

Who, busied in her Majesty's surveys
The singing masons building roofs of gold,
The civil citizens kneading up the honey;
The poor mechanic porters, crowding in
Their heavy burdens at her narrow gate;
The sad-eyed justice with his surly hum,
Delivering over to executors pale
The lazy yawning drone; I this infer,
That many things having full reference
To one consent, may work contrariously,
As many arrows loosed several ways
Come to one mark; as many ways meet in one town,
As many fresh streams meet in one salt sea;
As many lines close in the dial's center;
So may a thousand actions once afoot,
And in one purpose, and be all well borne
Without defeat. Therefore, to France, my Liege,
Divide your happy England into four,
Whereof, take you one quarter into France,
And you withal shall make all Gallia shake.
If we with thrice such powers left at home,
Cannot defend our own doors from the dog,
Let us be worried, and our nation lose
The name of hardiness and policy.

King Henry. Call in the messengers sent from the Dauphin.
Now are we well resolved, and by God's help
And yours, the noble sinews of our power,
France being ours, we'll bend it to our awe,
Or break it all to pieces. Or there we'll sit,
Ruling in large and ample empery,
Over France, and all her, almost, Kingly dukedoms,
Or lay these bones in an unworthy urn,
Tombless, with no remembrance over them;
Either our history shall with full mouth
Speak freely of our acts, or else our grave
Like Turkish mute, shall have a tongueless mouth,
Not worshipped with a waxen epitaph.

[*Enter Ambassadors of France*]

Now are we well prepared to know the pleasure
Of our fair cousin Dauphin; for we hear,
Your greeting is from him, not from the King.

French Ambassador. May it please your Majesty to give us leave

Freely to render what we have in charge;
Or shall we sparingly show you far off
The Dauphin's meaning, and our embassy.

King Henry. We are no tyrant, but a Christian King,
Unto whose grace our passion is as subject
As is our wretches fettered in our prisons,
Therefore with frank and with uncurbed plainness,
Tell us the Dauphin's mind.

French Ambassador. Thus then in few;
Your Highness lately sending into France,
Did claim some certain dukedoms, in the right
Of your great predecessor, King Edward the Third.
In answer of which claim, the Prince our Master
Says, that you savor too much of your youth,
And bids you be advised; there's nought in France,
That can be with a nimble galliard won;
You cannot revel into dukedoms there.
He therefore sends you meeter for your spirit
This tun of treasure; and in lieu of this,
Desires you let the dukedoms that you claim
Hear no more of you. This the Dauphin speaks.

King Henry. What treasure, Uncle?

Exeter. Tennis balls, my Liege.

King Henry. We are glad the Dauphin is so pleasant with us,
His present, and your pains we thank you for;
When we have matched our rackets to these balls,
We will in France, by God's grace, play a set,
Shall strike his father's Crown into the hazard.
Tell him, he has made a match with such a wrangler,
That all the courts of France will be disturbed
With chases. And we understand him well,
How he comes over us with our wilder days,
Not measuring what use we made of them.
We never valued this poor seat of England,
And therefore living hence, did give ourself
To barbarous license; as 'tis ever common,
That men are merriest, when they are from home.
But tell the Dauphin, I will keep my State,
Be like a King, and show my sail of greatness,
When I do rouse me in my Throne of France.
For that I have laid by my Majesty,

And plodded like a man for working days;
But I will rise there with so full a glory,
That I will dazzle all the eyes of France—
Yea strike the Dauphin blind to look on us,
And tell the pleasant Prince, this mock of his
Has turned his balls to gun-stones, and his soul
Shall stand sore charged, for the wasteful vengeance
That shall fly with them; for many a thousand widows
Shall this his mock, mock out of their dear husbands;
Mock mothers from their sons, mock castles down;
And some are yet ungotten and unborn,
That shall have cause to curse the Dauphin's scorn.
But this lies all within the will of God,
To whom I do appeal, and in whose name
Tell you the Dauphin, I am coming on,
To venge me as I may, and to put forth
My rightful hand in a well-hallowed cause.
So get you hence in peace; and tell the Dauphin,
His jest will savor but of shallow wit,
When thousands weep more than did laugh at it.
Convey them with safe conduct. Fare you well.

[*Exit Ambassadors*]

Exeter. This was a merry message.

King Henry. We hope to make the sender blush at it;
Therefore, my Lords, omit no happy hour,
That may give furtherance to our expedition;
For we have now no thought in us but France,
Save those to God, that run before our business.
Therefore let our proportions for these wars
Be soon collected, and all things thought upon,
That may with reasonable swiftness add
More feathers to our wings; for God before,
We'll chide this Dauphin at his father's door.
Therefore let every man now task his thought,
That this fair action may on foot be brought.

[*Exit All*]

Act Two

[Flourish]

[Enter Chorus]

Chorus. Now all the youth of England are on fire,
    And silken dalliance in the wardrobe lies;
    Now thrive the armorers, and honors thought
    Reigns solely in the breast of every man.
    They sell the pasture now, to buy the horse;
    Following the mirror of all Christian Kings,
    With winged heels, as English Mercuries.
    For now sits expectation in the air,
    And hides a sword, from hilts unto the point,
    With crowns imperial, crowns and coronets,
    Promised to Harry, and his followers.
    The French advised by good intelligence
    Of this most dreadful preparation,
    Shake in their fear, and with pale policy
    Seek to divert the English purposes.
    O, England; model to your inward greatness,
    Like little body with a mighty heart;
    What might you do, that honor would you do,
    Were all your children kind and natural;
    But see, your fault France has in you found out,
    A nest of hollow bosoms, which he fills
    With treacherous crowns, and three corrupted men;
    One, Richard Earl of Cambridge, and the second
    Henry Lord Scroop of Masham, and the third
    Sir Thomas Grey, Knight of Northumberland,
    Have for the gilt of France, O, guilt indeed,
    Confirmed conspiracy with fearful France,
    And by their hands, this grace of Kings must die.
    If Hell and treason hold their promises,

Before he take ship for France; and in Southampton.
Linger your patience on, and we'll digest
The abuse of distance; force a play;
The sum is paid, the traitors are agreed,
The King is set from London, and the scene
Is now transported, Gentles, to Southampton,
There is the playhouse now, there must you sit,
And thence to France shall we convey you safe,
And bring you back; charming the narrow seas
To give you gentle pass; for if we may,
We'll not offend one stomach with our play.
But till the King come forth, and not till then,
Unto Southampton do we shift our scene.

[*Exit*]

[*London. A Street*]

[*Enter Corporal Nym, and Lieutenant Bardolph*]

Lieutenant Bardolph. Well met, Corporal Nym.

Corporal Nym. Good morrow, Lieutenant Bardolph.

Lieutenant Bardolph. What, are ancient Pistol and you friends yet?

Corporal Nym. For my part, I care not; I say little; but when time
shall serve, there shall be smiles, but that shall be as it may.
I dare not fight, but I will wink and hold out my iron; it is a
simple one, but what though? It will toast cheese, and it will
endure cold, as another man's sword will; and there's an end.

Lieutenant Bardolph. I will bestow a breakfast to make you
friends, and we'll be all three sworn brothers to France; Let it
be so good Corporal Nym.

Corporal Nym. Faith, I will live so long as I may, that's the certain
of it; and when I cannot live any longer, I will do as I may; that
is my rest, that is the rendezvous of it.

Lieutenant Bardolph. It is certain Corporal, that he is married to
Nell Quickly, and certainly she did you wrong, for you were
truth-plight to her.

Corporal Nym. I cannot tell, things must be as they may; men may
sleep, and they may have their throats about them at that time,
and some say, knives have edges; It must be as it may, though
patience be a tired name, yet she will plod, there must be
conclusions, well, I cannot tell.

[*Enter Pistol and Quickly*]

Lieutenant Bardolph. Here comes ancient Pistol and his wife; good
Corporal be patient here. How now my host Pistol?

Pistol. Base tyke, call you me host, now by this hand I swear I
scorn the term; nor shall my Nell keep lodgers.

Hostess. No, by my truth, not long; for we cannot lodge and board
a dozen or fourteen gentlewomen that live honestly by the
prick of their needles, but it will be thought we keep a bawdy-
house straight.
[*Nym and Pistol draw swords*] O, welladay lady, if he
be not drawn now, we shall see willful adultery and

murder committed.

Lieutenant Bardolph. Good Lieutenant, good Corporal offer
nothing here.

Corporal Nym. Pish.

Pistol. Pish for you, Iceland dog; you prick-eared cur of Iceland.

Hostess. Good Corporal Nym, show your valor, and put
up your sword.

Corporal Nym. Will you shog off? I would have you solus.

Pistol. Solus, egregious dog? O, viper vile; the solus in your most
mervailous face, the solus in your teeth, and in your throat,
and in your hateful lungs, yea in your maw perdy; and which
is worse, within your nasty mouth. I do retort the solus in your
bowels, for I can take, and Pistol's cock is up, and flashing fire
will follow.

Corporal Nym. I am not Barbason, you cannot conjure me; I have
an humor to knock you indifferently well. If you grow foul
with me Pistol, I will scour you with my rapier, as I may, in fair
terms. If you would walk off, I would prick your guts a little in
good terms, as I may, and that's the humor of it.

Pistol. O, braggard vile, and damned furious wight, the grave does
gape, and doting death is never, therefore exhale.

Lieutenant Bardolph. Hear me, hear me what I say; he that strikes
the first stroke, I'll run him up to the hilts, as I am a soldier.

Pistol. An oath of mickle might, and fury shall abate. Give me your
fist, your forefoot to me give; your spirits are most tall.

Corporal Nym. I will cut your throat one time or other in fair
terms, that is the humor of it.

Pistol. Couple a gorge, that is the word. I defy you again. O,
hound of Crete, think you my spouse to get? No, to the spittle
go, and from the powdering tub of infamy, fetch forth the lazar
kite of Cressid's kind, Doll Tearsheet, she by name, and her
spouse. I have, and I will hold the quondam Quickly for the
only she; and pauca, there's enough to go to.

[Enter the Boy]

Boy. My host Pistol, you must come to my Mayster, and your
hostess; he is very sick, and would to bed. Good Bardolph, put
your face between his sheets, and do the office of a warming-
pan; faith, he's very ill.

Lieutenant Bardolph. Away you rogue.

Hostess. By my truth he'll yield the crow a pudding one of these days; the King has killed his heart. Good husband come home presently.

[*Exit Hostess*]

Lieutenant Bardolph. Come, shall I make you two friends. We must to France together; why the devil should we keep knives to cut one another's throats?

Pistol. Let floods over-swell, and fiends for food howl on.

Corporal Nym. You'll pay me the eight shillings I won of you at betting?

Pistol. Base is the slave that pays.

Corporal Nym. That now I will have; that's the humor of it.

Pistol. As manhood shall compound; push home.

[*They Draw*]

Lieutenant Bardolph. By this sword, he that makes the first thrust, I'll kill him; By this sword, I will.

Pistol. Sword is an oath, and oaths must have their course.

Lieutenant Bardolph. Coporal Nym, and you will be friends. be friends, and you will not, why then be enemies with me to; please, put up.

Pistol. A noble shall you have, and present pay, and liquor likewise will I give to you, and friendship shall combine, and brotherhood. I'll live by Nym, and Nym shall live by me, is not this just? For I shall sutler be unto the camp, and profits will accrue. Give me your hand.

Corporal Nym. I shall have my noble?

Pistol. In cash, most justly paid.

Corporal Nym. Well, then that's the humor of it.

[*Enter Hostess*]

Hostess. As ever you come of women, come in quickly to Sir John; a poor heart, he is so shaked of a burning quotidian tertian, that it is most lamentable to behold. Sweet men, come to him.

Corporal Nym. The King has run bad humors on the Knight, that's the even of it.

Pistol. Nym, you have spoke the right, his heart is fracted and corroborate.

Corporal Nym. The King is a good King, but it must be as it may;

he passes some humors, and careers.

Pistol. Let us condole the Knight, for, lambkins, we will live.

[*Exit All*]

2

[*Southampton. A Council Chamber*]

[*Enter Exeter, Bedford, and Westmoreland*]

Bedford. Before God, his Grace is bold to trust these traitors.

Exeter. They shall be apprehended by and by.

Westmoreland. How smooth and even they do bear themselves,
    as if allegiance in their bosom's sat, crowned with faith, and
    constant loyalty.

Bedford. The King has note of all that they intend, by interception,
    which they dream not of.

Exeter. Nay, but the man that was his bedfellow,
    Whom he has dulled and cloyed with gracious favors;
    That he should for a foreign purse, so sell
    His Sovereign's life to death and treachery.

[*Sound Trumpets*]

[*Enter the King, Scroop, Cambridge, and Lord Grey*]

King Henry. Now sits the wind fair, and we will aboard.
    My Lord of Cambridge, and my kind Lord of Masham,
    And you my gentle Knight, give me your thoughts;
    Think you not that the powers we bear with us
    Will cut their passage through the force of France?
    Doing the execution, and the act,
    For which we have in head assembled them.

Scroop. No doubt my Liege, if each man do his best.

King Henry. I doubt not that, since we are well persuaded
    We carry not a heart with us from hence,
    That grows not in a fair consent with ours;
    Nor leave not one behind, that does not wish
    Success and conquest to attend on us.

Cambridge. Never was Monarch better feared and loved,
    Than is your Majesty; there's not I think a subject
    That sits in heart-grief and uneasiness
    Under the sweet shade of your government.

Lord Grey. True; those that were your father's enemies,
    Have steeped their galls in honey, and do serve you
    With heart's create of duty, and of zeal.

King Henry. We therefore have great cause of thankfulness,
  And shall forget the office of our hand
  Sooner than quittance of desert and merit,
  According to the weight and worthiness.

Scroop. So service shall with steeled sinews toil,
  And labor shall refresh itself with hope
  To do your Grace incessant services.

King Henry. We judge no less. Uncle of Exeter,
  Enlarge the man committed yesterday,
  That railed against our person; we consider
  It was excess of wine that set him on,
  And on his more advice, we pardon him.

Scroop. That's mercy, but too much security;
  Let him be punished, Sovereign, lest example
  Breed, by his sufferance, more of such a kind.

King Henry. O, let us yet be merciful.

Cambridge. So may your Highness, and yet punish too.

Lord Grey. Sir, you show great mercy if you give him life,
  After the taste of much correction.

King Henry. Alas, your too much love and care of me,
  Are heavy orisons against this poor wretch;
  If little faults proceeding on distemper,
  Shall not be winked at, how shall we stretch our eyes
  When capital crimes, chewed, swallowed, and digested,
  Appear before us? We'll yet enlarge that man,
  Though Cambridge, Scroop, and Grey, in their dear care
  And tender preservation of our person
  Would have him punished. And now to our French causes,
  Who are the late commissioners?

Cambridge. I one my Lord,
  Your Highness bade me ask for it today.

Scroop. So did you me, my Liege.

Lord Grey. And I, my Royal Sovereign.

King Henry. Then Richard Earl of Cambridge, there is yours;
  There yours, Lord Scroop of Masham, and Sir Knight;
  Grey of Northumberland, this same is yours;
  Read them, and know I know your worthiness.
  My Lord of Westmoreland, and Uncle Exeter,
  We will aboard tonight. Why how now, Gentlemen?
  What see you in those papers, that you lose

So much complexion? Look you how they change;
Their cheeks are paper. Why, what read you there,
That have so cowarded and chased your blood
Out of appearance.

Cambridge. I do confess my fault,
And do submit me to your Highness mercy.

Lord Grey and Scroop. To which we all appeal.

King Henry. The mercy that was quick in us but late,
By your own counsel is suppressed and killed;
You must not dare, for shame, to talk of mercy,
For your own reasons turn into your bosoms,
As dogs upon their masters, worrying you;
See you my Princes, and my noble Peers,
These English monsters; my Lord of Cambridge here,
You know how apt our love was, to accord
To furnish with all appertinence
Belonging to his honor; and this man,
Has for a few light crowns, lightly conspired
And sworn unto the practices of France
To kill us here in Hampton. To the which,
This Knight no less for bounty bound to us
Than Cambridge is, has likewise sworne. But O,
What shall I say to you Lord Scroop, you cruel,
Ungrateful, savage, and inhumane creature?
You that did bear the key of all my counsels,
That knew the very bottom of my soul,
That, almost, might have coined me into gold,
Would you have practiced on me, for your use?
May it be possible, that foreign hire
Could out of you extract one sparke of evil
That might annoy my finger? 'Tis so strange,
That though the truth of it stands off as gross
As black and white, my eye will scarcely see it.
Treason, and murder, ever kept together,
As two-yoke devils sworn to either's purpose,
Working so grossly in an natural cause,
That admiration did not hoop at them.
But you, against all proportion, did bring in
Wonder to wait on treason, and on murder;
And whatsoever cunning fiend it was
That wrought upon you so preposterously,
Has got the voice in hell for excellence;

And other devils that suggest by treasons,
Do botch and bungle up damnation,
With patches, colors, and with forms being fetched
From glistering semblances of piety;
But he that tempered you, bade you stand up,
Gave you no instance why you should do treason,
Unless to dub you with the name of traitor.

King Henry. If that same demon that has gulled you thus,
Should with his lion-gate walk the whole world,
He might return to vasty Tartar back,
And tell the legions, I can never win
A soul so easy as that Englishman's.
Oh, how have you with jealousy infected
The sweetness of affiance? Show men dutiful?
Why so did you; seem they grave and learned?
Why so did you. Come they of noble family?
Why so did you. Seem they religious?
Why so did you. Or are they spare in diet,
Free from gross passion, or of mirth, or anger,
Constant in spirit, not swerving with the blood,
Garnished and decked in modest complement,
Not working with the eye, without the ear,
And but in purged judgment trusting neither,
Such and so finely boulted did you seem;
And thus, your fall has left a kind of blot,
To make you full fraught man, and best endued
With some suspicion, I will weep for you.
For this revolt of yours, I think is like
Another fall of man. Their faults are open,
Arrest them to the answer of the law,
And God acquit them of their practices.

Exeter. I arrest you of high treason, by the name of
Richard Earl of Cambridge.
I arrest you of high treason, by the name of Thomas
Lord Scroop of Marsham.
I arrest you of high treason, by the name of Thomas
Grey, Knight of Northumberland.

Scroop. Our purposes, God justly has discovered,
And I repent my fault more than my death,
Which I beseech your Highness to forgive,
Although my body pay the price of it.

Cambridge. For me, the gold of France did not seduce,

Although I did admit it as a motive,
The sooner to effect what I intended;
But God be thanked for prevention,
Which in sufferance heartily will rejoice,
Beseeching God, and you, to pardon me.

Lord Grey. Never did faithful subject more rejoice
At the discovery of most dangerous treason,
Than I do at this hour joy over myself,
Prevented from a damned enterprise;
My fault, but not my body, pardon Sovereign.

King Henry. God quit you in his mercy; Hear your sentence.
You have conspired against our Royal person,
Joined with an enemy proclaimed, and from his coffers,
Received the golden earnest of our death;
Wherein you would have sold your King to slaughter,
His Princes, and his Peers to servitude,
His subjects to oppression, and contempt,
And his whole kingdom into desolation;
Touching our person, seek we no revenge,
But we our Kingdom's safety must so tender,
Whose ruin you sought, that to her laws
We do deliver you. Get you therefore hence,
Poor miserable wretches, to your death;
The taste whereof, God of his mercy give
You patience to endure, and true repentance
Of all your dear offenses. Bear them hence.

[Exit as prisoners Cambridge, Scroop and Grey]

Now Lords, for France; the enterprise whereof
Shall be to you as us, like glorious.
We doubt not of a fair and lucky war,
Since God so graciously has brought to light
This dangerous treason, lurking in our way,
To hinder our beginnings. We doubt not now,
But every rub is smoothed on our way.
Then forth, dear countrymen; let us deliver
Our puissance into the hand of God,
Putting it straight in expedition.
Cheerily to sea, the signs of war advance,
No King of England, if not King of France.

[Flourish]

[Exit All]

[London. In front of a tavern]

[Enter Pistol, Nym, Bardolph, Boy, and Hostess]

Hostess. I beg you, honey sweet husband, let me bring you to Staines.

Pistol. No; for my manly heart does yearn. Bardolph, be blythe; Nym, rouse your vaunting veins; Boy, bristle your courage up; for Falstaff he is dead, and we must yearn therefore.

Lieutenant Bardolph. Would I were with him, wheresomever he is, either in Heaven, or in Hell.

Hostess. Nay sure, he's not in Hell; he's in Arthur's bosom, if ever man went to Arthur's bosom; a made a finer end, and went away and it had been any Christom child; a parted even just between twelve and one, even at the turning of the tide; for after I saw him fumble with the sheets, and play with flowers, and smile upon his finger's end, I knew there was but one way; for his nose was as sharp as a pen, and a table of green fields. "How now Sir John?" quoth I, "What man? be a good cheer." So a cried out, "God, God, God," three or four times; now I, to comfort him, bid him a should not think of God; I hoped there was no need to trouble himself with any such thoughts yet; so a bade me lay more clothes on his feet; I put my hand into the bed, and felt them, and they were as cold as any stone; then I felt to his knees, and so up-peered, and upward, and all was as cold as any stone.

Nym. They say he cried out of sack.

Hostess. Aye, that a did.

Lieutenant Bardolph. And of women.

Hostess. Nay, that a did not.

Boy. Yes that a did, and said they were devils incarnate.

Hostess. A could never abide carnation, 'twas a color he never liked.

Boy. A said once, the devil would have him about women.

Hostess. A did in some sort, indeed, handle women; but then he was rheumatic, and talked of the whore of Babylon.

Boy. Do you not remember a saw a flea stick upon Bardolph's nose, and a said it was a black soul burning in Hell.

Lieutenant Bardolph. Well, the fuel is gone that maintained that fire; that's all the riches I got in his service.

Nym. Shall we shog? the King will be gone from Southampton.

Pistol. Come, let's away. My love, give me your lips; look to my chattels, and my moveables; let senses rule; the world is, pitch and pay; trust none; for oaths are straws, men's faiths are wafer-cakes, and hold-fast is the only dog; my duck, therefore Caveto be your counselor. Go, clear your crystals. Yokefellows in arms, let us to France, like horseleeches my boys, to suck, to suck, the very blood to suck.

Boy. And that's but unwholesome food, they say.

Pistol. Touch her soft mouth, and march.

Lieutenant Bardolph. Farewell Hostess.

Nym. I cannot kiss, that is the humor of it; but adieu.

Pistol. Let huswifery appear; keep close, I you command.

Hostess. Farewell; adieu.

[*Exit All*]

[*France. French King's Palace*]

[*Enter the French King, the Dauphin, the Dukes of Berry and Brittany, Constable of France*]

French King. Thus comes the English with full power upon us,
And more than carefully it us concerns,
To answer royally in our defenses.
Therefore the Dukes of Berry and of Brittany,
Of Brabant and of Orleans, shall make forth,
And you Prince Dauphin, with all swift dispatch
To line and new repair our towns of war
With men of courage, and with means defendant;
For England his approaches makes as fierce,
As waters to the sucking of a gulf.
It fits us then to be as provident,
As fear may teach us, out of late examples
Left by the fatal and neglected English,
Upon our fields

Dauphin. My most redoubted father,
It is most meet we arm us against the foe;
For peace itself should not so dull a kingdom,
Though war nor no known quarrel were in question,
But that defenses, musters, preparations,
Should be maintained, assembled, and collected,
As were a war in expectation.
Therefore I say, 'tis meet we all go forth,
To view the sick and feeble parts of France;
And let us do it with no show of fear,
No, with no more than if we heard that England
Were busied with a Whitsun morris-dance;
For, my good Liege, she is so idly Kinged,
Her scepter so fantastically borne,
By a vain, giddy, shallow, humorous youth,
That fear attends her not.

Constable. O, peace, Prince Dauphin,
You are too much mistaken in this King;
Question your Grace the late Ambassadors,
With what great State he heard their embassy,
How well supplied with noble counselors,

How modest in exception; and withal,
How terrible in constant resolution;
And you shall find, his vanities fore-spent,
Were but the outside of the Roman Brutus,
Covering discretion with a coat of folly;
As gardeners do with ordure hide those roots
That shall first spring, and be most delicate.

Dauphin. Well, 'tis not so, my Lord High Constable.
But though we think it so, it is no matter;
In cases of defense, 'tis best to weigh
The enemy more mighty than he seems,
So the proportions of defense are filled;
Which of a weak and niggardly projection,
Does like a miser spoil his coat, with scanting
A little cloth.

French King. Think we King Harry strong;
And Princes, look you strongly arm to meet him.
The kindred of him has been fleshed upon us;
And he is bred out of that bloody strain,
That haunted us in our familiar paths;
Witness our too much memorable shame,
When Cressy Battle fatally was struck,
And all our Princes captived, by the hand
Of that black name, Edward, Black Prince of Wales;
While that his mountain sire, on mountain standing
Up in the air, crowned with the golden sun,
Saw his heroical seed, and smiled to see him
Mangle the work of nature, and deface
The patterns, that by God and by French fathers
Had twenty years been made. This is a stem
Of that victorious stock; and let us fear
The native mightiness and fate of him.

[*Enter a Messenger*]

Messenger. Ambassadors from Harry King of England,
Do crave admittance to your Majesty.

French King. We'll give them present audience.
Go, and bring them.
You see this chase is hotly followed, friends.

Dauphin. Turn head, and stop pursuit; for coward dogs
Most spend their mouths, when what they seem to threaten
Runs far before them. Good my Sovereign

Take up the English short, and let them know
Of what a Monarchy you are the head;
Self-love, my Liege, is not so vile a sin,
As self-neglecting.

[*Enter Exeter*]

French King. From our brother of England?

Exeter. From him, and thus he greets your Majesty;
He wills you in the name of God Almighty,
That you divest yourself, and lay apart
The borrowed glories, that by gift of Heaven,
By law of nature, and of nations, belongs
To him and to his heirs, namely, the Crown,
And all wide-stretched honors, that pertain
By custom, and the ordnance of times,
Unto the Crown of France; that you may know
'Tis no sinister, nor no awkward claim,
Picked from the worm-holes of long-vanished days,
Nor from the dust of old oblivion raked,
He sends you this most memorable line,
In every branch truly demonstrative;
Willing you over-look this pedigree;
And when you find him evenly derived
From his most famed, of famous ancestors,
Edward the Third; he bids you then resign
Your Crown and Kingdom, indirectly held
From him, the native and true challenger.

French King. Or else what follows?

Exeter. Bloody constraint; for if you hide the Crown
Even in your hearts, there will he rake for it.
Therefore in fierce tempest is he coming,
In thunder and in earthquake, like a Jove;
That if requiring fail, he will compel.
And bids you, in the bowels of the Lord,
Deliver up the Crown, and to take mercy
On the poor souls, for whom this hungry war
Opens his vasty jaws; and on your head
Turning the widows' tears, the orphans' cries,
The dead-men's blood, the privy maidens' groans,
For husbands, fathers, and betrothed lovers,
That shall be swallowed in this controversy.
This is his claim, his threatening, and my message;

Unless the Dauphin be in presence here;
To whom expressely I bring greeting too.

French King. For us, we will consider of this further;
Tomorrow shall you bear our full intent
Back to our brother of England.

Dauphin. For the Dauphin,
I stand here for him; what to him from England?

Exeter. Scorn and defiance, slight regard, contempt,
And anything that may not mis-become
The mighty sender, does he prize yet.
Thus says my King; and if your father's Highness
Doe not, in grant of all demands at large,
Sweeten the bitter mock you sent his Majesty;
He'll call you to so hot an answer of it,
That caves and womby vaultages of France
Shall chide your trespass, and return your mock
In second accent of his ordinance.

Dauphin. Say; if my father render fair return,
It is against my will; for I desire
Nothing but odds with England.
To that end, as matching to his youth and vanity,
I did present him with the Paris-Balls.

Exeter. He'll make your Paris lover shake for it,
Were it the Mistress Court of mighty Europe;
And be assured, you'll find a difference,
As we his subjects have in wonder found,
Between the promise of his greener days,
And these he masters now; now he weighs time
Even to the utmost grain; that you shall read
In your own losses, if he stay in France.

French King. Tomorrow shall you know our mind at full.

Exeter. Dispatch us with all speed, lest that our King
Come here himself to question our delay;
For he is footed in this land already.

French King. You shall be soon dispatched, with fair conditions.
A night is but small breath, and little pause,
To answer matters of this consequence.

[*Exit All*]

Act Three

[Flourish]

[Enter Chorus]

Chorus. Thus with imagined wing our swift scene flies,
In motion of no less celerity than that of thought.
Suppose, that you have seen
The well-appointed King at Dover Pier,
Embark his Royalty; and his brave fleet,
With silken streamers, the young Phebus faining;
Play with your fancies; and in them behold,
Upon the hempen tackle, ship-boys climbing;
Hear the shrill whistle, which does order give
To sounds confused; behold the threaded sails,
Borne with the invisible and creeping wind,
Draw the huge bottoms through the furrowed sea,
Breasting the lofty surge. O, do but think
You stand upon the rivage, and behold
A city on the inconstant billows dancing;
For so appears this fleet Majestical,
Holding due course to Harfleur. Follow, follow;
Grapple your minds to sternage of this navy,
And leave your England as dead midnight, still,
Guarded with grandsires, babies, and old women,
Either passed, or not arrived to pith and puissance;
For who is he, whose chin is but enriched
With one appearing hair, that will not follow
These culled and choice-drawn cavaliers to France?
Work, work your thoughts, and therein see a siege;
Behold the ordnance on their carriages,
With fatal mouths gaping on girded Harfleur.
Suppose the Ambassador from the French comes back;
Tells Harry, that the King does offer him
Katherine his daughter, and with her to dowry,

Some petty and unprofitable dukedoms.
The offer likes not; and the nimble gunner
With linstock now the devilish cannon touches,

[Alarm, and Artillery fires]

And down goes all before them. Still be kind,
And etch out our performance with your mind.

[Exit Chorus]

1

[*Before Harfleur*]

[*Alarm; Scaling Ladders against the Castle Wall*]

[*Enter the King, Exeter, Bedford, Gloucester, Soldiers*]

King Henry. Once more unto the breach,
   Dear friends, once more;
   Or close the wall up with our English dead;
   In peace, there's nothing so becomes a man,
   As modest stillness, and humility;
   But when the blast of war blows in our ears,
   Then imitate the action of the tiger;
   Stiffen the sinews, commune up the blood,
   Disguise fair nature with hard-favored rage;
   Then lend the eye a terrible aspect;
   Let it pry through the portage of the head,
   Like the brass cannon; let the brow overwhelm it,
   As fearfully, as does a galled rock
   Overhang and jutty his confounded base,
   Swilled with the wild and wastful ocean.
   Now set the teeth, and stretch the nostril wide,
   Hold hard the breath, and bend up every spirit
   To his full height. On, on, you noblish English,
   Whose blood is fed from fathers of war-proof;
   Fathers, that like so many Alexanders,
   Have in these parts from morn till evening fought,
   And sheathed their swords, for lack of argument.
   Dishonor not your mothers; now attest,
   That those whom you called fathers, did beget you.
   Be copy now to men of grosser blood,
   And teach them how to war. And you good yeomen,
   Whose limbs were made in England; show us here
   The mettle of your pasture; let us swear,
   That you are worth your breeding; which I doubt not;
   For there is none of you so mean and base,
   That has not noble luster in your eyes.
   I see you stand like greyhounds in the slips,
   Straying upon the start. The game's afoot;

Follow your spirit; and upon this charge,
Cry, God for Harry, England, and St. George.

[*Alarm, and Cannons go off*]

[*Exit All*]

[*At Harfleur*]

[*Enter Nym, Bardolph, Pistol, and Boy*]

Bardolph. On, on, on, on, on, to the breach, to the breach.

Nym. May you, Corporal, stay, the knocks are too hot; and for my own part, I have not a case of lives; the humor of it is too hot, that is the very plain-song of it.

Pistol. The plain-song is most just; for humors do abound. Knocks go and come; God's vassals drop and die; and sword and shield, in bloody Field, does win immortal fame.

Boy. Would I were in a ale-house in London, I would give all my fame for a pot of ale, and safety.

Pistol. And I; If wishes would prevail with me, my purpose should not fail with me; but there would I hie.

Boy. As duly, but not as truly, as bird does sing on bough.

[*Enter Fluellen*]

Fluellen. Up to the breach, you dogs; avaunt you cullions.

Pistol. Be merciful great Duke to men of mold; abate thy rage, abate your manly rage; abate your rage, great Duke. Good bawcock bate your rage; use lenity, sweet Chuck.

Nym. These be good humors; your Honor wins bad humors.

[*Exit all but the Boy*]

Boy. As young as I am, I have observed these three Swashers; I am boy to them all three, but all they three, though they would serve me, could not be man to me; for indeed three such antiques do not amount to a man; for Bardolph, he is white-livered, and red-faced; by the means whereof, a faces it out, but fights not; for Pistol, he has a killing tongue, and a quiet sword; by the means whereof, a breaks words, and keeps whole weapons; for Nym, he has heard, that men of few words are the best men, and therefore he scorns to say his prayers, lest a should be thought a coward; but his few bad words are matched with as few good deeds; for a never broke any man's head but his own, and that was against a post, when he was drunk. They will steal anything, and call it purchase. Bardolph stole a lute-case, bore it twelve leagues, and sold it

for three half-pence. Nym and Bardolph are sworn brothers
in filching; and in Calais they stole a fire-shovel. I knew by
that piece of service, the men would carry coals. They would
have me as familiar with men's pockets, as their gloves or
their handkerchers; which makes much against my manhood,
if I should take from another's pocket, to put into mine; for
it is plain pocketing up of wrongs. I must leave them, and
seek some better service; their villainy goes against my weak
stomach, and therefore I must cast it up.

[*Exit Boy*]

[*Enter Fluellen and Gower*]

Gower. Captain Fluellen, you must come presently to the mines; the
Duke of Gloucester would speak with you.

Fluellen. To the mines? Tell you the Duke, it is not so good to come
to the mines; for look you, the mines is not according to the
disciplines of the war; the concavities of it is not sufficient;
for look you, the athversary, you may discuss unto the Duke,
look you, is digged himself four yard under the countermines;
by Cheshu, I think a will plow up all, if there is not better
directions.

Gower. The Duke of Gloucester, to whom the order of the siege
is given, is altogether directed by an Irishman, a very valiant
gentleman, truly.

Fluellen. It is Captain Macmorris, is it not?

Gower. I think it be.

Fluellen. By Cheshu he is an ass, as in the world, I will verify as
much in his beard; he has no more directions in the true
disciplines of the wars, look you, of the Roman disciplines,
than is a puppy-dog.

[*Enter Macmorris, and Captain Jamy.*]

Gower. Here a comes, and the Scots Captain, Captain Jamy, with
him.

Fluellen. Captain Jamy is a marvellous falorous gentleman,
that is certain, and of great expedition and knowledge in
the aunchiant wars, upon my particular knowledge of his
directions; by Cheshu he will maintain his argument as well as
any military man in the world, in the disciplines of the pristine
wars of the Romans.

Scots Captain. I say gudday, Captain Fluellen.

Fluellen. Godden to your worship, good Captain James.

Gower. How now Captain Macmorris, have you quit the mines?
have the pioners given over?

Irishman. By Chrish law tish ill done; the work ish give over, the
trompet sound the retreat. By my hand I swear, and my father's
soul, the work ish ill done; it ish give over; I would have
blowed up the town, so Chrish save me law, in an hour. O, tish
ill done, tish ill done; by my hand tish ill done.

Fluellen. Captain Macmorris, I beseech you now, will you voutsafe
me, look you, a few disputations with you, as partly touching
or concerning the disciplines of the war, the Roman wars, in
the way of argument, look you, and friendly communication;
partly to satisfy my opinion, and partly for the satisfaction,
look you, of my mind; as touching the direction of the military
discipline, that is the point.

Scots Captain. It sall be vary gud, gud feith, gud Captens bath, and
I sall quit you with gud leve, as I may pick occasion; that sall I
mary.

Irishman. It is no time to discourse, so Chrish save me; the day
is hot, and the weather, and the wars, and the King, and the
Dukes; it is no time to discourse, the town is beseeched; and
the trumpet call us to the breech, and we talk, and be Chrish
do nothing, tis shame for us all; so God sa'me tis shame to
stand still, it is shame by my hand; and there is throats to be
cut, and works to be done, and there ish nothing done, so
Christ sa'me law.

Scots Captain. By the mes, before these eyes of mine take themselves
to slomber, a'll de gud service, or I'll lig in the grund for it; ay,
or go to death; and I'll pay it as valorously as I may, that sal I
suerly do, that is the breff and the long; mary, I wad full fain
heard some question
tween you tway.

Fluellen. Captain Macmorris, I think, look you, under your
correction, there is not many of your nation.

Irishman. Of my nation? What ish my nation? Ish a villain, and a
basterd, and a knave, and a rascal. What ish my nation? Who
talks of my nation?

Fluellen. Look you, if you take the matter otherwise then is meant,
Captain Macmorris, peradventure I shall think you do not
use me with that affability, as in discretion you ought to use

me, look you, being as good a man as yourself, both in the disciplines of war, and in the derivation of my birth, and in other particularities.

Irishman. I do not know you so good a man as myself; so Chrish save me, I will cut off your head.

Gower. Gentlemen both, you will mistake each other.

Scots Captain. A, that's a foul fault.

[A Parley sounds]

Gower. The town sounds a parley.

Fluellen. Captain Macmorris, when there is more better opportunity to be required, look you, I will be so bold as to tell you, I know the disciplines of war; and there is an end.

[Exit All]

[*Before the Gates of the City*]

[*Enter King Henry and all his train*]

King Henry. How yet resolves the Governor of the town?
This is the latest parle we will admit;
Therefore to our best mercy give yourselves,
Or like to men proud of destruction,
Defy us to our worst; for as I am a soldier,
A name that in my thoughts becomes me best;
If I begin the battery once again,
I will not leave the half-achieved Harfleur,
Till in her ashes she lie buried.
The gates of mercy shall be all shut up,
And the fleshed soldier, rough and hard of heart,
In liberty of bloody hand, shall range
With conscience wide as Hell, mowing like grass
Your fresh fair virgins, and your flowering infants.
What is it then to me, if impious war,
Arrayed in flames like to the Prince of fiends,
Do with his smirched complexion all fell feats,
Enlinked to waste and desolation?
What is it to me, when you yourselves are cause,
If your pure maidens fall into the hand
Of hot and forcing violation?
What rein can hold licentious wickedness,
When down the hill he holds his fierce career?
We may as bootless spend our vain command
Upon the enraged soldiers in their spoil,
As send precepts to the Leviathan, to come ashore.

King Henry. Therefore, you men of Harfleur,
Take pity of your town and of your people,
While yet my soldiers are in my command,
While yet the cool and temperate wind of grace
Over-blows the filthy and contagious clouds
Of heady murder, spoil, and villainy.
If not; why in a moment look to see
The blind and bloody soldier, with foul hand
Desire the locks of your shrill-shrieking daughters;
Your fathers taken by the silver beards,

And their most reverend heads dashed to the walls;
Your naked infants spitted upon pikes,
While the mad mothers, with their howls confused,
Do break the clouds; as did the wives of Jewry,
At Herod's bloody-hunting slaughter-men.
What say you? Will you yield, and this avoid?
Or guilty in defense, be thus destroyed.

[*Enter Governor*]

Governor. Our expectation has this day an end;
The Dauphin, whom of succors we entreated,
Returns us, that his powers are yet not ready,
To raise so great a siege; therefore great King,
We yield our town and lives to your soft mercy;
Enter our gates, dispose of us and ours,
For we no longer are defensible.

King Henry. Open your gates; come Uncle Exeter,
Go you and enter Harfleur; there remain,
And fortify it strongly against the French;
Use mercy to them all for us, dear Uncle.
The winter coming on, and sickness growing
Upon our soldiers, we will retire to Calais.
Tonight in Harfleur will we be your guest,
Tomorrow for the march are we addressed.

[*Flourish*]

[*Exit All,* as *King and company enter the town*]

[*A Room in the French King's Palace*]

[*Enter Katherine and an old Gentlewoman*]

Katherine. Alice, tu as eté en Angleterre, and tu bien parles le
  language

Alice. Un peu, Madame

Katherine. Je te prie m'ensigniez, il faut que j'apprenne a parler;
  Comment appellez-vous la main en Anglois?

Alice. La main? Elle est appelée de hand

Katherine. De hand. E le doigts?

Alice. Le doigts, ma foi j'oublie les doigts, mais je me souviendrai le
  doigts je pense qu'ils sont appelée de fingres. Oui, de fingres.

Katherine. La main de hand, le doigts le fingres, je pense que je
  suis le bon écolier. J'ai gagné deux mots d'Anglois vitement.
  Comment appelez-vous le ongles?

Alice. Le ongles, nous les appelons de nails.

Katherine. De nails. Écoutez: dites moi, si je parle bien; de hand, de
  fingres, e de nails.

Alice. C'est bien dit Madame. Il est fort bon Anglois.

Katherine. Dites-moi l'Anglois pour le bras.

Alice. De arm, Madame

Katherine. E de coude?

Alice. De elbow

Katherine. De elbow; Je m'en fais le répétition de touts les mots que
  vous m'avez, appris dès á present.

Alice. Il est trop difficile, Madame, comme je pense.

Katherine. Excusez-moi, Alice; écoutez, de hand, de fingre, de nails,
  de arma, de bilbow.

Alice. De elbow, Madame.

Katherine. O, Seigneur Dieu, je m'en oublie! De elbow, comment
  appelez-vous le col?

Alice. De nick, Madame.

Katherine. De nick. E le menton?

Alice. De chin.

Katherine. De sin; le col de nick, le menton de sin.

Alice. Oui. Sauf votre honneur en vérité vous prononcez
les mots aussi droit, que le natifs d'Angleterre.

Katherine. Je ne doute point d'apprendre, par la grace de Dieu, et en
peu de temps.

Alice. N'avez vous pas déjà oublié ce que je vous ai enseigné?

Katherine. Non, je reciterai à vous promptement, de hand, de fingre,
de mails.

Alice. De nails, Madame.

Katherine. De nails, de arm, de ilbow.

Alice. Sauf votre honneur, de elbow.

Katherine. Ainsi dis-je; de elbow, de nick, et de sin; comment
appelez-vous le pied et la robe?

Alice. De foot Madame, et de coun.

Katherine. De foot, and le coun! O, Seignieur Dieu! ce sont mots
de son mauvais, corruptible, gros et impudique, et non pour
le dames de honneur d'user. Je ne voudrai prononcer ce mots
devant le seigneurs de France, pour toute le monde. Foh! le
foot and le coun! Néanmoins, je reciterai une autre fois ma
leçon ensemble: De hand, de fingres, de nails, d'arm, d'elbow,
de nick, de sin, de foot, le coun.

Alice. Excellent, Madame.

Katherine. C'est assez pour une fois, allons nous à diner.

[*Exit All*]

[*A Room in the French King's Palace*]

[*Enter the King of France, the Dauphin, Constable of France,
and others*]

French King. 'Tis certain he has passed the river Somme

Constable. And if he be not fought withal, my Lord,
Let us not live in France; let us quit all,
And give our vineyards to a barbarous people.

Dauphin. O, Dieu vivant; shall a few sprays of us,
The emptying of our fathers' luxury,
Our scions, put in wild and savage stock,
Spurt up so suddenly into the clouds,
And over-look their grafters?

Duke of Brittany. Normans, but bastard Normans, Norman
bastards;
Mort du ma vie, if they march along
Unfought withal, but I will sell my dukedom,
To buy a slobbery and a dirty farm
In that nook-shotten Isle of Albion.

Constable. Dieu de battles, where have they this mettle?
Is not their climate foggy, raw, and dull?
On whom, as in despite, the sun looks pale,
Killing their fruit with frowns. Can sodden water,
A drench for sur-reined jades, their barley broth,
Decoct their cold blood to such valiant heat?
And shall our quick blood, spirited with wine,
Seem frosty? O, for honor of our land,
Let us not hang like roping icicles
Upon our houses' thatch, while a more frosty people
Sweat drops of gallant youth in our rich fields;
Poor we call them, in their native Lords.

Dauphin. By faith and honor,
Our Madames mock at us, and plainly say,
Our mettle is bred out, and they will give
Their bodies to the lust of English youth,
To new-store France with bastard warriors.

Duke of Brittany. They bid us to the English dancing-schools,
And teach Lavolta's high, and swift Corantos,

Saying, our Grace is only in our heels,
And that we are most lofty runaways.

French King. Where is Montjoy the Herald? speed him hence,
Let him greet England with our sharp defiance.
Up Princes, and with spirit of honor edged,
More sharper than your swords, hie to the field;
Charles Delabreth, High Constable of France,
You Dukes of Orleans, Bourbon, and of Berry,
Alanson, Brabant, Bar, and Burgundy,
Jaques Chattillion, Rambures, Vandemont,
Beumont, Grandpre, Roussi, and Faulconbridge,
Foix, Lestrale, Bouciquall, and Charolois,
High Dukes, great Princes, Barons, Lords, and Kings;
For your great Seats, now quit you of great shames;
Bar Harry England, that sweeps through our land
With pennons painted in the blood of Harfleur;
Rush on his host, as does the melted snow
Upon the valleys, whose low vassal seat,
The Alps does spit, and void his rheum upon.
Go down upon him, you have power enough,
And in a captive chariot, into Rouen
Bring him our prisoner.

Constable. This becomes the great.
Sorry am I his numbers are so few,
His soldiers sick, and famished in their march;
For I am sure, when he shall see our army,
He'll drop his heart into the sink of fear,
And for achievement, offer us his ransom.

*French King.*Therefore Lord Constable, have on Montjoy,
And let him say to England, that we send,
To know what willing ransom he will give.
Prince Dauphin, you shall stay with us in Rouen.

Dauphin. Not so, I do beseech your Majesty.

French King. Be patient, for you shall remain with us.
Now forth Lord Constable, and Princes all,
And quickly bring us word of England's fall.

[*Exit All*]

[*The English camp in Picardy*]

[*Enter Captains Gower and Fluellen*]

Gower. How now, Captain Fluellen, come you from
  the bridge?

Fluellen. I assure you, there is very excellent services committed at
  the bridge.

Gower. Is the Duke of Exeter safe?

Fluellen. The Duke of Exeter is as magnanimous as Agamemnon,
  and a man that I love and honor with my soul, and my heart,
  and my duty, and my life, and my living, and my uttermost
  power. He is not, God be praised and blessed, any hurt in
  the world, but keeps the bridge most valiantly, with excellent
  discipline. There is an aunchient Lieutenant there at the pridge,
  I think in my very conscience he is as valiant a man as Mark
  Anthony, and he is a man of no estimation in the world, but I
  did see him do as gallant service.

Gower. What do you call him?

Fluellen. He is called aunchient Pistol.

Gower. I know him not.

[*Enter Pistol*]

Fluellen. Here is the man.

Pistol. Captain, I you beseech to do me favors; the Duke of Exeter
  does love you well.

Fluellen. Aye, I praise God, and I have merited some love at his
  hands.

Pistol. Bardolph, a soldier firm and sound of heart, and of buxom
  valor, has by cruel fate, and giddy Fortune's furious fickle
  wheel, that Goddess blind, that stands upon the rolling restless
  stone...

Fluellen. By your patience, aunchient Pistol; fortune is painted blind,
  with a muffler afore her eyes, to signify to you, that fortune is
  blind; and she is painted also with a wheel, to signify to you,
  which is the moral of it, that she is turning and inconstant, and
  mutability, and variation; and her foot, look you, is fixed upon
  a spherical stone, which rolls, and rolls, and rolls; in good

truth, the poet makes a most excellent description of it; fortune is an excellent moral.

Pistol. Fortune is Bardolph's foe, and frowns on him; for he has stolen a pax, and hanged must a be; a damned death; let gallows gape for dog, let man go free, and let not hemp his wind-pipe suffocate; but Exeter has given the doom of death, for pax of little price. Therefore go speak, the Duke will hear your voice; and let not Bardolph's vital thread be cut with edge of penny-cord, and vile reproach. Speak, Captain for his life, and I will you requite.

Fluellen. Aunchient Pistol, I do partly understand your meaning.

Pistol. Why then, rejoice therefore.

Fluellen. Certainly Aunchient, it is not a thing to rejoice at; for if, look you, he were my brother, I would desire the Duke to use his good pleasure, and put him to execution; for discipline ought to be used.

Pistol. Die, and be damned, and figo for your friendship.

Fluellen. It is well.

Pistol. The fig of Spain.

[*Exit Pistol*]

Fluellen. Very good.

Gower. Why, this is an arrant counterfeit rascal, I remember him now; a bawd, a cut-purse.

Fluellen. I'll assure you, a uttered as prave words at the Pridge, as you shall see in a summer's day; but it is very well; what he has spoke to me, that is well I warrant you, when time is serve.

Gower. Why 'tis a gull, a fool, a rogue, that now and then goes to the wars, to grace himself at his return into London, under the form of a soldier; and such fellows are perfect in the great commanders' names, and they will learn you by rote where services were done; at such and such a sconce, at such a breach, at such a convoy; who came off bravely, who was shot, who disgraced, what terms the enemy stood on; and this they con perfectly in the phrase of war; which they trick up with new-tuned oaths; and what a beard of the generals cut, and a horrid suit of the camp, will do among foaming bottles, and ale-washed wits, is wonderful to be thought on; but you must learn to know such slanders of the age, or else you may be marvellously mistook.

Fluellen. I tell you what, Captain Gower; I do perceive he is not the man that he would gladly make show to the world he is; if I find a hole in his coat, I will tell him my mind; hark you, the King is coming, and I must speak with him from the pridge.

[*Drum and Colors*]

[*Enter the King and his poor Soldiers, and Gloucester*]

Fluellen. God pless your Majesty.

King Henry. How now, Fluellen, came you from the bridge?

Fluellen. Aye, so please your Majesty; the Duke of Exeter has very gallantly maintained the pridge; the French is gone off, look you, and there is gallant and most prave passages; marry, the athversary would have possession of the pridge, but he is enforced to retire, and the Duke of Exeter is Master of the pridge; I can tell your Majesty, the Duke is a prave man.

King Henry. What men have you lost, Fluellen?

Fluellen. The perdition of the athversary has been very great, reasonable great; well, for my part, I think the Duke has lost never a man, but one that is like to be executed for robbing a church, one Bardolph, if your Majesty know the man; his face is all bubukles and whelks, and knobs, and flames a fire, and his lips blows at his nose, and it is like a coal of fire, sometimes plew, and sometimes red, but his nose is executed, and his fire's out.

King Henry. We would have all such offendors so cut off; and we give express charge, that in our marches through the country, there be nothing compelled from the villages; nothing taken, but paid for; none of the French upbraided or abused in disdainful language; for when levity and cruelty play for a kingdom, the gentler gamester is the soonest winner.

[*Tucket*]

[*Enter Montjoy*]

Montjoy. You know me by my habit.

King Henry. Well then, I know you; what shall I know of you?

Montjoy. My Master's mind.

King Henry. Unfold it.

Montjoy. Thus says my King; say you to Harry of England, though we seemed dead, we did but sleep; advantage is a better soldier than rashness. Tell him, we could have rebuked him at Harfleur, but that we thought not good to bruise an injury, till it were full ripe. Now we speak upon our cue, and our voice is imperial; England shall repent his folly, see his weakness, and admire our sufferance. Bid him therefore consider of his ransom, which must proportion the losses we have borne, the subjects we have lost, the disgrace we have digested; which in weight to re-answer, his pettiness would bow under. For our losses, his Exchequer is too poor; for the effusion of our blood, the muster of his kingdom too faint a number; and for our disgrace, his own person kneeling at our feet, but a weak and worthless satisfaction. To this add defiance; and tell him for conclusion, he has betrayed his followers, whose condemnation is pronounced; so far my King and Master; so much my office.

King Henry. What is your name? I know your quality.

Montjoy. Montjoy.

King Henry. You do your office fairly. Turn you back,
And tell your King, I do not seek him now,
But could be willing to march on to Calais,
Without impeachment; for to say the sooth,
Though 'tis no wisdom to confess so much
Unto an enemy of craft and vantage,
My people are with sickness much enfeebled,
My numbers lessened; and those few I have,
Almost no better than so many French;
Who when they were in health, I tell you Herald,
I thought, upon one pair of English legs
Did march three Frenchmen. Yet forgive me God,
That I do brag thus; this your air of France
Has blown that vice in me. I must repent;
Go therefore tell your Master, here I am;
My ransom, is this frail and worthless trunk;
My army, but a weak and sickly guard;
Yet God before, tell him we will come on,
Though France himself, and such another neighbor
Stand in our way. There's for your labor Montjoy.
Go bid your Master well advise himself.
If we may pass, we will; if we be hindered,
We shall your tawny ground with your red blood
Discolor; and so Montjoy, fare you well.
The sum of all our answer is but this;

We would not seek a battle as we are,
Nor as we are, we say we will not shun it;
So tell your Master.

Montjoy. I shall deliver so; thanks to your Highness.

Duke of Gloucester. I hope they will not come upon us now.

King Henry. We are in God's hand, brother, not in theirs;
March to the bridge, it now draws toward night,
Beyond the river we'll encamp our selves,
And on tomorrow bid them march away.

[Exit All]

[French camp, near Agincourt]

[Enter the Constable of France, Lord Rambures, Orleans, Dauphin, others]

Constable. Tut, I have the best armor of the world; would it were day.

Orleans. You have an excellent armor; but let my horse have his due.

Constable. It is the best horse of Europe.

Orleans. Will it never be morning?

Dauphin. My Lord of Orleans, and my Lord High Constable, you talk of horse and armor?

Orleans. You are as well provided of both, as any Prince in the world.

Dauphin. What a long night is this? I will not change my horse with any that treads but on four pasterns; Ça ha; he bounds from the Earth, as if his entrails were hairs; le cheval volante, the Pegasus, chez les narines de feu. When I bestride him, I soar, I am a hawk; he trots the air; the Earth sings, when he touches it; the basest horn of his hoof, is more musical than the pipe of Hermes.

Orleans. He's of the color of the nutmeg.

Dauphin. And of the heat of the ginger. It is a beast for Perseus; he is pure air and fire; and the dull elements of Earth and water never appear in him, but only in patient stillness while his rider mounts him; he is indeed a horse, and all other jades you may call beasts.

Constable. Indeed my Lord, it is a most absolute and excellent horse.

Dauphin. It is the Prince of palfreys, his neigh is like the bidding of a Monarch, and his countenance enforces homage.

Orleans. No more cousin.

Dauphin. Nay, the man has no wit, that cannot from the rising of the lark to the lodging of the lamb, vary deserved praise on my palfrey; it is a theme as fluent as the sea; turn the sands into eloquent tongues, and my horse is argument for them all; 'tis a subject for a Sovereign to reason on, and for a Sovereign's Sovereign to ride on; and for the world, familiar to us, and unknown, to lay apart their particular functions, and wonder at him. I once writ a sonnet in his praise, and began thus, "Wonder of nature."

Orleans. I have heard a sonnet begin so to one's mistress.

Dauphin. Then did they imitate that which I composed to my courser, for my horse is my mistress.

Orleans. Your mistress bears well.

Dauphin. Me well, which is the prescript praise and perfection of a good and particular mistress.

Constable. Nay, for I thought yesterday your mistress shrewdly shook your back.

Dauphin. So perhaps did yours.

Constable. Mine was not bridled.

Dauphin. O, then belike she was old and gentle, and you rode like a kern of Ireland, your French hose off, and in your straight trousers.

Constable. You have good judgment in horsemanship.

Dauphin. Be warned by me then; they that ride so, and ride not warily, fall into foul bogs; I had rather have my horse to my mistress.

Constable. I had as lief have my mistress a jade.

Dauphin. I tell you Constable, my mistress wears his own hair.

Constable. I could make as true a boast as that, if I had a sow to my mistress.

Dauphin. Le chien est retourné a son propre vomissement et la truie lavée au bourbier; you make use of anything.

Constable. Yet do I not use my horse for my mistress, or any such proverb, so little kin to the purpose.

Rambures. My Lord Constable, the armor that I saw in your tent tonight, are those stars or suns upon it?

Constable. Stars my Lord.

Dauphin. Some of them will fall tomorrow, I hope.

Constable. And yet my sky shall not want.

Dauphin. That may be, for you bear a many superfluously, and 'twere more honor some were away.

Constable. Even as your horse bears your praises, who would trot as well, were some of your brags dismounted.

Dauphin. Would I were able to load him with his desert. Will it never be day? I will trot tomorrow a mile, and my way shall be paved with English faces.

Constable. I will not say so, for fear I should be faced out of my way; but I would it were morning, for I would fain be about the ears of the English.

Rambures. Who will go to hazard with me for twenty prisoners?

Constable. You must first go yourself to hazard, before you have them.

Dauphin. 'Tis midnight, I'll go arm myself.

[*Exit the Dauphin*]

Orleans. The Dauphin longs for morning.

Rambures. He longs to eat the English.

Constable. I think he will eat all he kills.

Orleans. By the white hand of my lady, he's a gallant Prince.

Constable. Swear by her foot, that she may tread out the oath.

Orleans. He is simply the most active gentleman of France.

Constable. Doing is activity, and he will still be doing.

Orleans. He never did harm, that I heard of.

Constable. Nor will do none tomorrow; he will keep that good name still.

Orleans. I know him to be valiant.

Constable. I was told that, by one that knows him better then you.

Orleans. What's he?

Constable. Well, he told me so himself, and he said he cared not who knew it.

Orleans. Hee needs not, it is no hidden virtue in him.

Constable. By my faith Sir, but it is; never anybody saw it, but his lackey; 'tis a hooded valor, and when it appears, it will abate.

Orleans. Ill will never said well.

Constable. I will cap that proverb with, There is flattery in friendship.

Orleans. And I will take up that with, Give the devil his due.

Constable. Well placed; there stands your friend for the Devil; have at the very eye of that proverb with, A pox of the Devil.

Orleans. You are the better at proverbs, by how much a fool's bolt is soon shot.

Constable. You have shot over.

Orleans. 'Tis not the first time you were over-shot.

[*Enter a Messenger*]

Messenger. My Lord high Constable, the English lie within fifteen hundred paces of your tents.

Constable. Who has measured the ground?

Messenger. The Lord Grandpre.

Constable. A valiant and most expert gentleman. Would it were day? Alas, poor Harry of England; he longs not for the dawning, as we do.

Orleans. What a wretched and peevish fellow is this King of England, to mope with his fat-brained followers so far out of his knowledge.

Constable. If the English had any apprehension, they would run away.

Orleans. That they lack; for if their heads had any intellectual Armor, they could never wear such heavy head-pieces.

Rambures. That island of England breeds very valiant creatures; their mastiffs are of unmatchable courage.

Orleans. Foolish curs, that run winking into the mouth of a Russian bear, and have their heads crushed like rotten apples; you may as well say, that's a valiant flea, that dare eat his breakfast on the lip of a lion.

Constable. Just, just; and the men do sympathize with the mastiffs, in robustious and rough coming on, leaving their wits with their wives; and then give them great meals of beef, and iron and steel; they will eat like wolves, and fight like devils.

Orleans. Aye, but these English are shrewdly out of beef.

Constable. Then shall we find tomorrow, they have only stomachs to eat, and none to fight. Now is it time to arm; come, shall we about it?

Orleans. It is now two o'clock; but let me see, by ten we shall have each a hundred English men.

[*Exit All*]

Act Four

[Enter Chorus]

Chorus. Now entertain conjecture of a time,
    When creeping murmur and the poring dark
    Fills the wide vessel of the Universe.
    From camp to camp, through the foul womb of night
    The hum of either army stilly sounds;
    That the fixed sentinels almost receive
    The secret whispers of each other's watch.
    Fire answers fire, and through their pale flames
    Each battle sees the others umbered face.
    Steed threatens steed, in high and boastful neighs
    Piercing the night's dull ear; and from the tents,
    The armorers accomplishing the knights,
    With busy hammers closing rivets up,
    Give dreadful note of preparation.
    The country cocks do crow, the clocks do toll;
    And the third hour of drowsy morning named,
    Proud of their numbers, and secure in soul,
    The confident and over-lusty French,
    Do the low-rated English play at dice;
    And chide the cripple tardy-gated night,
    Who like a foul and ugly witch does limp
    So tediously away. The poor condemned English,
    Like sacrifices, by their watchful fires
    Sit patiently, and inly ruminate
    The morning's danger; and their gesture sad,
    Investing lank-lean cheeks, and war-worn coats,
    Presented them unto the gazing moon
    So many horrid ghosts. O, now, who will behold
    The Royal Captain of this ruined band
    Walking from watch to watch, from tent to tent;
    Let him cry, praise and glory on his head;

For forth he goes, and visits all his host,
Bids them good morrow with a modest smile,
And calls them brothers, friends, and countrymen.
Upon his Royal face there is no note,
How dread an army has enrounded him;
Nor does he dedicate one jot of color
Unto the weary and all-watched night;
But freshly looks, and over-bears attaint,
With cheerful semblance, and sweet Majesty;
That every wretch, pining and pale before,
Beholding him, plucks comfort from his looks.
A largesse universal, like the sun,
His liberal eye does give to everyone,
Thawing cold fear, that mean and gentle all
Behold, as may unworthiness define.
A little touch of Harry in the night,
And so our scene must to the battle fly;
Where, O, for pity, we shall much disgrace,
With four or five most vile and ragged foils,
Right ill disposed, in brawl ridiculous,
The name of Agincourt; Yet sit and see,
Minding true things, by what their mockeries be.

[*Exit Chorus*]

[*The English camp at Agincourt*]

[*Enter the King, Bedford, and Gloucester*]

King Henry. Gloucester, 'tis true that we are in great danger,
The greater therefore should our courage be.
Good morrow brother Bedford; God Almighty,
There is some soul of goodness in things evil,
Would men observingly distill it out.
For our bad neighbor makes us early stirrers,
Which is both healthful, and good husbandry.
Besides, they are our outward consciences,
And preachers to us all; admonishing,
That we should dress us fairly for our end.
Thus may we gather honey from the weed,
And make a moral of the Devil himself.

[*Enter Erpingham*]

Good morrow old Sir Thomas Erpingham;
A good soft pillow for that good white head,
Were better than a churlish turf of France.

Erpingham. Not so, my Liege, this lodging likes me better,
Since I may say, now lie I like a King.

King Henry. 'Tis good for men to love their present pains,
Upon example, so the spirit is eased;
And when the mind is quickened, out of doubt
The organs, though defunct and dead before,
Break up their drowsy grave, and newly move
With casted slough, and fresh legerity.
Lend me your cloak, Sir Thomas; brothers both,
Commend me to the Princes in our camp;
Do my good morrow to them, and anon
Desire them all to my pavilion.

Gloucester. We shall, my Liege.

Erpingham. Shall I attend your Grace?

King Henry. No, my good Knight;
Go with my brothers to my Lords of England;
I and my bosom must debate a while,
And then I would no other company.

Erpingham. The Lord in Heaven bless you, noble Harry.

[Exit All but the King]

King Henry. God a mercy old heart, you speak cheerfully.

[Enter Pistol]

Pistol. Qui va là?

King Henry. A friend.

Pistol. Discuss unto me, are you Officer, or are you base, common, and popular?

King Henry. I am a gentleman of a company.

Pistol. Trail you the puissant pike?

King Henry. Even so; what are you?

Pistol. As good a gentleman as the Emperor.

King Henry. Then you are a better than the King.

Pistol. The King's a bawcock, and a heart of gold, a lad of life, an imp of fame, of parents good, of fist most valiant; I kiss his dirty shoe, and from heartstring I love the lovely bully. What is your name?

King Henry. Harry le Roy.

Pistol. Le Roy? a Cornish name; are you of Cornish crew?

King Henry. No, I am a Welshman.

Pistol. Know you Fluellen?

King Henry. Yes.

Pistol. Tell him I'll knock his leek about his pate upon St. Davy's day.

King Henry. Do not you wear your dagger in your cap that day, lest he knock that about yours.

Pistol. Are you his friend?

King Henry. And his kinsman too.

Pistol. The figo for you then.

King Henry. I thank you; God be with you.

Pistol. My name is Pistol called.

[Exit Pistol]

King Henry. It sorts well with your fierceness.

[Enter Fluellen and Gower]

Gower. Captain Fluellen.

Fluellen. So, in the name of Jesus Christ, speak lower; it is the
greatest admiration in the universal world, when the true and
aunchient prerogatifes and laws of the wars is not kept; if you
would take the pains but to examine the wars of Pompey the
Great, you shall find, I warrant you, that there is no tiddle
taddle nor pibble babble in Pompey's camp; I warrant you, you
shall find the ceremonies of the wars, and the cares of it, and
the forms of it, and the sobriety of it, and the modesty of it, to
be otherwise.

Gower. Why the enemy is loud, you hear him all night.

Fluellen. If the enemy is an ass and a fool, and a prating coxcomb;
is it meet, think you, that we should also, look you, be an ass
and a fool, and a prating coxcomb, in your own conscience
now?

Gower. I will speak lower.

Fluellen. I pray you, and beseech you, that you will.

[*Exit Gower and Fluellen*]

King Henry. Though it appear a little out of fashion,
There is much care and valor in this Welshman.

[*Enter Soldiers, John Bates, Alexander Court, and Michael Williams*]

Court. Brother John Bates, is not that the morning which breaks
yonder?

Bates. I think it be; but we have no great cause to desire the
approach of day.

Williams. We see yonder the beginning of the day, but I think we
shall never see the end of it. Who goes there?

King Henry. A friend.

Williams. Under what Captain serve you?

King Henry. Under Sir John Erpingham.

Williams. A good old commander, and a most kind gentleman; I
pray you, what thinks he of our estate?

King Henry. Even as men wracked upon a sand, that look to be
washed off the next tide.

Bates. He has not told his thought to the King?

King Henry. No; nor it is not meet he should; for though I speak it
to you, I think the King is but a man, as I am; the violet smells
to him, as it does to me; the element shows to him, as it does
to me; all his senses have but human conditions; his ceremonies

laid by, in his nakedness he appears but a man; and though his affections are higher mounted than ours, yet when they stoop, they stoop with the like wing; therefore, when he sees reason of fears, as we do; his fears, out of doubt, be of the same relish as ours are; yet in reason, no man should possess him with any appearance of fear; lest he, by showing it, should dishearten his army.

Bates. He may show what outward courage he will; but I believe, as cold a night as 'tis, he could wish himself in Thames up to the neck; and so I would he were, and I by him, at all adventures, so we were quit here.

King Henry. By my truth, I will speak my conscience of the King; I think he would not wish himself anywhere, but where he is.

Bates. Then I would he were here alone; so should he be sure to be ransomed, and a many poor men's lives saved.

King Henry. I dare say, you love him not so ill, to wish him here alone; howsoever you speak this to feel other men's minds, I think I could not die anywhere so contented, as in the King's company; his cause being just, and his quarrel honorable.

Williams. That's more than we know.

Bates. Aye, or more than we should seek after; for we know enough, if we know we are the King's subjects; if his cause be wrong, our obedience to the King wipes the crime of it out of us.

Williams. But if the cause be not good, the King himself has a heavy reckoning to make, when all those legs, and arms, and heads, chopped off in a battle, shall join together at the latter day, and cry all, "We died at such a place," some swearing, some crying for a surgeon; some upon their wives, left poor behind them; some upon the debts they owe, some upon their children rawly left; I am afeard, there are few die well, that die in a battle; for how can they charitably dispose of any thing, when blood is their argument? Now, if these men do not die well, it will be a black matter for the King, that led them to it; who to disobey, were against all proportion of subjection.

King Henry. So, if a son that is by his father sent about merchandise, do sinfully miscarry upon the sea; the imputation of his wickedness, by your rule, should be imposed vpon his father that sent him; or if a servant, under his master's command, transporting a sum of money, be assaild by robbers, and die in many irreconciled iniquities; you may call the business of the master the author of the servant's damnation;

but this is not so; The King is not bound to answer the particular endings of his soldiers, the father of his son, nor the master of his servant; for they purpose not their death, when they purpose their services. Besides, there is no King, be his cause never so spotless, if it come to the arbitrement of swords, can try it out with all unspotted soldiers; some, peradventure, have on them the guilt of premeditated and contrived murder; some, of beguiling virgins with the broken seals of perjury; some, making the wars their bulwark, that have before gored the gentle bosom of peace with pillage and robbery. Now, if these men have defeated the law, and outrun native punishment; though they can out-strip men, they have no wings to fly from God. War is his beadle, war is his vengeance; so that here men are punished, for before breach of the King's laws, in now the King's quarrel; where they feared the death, they have borne life away; and where they would be safe, they perish. Then if they die unprovided, no more is the King guilty of their damnation, than he was before guilty of those impieties, for the which they are now visited. Every subject's duty is the King's, but every subject's soul is his own. Therefore should every soldier in the wars do as every sick man in his bed, wash every moth out of his conscience; and dying so, death is to him advantage; or not dying, the time was blessedly lost, wherein such preparation was gained; and in him that escapes, it were not sin to think, that making God so free an offer, he let him outlive that day, to see his greatness, and to teach others how they should prepare.

Williams. 'Tis certain, every man that dies ill, the ill upon his own head, the King is not to answer it.

Bates. I do not desire he should answer for me, and yet I determine to fight lustily for him.

King Henry. I myself heard the King say he would not be ransomed.

Williams. Aye, he said so, to make us fight cheerfully; but when our throats are cut, he may be ransomed, and we never the wiser.

King Henry. If I live to see it, I will never trust his word after.

Williams. You pay him then; that's a perilous shot out of an elder gun, that a poor and a private displeasure can do against a Monarch; you may as well go about to turn the sun to ice, with fanning in his face with a peacock's feather; You'll never trust his word after; come, 'tis a foolish saying.

King Henry. Your reproof is something too round, I should be angry with you, if the time were convenient.

Williams. Let it be a quarrel between us, if you live.

King Henry. I embrace it.

Williams. How shall I know you again?

King Henry. Give me any gage of yours, and I will wear it in my
bonnet; then if ever you dare acknowledge it, I will make it my
quarrel.

Williams. Here's my glove; give me another of yours.

King Henry. There.

Williams. This will I also wear in my cap; if ever you come to me,
and say, after tomorrow, this is my glove, by this hand I will
take you a box on the ear.

King Henry. If ever I live to see it, I will challenge it.

Williams. You dare as well be hanged.

King Henry. Well, I will do it, though I take you in the King's
company.

Williams. Keep your word; fare you well.

Bates. Be friends, you English fools, be friends, we have French
quarrels enough, if you could tell how to reckon.

[Exit Soldiers]

King Henry. Indeed the French may lay twenty French
crowns to one, they will beat us, for they bear them
on their shoulders; but it is no English treason to cut
French crowns, and tomorrow the King himself will
be a clipper.
Upon the King, let us our lives, our souls,
Our debts, our careful wives,
Our children, and our sins, lay on the King;
We must bear all.
O, hard condition, twin-born with greatness,
Subject to the breath of every fool, whose sense
No more can feel, but his own wringing.
What infinite heart's-ease must Kings neglect,
That private men enjoy?
And what have Kings, that privates have not too,
Save ceremony, save general ceremony?
And what are you, you idol ceremony?
What kind of God are you? that suffer more
Of mortal griefs, than do your worshippers.
What are your rents? What are your comings in?
O, ceremony, show me but your worth.

What? is your soul of odoration?
Are you ought else but place, degree, and form,
Creating awe and fear in other men?
Wherein you are less happy, being feared,
Than they in fearing.
What drink you oft, instead of homage sweet,
But poisoned flattery? O, be sick, great greatness,
And bid your ceremony give you cure.
Thinks you the fiery fever will go out
With titles blown from adulation?
Will it give place to flexure and low bending?
Can you, when you command the beggar's knee,
Command the health of it? No, you proud dream,
That play so subtly with a King's repose.

King Henry. I am a King that find you; and I know,
'Tis not the balm, the scepter, and the ball,
The sword, the mace, the crown imperial,
The inter-tissued robe of gold and pearl,
The farced title running afore the King,
The throne he sits on; nor the tide of pomp,
That beats upon the high shore of this world;
No, not all these, thrice-gorgeous ceremony;
Not all these, laid in bed Majestical,
Can sleep so soundly, as the wretched slave;
Who with a body filled, and vacant mind,
Gets him to rest, crammed with distressful bread,
Never sees horrid night, the child of Hell;
But like a lackey, from the rise to set,
Sweats in the eye of Phebus; and all night
Sleeps in Elysium; next day after dawn,
Does rise and help Hyperion to his horse,
And follows so the ever-running year
With profitable labor to his grave;
And but for ceremony, such a wretch,
Winding up days with toil, and nights with sleep,
Had the forehand and vantage of a King Henry.
The slave, a member of the country's peace,
Enioys it; but in gross brain little wots,
What watch the King keeps, to maintain the peace;
Whose hours, the peasant best advantages.

[*Enter Erpingham*]

Erpingham. My Lord, your nobles jealous of your absence,

Seek through your camp to find you.

King Henry. Good old Knight, collect them all together
At my tent; I'll be before you.

Erpingham. I shall do it, my Lord.

[*Exit Erpingham*]

King Henry. O, God of battles, steel my soldiers' hearts,
Possess them not with fear; take from them now
The sense of reckoning of the opposed numbers;
Pluck their hearts from them. Not today, O, Lord,
O, not today, think not upon the fault
My father made, in compassing the Crown.
I Richard's body have interred anew,
And on it have bestowed more contrite tears,
Than from it issued forced drops of blood.
Five hundred poor I have in yearly pay,
Who twice a day their withered hands hold up
Toward Heaven, to pardon blood;
And I have built two chantries,
Where the sad and solemn priests sing still
For Richard's soul. More will I do;
Though all that I can do, is nothing worth;
Since that my penitence comes after all,
Imploring pardon.

[*Enter Gloucester*]

Duke of Gloucester. My Liege.

King Henry. My brother Gloucester's voice? Aye,
I know your errand, I will go with you;
The day, my friend, and all things stay for me.

[*Exit All*]

[*The French camp*]

[*Enter the Dauphin, Orleans, Rambures, and Beaumont*]

Orleans. The sun does gild our armor up, my Lords.

Dauphin. Montez à cheval; my horse, varlot lackey; Ha.

Orleans. Oh brave spirit.

Dauphin. Via! les eaux et la terre.

Orleans. Rien puis? L'air et le feu.

Dauphin. Ceil, cousin Orleans.

[*Enter Constable*]

Now my Lord Constable?

Constable. Hark how our steeds, for present service neigh.

Dauphin. Mount them, and make incision in their hides,
That their hot blood may spin in English eyes,
And doubt them with superfluous courage; ha.

Rambures. What, will you have them weep our horses' blood?
How shall we then behold their natural tears?

[*Enter Messenger*]

Messenger. The English are embattled, you French
Peers.

Constable. To horse, you gallant Princes, straight to horse.
Do but behold yond poor and starved band,
And your fair show shall suck away their souls,
Leaving them but the shells and husks of men.
There is not work enough for all our hands,
Scarce blood enough in all their sickly veins,
To give each naked curtleaxe a stain,
That our French gallants shall today draw out,
And sheath for lack of sport. Let us but blow on them,
The vapor of our valor will over-turn them.
'Tis positive against all exceptions, Lords,
That our superfluous lackies, and our peasants,
Who in unnecessary action swarm
About our squares of battle, were enough
To purge this field of such a hilding foe;

Though we upon this mountain's base by,
Took stand for idle speculation;
But that our honors must not. What's to say?
A very little little let us do,
And all is done; then let the trumpets sound
The tucket sonance, and the note to mount;
For our approach shall so much dare the field,
That England shall couch down in fear, and yield.

[*Enter Grandpre*]

Grandpre. Why do you stay so long, my Lords of France?
　Yond Island carrions, desperate of their bones,
　Ill-favoredly become the morning field;
　Their ragged curtains poorly are let loose,
　And our air shakes them passing scornfully.
　Big Mars seems bankrupt in their beggared host,
　And faintly through a rusty beaver peeps.
　The horsemen sit like fixed candlesticks,
　With torch-staves in their hand; and their poor jades
　Lob down their heads, dropping the hides and hips;
　The gum down roping from their pale-dead eyes,
　And in their pale dull mouths the gimmal bit
　Lies foul with chewed grass, still and motionless.
　And their executors, the knavish crows,
　Fly over them all, impatient for their hour.
　Description cannot suit itself in words,
　To demonstrate the life of such a battle,
　In life so lifeless, as it shows itself.

Constable. They have said their prayers,
　And they stay for death.

Dauphin. Shall we go send them dinners, and fresh suits,
　And give their fasting horses provender,
　And after fight with them?

Constable. I stay but for my guard; on
　To the field, I will the banner from a trumpet take,
　And use it for my haste. Come, come away,
　The sun is high, and we out-wear the day.

[*Exit All*]

[The English Camp]

[Enter Gloucester, Bedford, Exeter, Erpingham and troops;
Salisbury and Westmoreland]

Duke of Gloucester. Where is the King?

Bedford. The King himself is rode to view their battle.

Westmoreland. Of fighting men they have full threescore thousand.

Exeter. There's five to one, besides, they all are fresh.

Salisbury. God's arm strike with us, 'tis a fearful odds.
    God be wi' you Princes all; I'll to my charge;
    If we no more meet, till we meet in Heaven;
    Then joyfully, my noble Lord of Bedford,
    My dear Lord Gloucester, and my good Lord Exeter,
    And my kind kinsman, warriors all, adieu.

Bedford. Farewell good Salisbury, and good luck go with you;
    And yet I do you wrong, to mind you of it,
    For you are framed of the firm truth of valor.

Exeter. Farewell, kind Lord; fight valiantly today.

[Exit Salisbury]

Bedford. He is as full of valor as of kindness,
    Princely in both.

[Enter the King]

Westmoreland. O, that we now had here
    But one ten thousand of those men in England,
    That do no work today.

King Henry. What's he that wishes so?
    My cousin Westmoreland. No, my fair cousin;
    If we are marked to die, we are enough
    To do our country loss; and if to live,
    The fewer men, the greater share of honor.
    God's will, I pray you wish not one man more.
    By Jove, I am not covetous for gold,
    Nor care I who does feed upon my cost;
    It yearns me not, if men my garments wear;
    Such outward things dwell not in my desires.
    But if it be a sin to covet honor,

I am the most offending soul alive.
No, in faith, my coz, wish not a man from England;
God's peace, I would not lose so great an honor,
As one man more I think would share from me,
For the best hope I have. O, do not wish one more;
Rather proclaim it, Westmoreland, through my host,
That he which has no stomach to this fight,
Let him depart, his passport shall be made,
And crowns for convoy put into his purse;
We would not die in that man's company,
That fears his fellowship, to die with us.
This day is called the Feast of Crispian;
He that outlives this day, and comes safe home,
Will stand a tiptoe when this day is named,
And rouse him at the name of Crispian.
He that shall see this day, and live old age,
Will yearly on the vigil feast his neighbors,
And say, tomorrow is Saint Crispian.
Then will he strip his sleeve, and show his scars;
Old men forget; yet all shall be forgot;
But he'll remember, with advantages,
What feats he did that day. Then shall our names,
Familiar in his mouth as household words,
Harry the King, Bedford and Exeter,
Warwick and Talbot, Salisbury and Gloucester,
Be in their flowing cups freshly remembered.

King Henry. This story shall the good man teach his son;
And crispine Crispian shall never go by,
From this day to the ending of the world,
But we in it shall be remembered;
We few, we happy few, we band of brothers;
For he today that sheds his blood with me,
Shall be my brother; be he never so vile,
This day shall gentle his condition.
And gentlemen in England, now abed,
Shall think themselves accursed they were not here;
And hold their manhood's cheap, while any speaks,
That fought with us upon Saint Crispins day.

[*Enter Salisbury*]

Salisbury. My Sovereign Lord, bestow yourself with speed;
The French are bravely in their battles set,
And will with all expedience charge on us.

King Henry. All things are ready, if our minds be so.

Westmoreland. Perish the man, whose mind is backward now.

King Henry. You do not wish more help from England,
    coz?

Westmoreland. God's will, my Liege, would you and I alone,
    Without more help, could fight this Royal battle

King Henry. Why now you have unwished five thousand men;
    Which likes me better, than to wish us one.
    You know your places; God be with you all.

[*Tucket*]

[*Enter Montjoy*]

Montjoy. Once more I come to know of you King Harry,
    If for your ransom you will now compound,
    Before your most assured overthrow;
    For certainly, you are so near the gulf,
    You needs must be englutted. Besides, in mercy
    The Constable desires you, you will mind
    Your followers of repentance; that their souls
    May make a peaceful and a sweet retire
    From off these fields; where, wretches, their poor bodies
    Must lie and fester.

King Henry. Who has sent you now?

Montjoy. The Constable of France

King Henry. I pray you bear my former answer back;
    Bid them achieve me, and then sell my bones.
    Good God, why should they mock poor fellows thus?
    The man that once did sell the lion's skin
    While the beast lived, was killed with hunting him.
    A many of our bodies shall no doubt
    Find native graves; upon the which, I trust
    Shall witness live in brass of this day's work.
    And those that leave their valiant bones in France,
    Dying like men, though buried in your dunghills,
    They shall be famed; for there the sun shall greet them,
    And draw their honors reeking up to Heaven,
    Leaving their earthly parts to choke your clime,
    The smell whereof shall breed a plague in France.
    Mark then abounding valor in our English;
    That being dead, like to the bullets grazing,

Break out into a second course of mischief,
Killing in relapse of mortality.
Let me speak proudly; tell the Constable,
We are but warriors for the working day;
Our gayness and our gilt are all besmirched
With rainy marching in the painful field.
There's not a piece of feather in our host;
Good argument, I hope, we will not fly;
And time has worn us into slovenry.
But by the mass, our hearts are in the trim;
And my poor soldiers tell me, yet before night,
They'll be in fresher robes, or they will pluck
The gay new coats over the French soldiers' heads,
And turn them out of service. If they do this,
As if God please, they shall; my ransom then
Will soon be levied.
Herald, save you your labor;
Come you no more for ransom, gentle herald,
They shall have none, I swear, but these my joints;
Which if they have, as I will leave 'em them,
Shall yield them little, tell the Constable

Montjoy. I shall, King Harry. And so fare you well;
You never shall hear Herald any more.

[*Exit Montjoy*]

King Henry. I fear you will once more come again for a
Ransom.

[*Enter Duke of York*]

Duke of York. My Lord, most humbly on my knee I beg
The leading of the vaward.
King Henry. Take it, brave Duke of York.
Now soldiers march away,
And how you please God, dispose the day.

[*Exit All*]

[The Battlefield]

[Alarm. Excursions]

[Enter Pistol, French Soldier, Boy]

Pistol. Yield cur.

French Soldier. Je pense que vous etes un gentilhomme de bon qualité.

Pistol. Qualtity calmy custure me. Are you a gentleman? What is your name? Discuss.

French Soldier. O, Seigneur Dieu.

Pistol. O, Signieur Dew should be a gentleman; perpend my words O, Signieur Dew, and mark; O, Signieur Dew, you die on point of Fox, except O, Signieur you do give to me egregious ransom.

French Soldier. O, prennez miséricord! Ayez pitié de moi.

Pistol. Mwa shall not serve, I will have forty mwas; for I will fetch your rim out at your throat, in drops of crimson blood.

French Soldier. Est-il impossible d'échapper le force de ton bras?

Pistol. Brass, cur? You damned and luxurious mountain goat, offer me brass?

French Soldier. O, pardonnez moi!

Pistol. Say you me so? is that a ton of mwas? Come here boy, ask me this slave in French what is his name.

Boy. Écoutez: Comment étes-vous appelé?

French Soldier. Monsieur le Fer.

Boy. He says his name is M. Fer.

Pistol. M. Fer; I'll fer him, and firk him, and ferret him; discusse the same in French unto him.

Boy. I do not know the French for fer, and ferret, and firk.

Pistol. Bid him prepare, for I will cut his throat.

French Soldier. Que dit-il Monsieur?

Boy. Il me commande de vous dire que vous faite vous pret, car ce soldat ici est disposée tout à cette heur de couper votre gorge.

Pistol. Oui, cuppe le gorge permafoy. Peasant, unless you give me crowns, brave crowns; or mangled shalt you be by this my sword.

French Soldier. O, je vous supplié pour l'amour de Dieu; me pardonner. Je suis un gentilhomme de bon maison. Gardez ma vie, and je vous donnerai deux cent écus.

Pistol. What are his words?

Boy. He prays you to save his life, he is a gentleman.
of a good house, and for his ransom he will give you two hundred crowns.

Pistol. Tell him my fury shall abate, and I the crowns will take.

French Soldier. Petit Monsieur que dit-il?

Boy. Encore qu'il est contra son jurement, de pardonner aucune prisonnier; néanmoins pour les écues que vous l'avez promis, il est content de vous donner la liberté, le franchisement.

French Soldier. Sur mes genoux se vous donnes milles remercimens, et je me estime heurex que je suis tombé, entre les mains d'un chevalier, je pense le plus brave, valliant, et très distingué signieur d'Angleterre.

Pistol. Expound unto me boy.

Boy. He gives you upon his knees a thousand thanks, and he esteems himself happy, that he has fallen into the hands of one, as he thinks, the most brave, valorous and thrice-worthy signeur of England.

Pistol. As I suck blood, I will some mercy show. Follow me.

Boy. Suivez-vous le grand capitaine?

[*Exit Pistol and French soldier*]

I did never know so full a voice issue from so empty a heart; but the saying is true, the empty vessel makes the greatest sound. Bardolph and Nym had ten times more valor, than this roaring devil in the old play, that everyone may pare his nails with a wooden dagger, and they are both hanged, and so would this be, if he dared steal anything adventurously. I must stay with the lackies with the luggage of our camp, the French might have a good prey of us, if he knew of it, for there is none to guard it but boys.

[*Exit Boy*]

[*Another part of the Field*]

[*Enter Constable, Orleans, Bourbon, Dauphin, and Rambures*]

Constable. O, Diable.

Orleans. O, signeur le jour est perdu, toute est perdu.

Dauphin. Mort de ma vie, all is confounded, all.
    Reproach, and everlasting shame
    Sits mocking in our plumes. O, méchante fortune!

                    [*A short Alarm*]

    Do not run away.

Constable. Why, all our ranks are broke.

Dauphin. O, perdurable shame, let's stab ourselves;
    Be these the wretches that we played at dice for?

Orleans. Is this the King we sent too, for his ransom?

Bourbon. Shame, and eternal shame, nothing but shame,
    Let us die in honor — once more back again,
    And he that will not follow Bourbon now,
    Let him go hence, and with his cap in hand
    Like a base pander hold the chamber door,
    While a base slave, no gentler than my dog,
    His fairest daughter is contaminated.

Constable. Disorder, that has spoiled us, friend us now!
    Let us on heaps go offer up our lives.

Orleans. We are enough yet living in the field,
    To smother up the English in our throngs,
    If any order might be thought upon

Bourbon. The devil take order now, I'll to the throng;
    Let life be short, else shame will be too long.

                    [*Exit All*]

[*Another part of the Field*]

[*Alarm*]

[*Enter King Henry and his train, with Prisoners*]

King Henry. Well have we done, thrice-valiant countrymen,
But all's not done, yet keep the French the field.

Exeter. The Duke of York commends him to your Majesty

King Henry. Lives he, good Uncle; thrice within this hour
I saw him down; thrice up again, and fighting,
From helmet to the spur, all blood he was.

Exeter. In which array, brave soldier, does he lie,
Larding the plain; and by his bloody side,
Yoke-fellow to his honor-owing-wounds,
The noble Earl of Suffolk also lies.
Suffolk first died, and York all haggled over
Comes to him, where in gore he lay insteeped,
And takes him by the beard, kisses the gashes
That bloodily did yawn upon his face.
He cries aloud; tarry my cousin Suffolk,
My soul shall yours keep company to heaven;
Tarry, sweet soul, for mine, then fly abreast;
As in this glorious and well-fought field
We kept together in our chivalry.

Exeter. Upon these words I came, and cheered him up,
He smiled me in the face, reached me his hand,
And with a feeble grip, says, "Dear my Lord,
Commend my service to my Sovereign,
So did he turn, and over Suffolk's neck
He threw his wounded arm, and kissed his lips,
And so espoused to death, with blood he sealed
A testament of noble-ending-love;
The pretty and sweet manner of it forced
Those waters from me, which I would have stopped,
But I had not so much of man in me,
And all my mother came into my eyes,
And gave me up to tears

King Henry. I blame you not,

For hearing this, I must perforce compound
With mistful eyes, or they will issue to.

[*Alarm*]

But hark, what new alarm is this same?
The French have re-inforced their scattered men;
Then every soldier kill his prisoners,
Give the word through.

[*Exit All*]

[Another part of the Field]

[Enter Fluellen and Gower]

Fluellen. Kill the poys and the luggage, 'Tis expressely against the law of arms, 'tis as arrant a piece of knavery mark you now, as can be offert in your conscience now, is it not?

Gower. 'Tis certain, there's not a boy left alive, and the cowardly rascals that ran from the battle ha' done this slaughter; besides they have burned and carried away all that was in the King's tent, wherefore the King most worthily has caused every soldier to cut his prisoners' throat. O, 'tis a gallant King.

Fluellen. Aye, he was porne at Monmouth, Captain Gower;
What call you the town's name where Alexander the pig was borne?

Gower. Alexander the Great.

Fluellen. Why I pray you, is not pig, great? The pig, or the great, or the mighty, or the huge, or the magnanimous, are all one reckonings, save the phrase is a little variations.

Gower. I think Alexander the Great was borne in Macedon, his father was called Phillip of Macedon, as I take it.

Fluellen. I think it is in Macedon where Alexander is porne; I tell you Captain, if you look in the maps of the 'orld, I warrant you sall find in the comparisons between Macedon and Monmouth, that the situations look you, is both alike. There is a river in Macedon, and there is also moreover a river at Monmouth, it is called Wye at Monmouth; but it is out of my prains, what is the name of the other river; but 'tis all one, 'tis alike as my fingers is to my fingers, and there is salmons in both. If you mark Alexander's life well, Harry of Monmouth's life is come after it indifferent well, for there is figures in all things. Alexander, God knows, and you know, in his rages, and his furies, and his wraths, and his cholers, and his moods, and his displeasures, and his indignations, and also being a little intoxicates in his prains, did in his ales and his angers, look you, kill his best friend Clytus.

Gower. Our King is not like him in that, he never killed any of his friends.

Fluellen. It is not well done, mark you now, to take the tales out
  of my mouth, before it is made and finished. I speak but in
  the figures, and comparisons of it; as Alexander killed his
  friend Clytus, being in his ales and his cups; so also Harry
  Monmouth being in his right wits, and his good judgments,
  turned away the fat knight with the great belly doublet; he was
  full of jests, and gipes, and knaveries, and mocks, I have forgot
  his name.

Gower. Sir John Falstaff.

Fluellen. That is he; I'll tell you, there is good men porne
  at Monmouth.

Gower. Here comes his Majesty.

[*Alarm*]

[*Exit Gower*]

[*Enter King Harry, Warwick, Gloucester, Exeter, others*]

King Henry. I was not angry since I came to France,
  Until this instant. Take a trumpet, Herald,
  Ride you unto the horsemen on yond hill;
  If they will fight with us, bid them come down,
  Or void the field; they do offend our sight.
  If they'll do neither, we will come to them,
  And make them skirr away, as swift as stones
  Enforced from the old Assyrian slings;
  Besides, we'll cut the throats of those we have,
  And not a man of them that we shall take,
  Shall taste our mercy. Go and tell them so.

[*Enter Montjoy*]

Exeter. Here comes the Herald of the French, my Liege.

Duke of Gloucester. His eyes are humbler than they used to be.

King Henry. How now, what means this, Herald? Know
  you not,
  That I have fined these bones of mine for ransom?
  Come you again for ransom?

Herald. No great King;
  I come to you for charitable license,
  That we may wander over this bloody field,
  To book our dead, and then to bury them,
  To sort our nobles from our common men.

For many of our Princes, woe the while,
Lie drowned and soaked in mercenary blood;
So do our vulgar drench their peasant limbs
In blood of Princes, and with wounded steeds
Fret fetlock deep in gore, and with wild rage
Jerk out their armed heels at their dead masters,
Killing them twice. O, give us leave, great King,
To view the field in safety, and dispose
Of their dead bodies.

King Henry. I tell you truly, Herald,
I know not if the day be ours or no,
For yet a many of your horsemen peer,
And gallop over the field.

Herald. The day is yours.

King Henry. Praised be God, and not our strength for it;
What is this castle called that stands hard by?

Herald. They call it Agincourt.

King Henry. Then call we this the field of Agincourt,
Fought on the day of Crispin Crispianus.

Fluellen. Your grandfather of famous memory, if it please your
Majesty, and your great Uncle Edward the Plack Prince of
Wales, as I have read in the Chronicles, fought a most prave
pattle here in France.

King Henry. They did, Fluellen.

Fluellen. Your Majesty says very true; If your Majesty is
remembered of it, the Welshmen did good service in a garden
where leeks did grow, wearing leeks in their Monmouth caps,
which your Majesty know to this hour is an honorable badge
of the service; and I do believe your Majesty takes no scorn to
wear the leek uppon St. Tavy's day.

King Henry. I wear it for a memorable honor;
For I am Welsh you know, good countryman.

Fluellen. All the water in Wye, cannot wash your Majesty's Welsh
plood out of your pody, I can tell you that; God pless it, and
preserve it, as long as it pleases his Grace, and his Majesty too

King Henry. Thanks good, my countryman.

Fluellen. By Yeshu, I am your Majestys countryman, I care not
who know it; I will confess it to all the 'orld, I need not to
be ashamed of your Majesty, praised be God so long as your
Majesty is an honest man.

King Henry. God keep me so.

[*Enter Williams*]

Our Heralds go with him,
Bring me just notice of the numbers dead
On both our parts. Call yonder fellow here.

[*Exit Heralds and Montjoy*]

Exeter. Soldier, you must come to the King.

King Henry. Soldier, why wear you that glove in your
cap?

Williams. If it please your Majesty, 'tis the gage of one
that I should fight withal, if he be alive.

King Henry. An Englishman?

Williams. If it please your Majesty, a rascal that swaggered with me
last night; who if alive, and ever dare to challenge this glove, I
have sworn to take him a box a'the ear; or if I can see my glove
in his cap, which he swore as he was a soldier he would wear,
if alive, I will strike it out soundly

King Henry. What think you, Captain Fluellen, is it fit this soldier
keep his oath?

Fluellen. He is a craven and a villain else, and it please your Majesty
in my conscience.

King Henry. It may be, his enemy is a gentleman of great sort quite
from the answer of his degree.

Fluellen. Though he be as good a yentleman as the devil is, as
Lucifer and Belzebub himself, it is necessary, look your Grace,
that he keep his vow and his oath. If he be perjured, see you
now, his reputation is as arrant a villain and a jack sauce, as
ever his black shoe trod upon God's ground, and his earth, in
my conscience law.

King Henry. Then keep your vow, sirrah, when you met the fellow.

Williams. So, I will my Liege, as I live.

King Henry. Who serve you under?

Williams. Under Captain Gower, my Liege.

Fluellen. Gower is a good Captain, and is good knowledge and
literatured in the wars.

King Henry. Call him here to me, soldier

Williams. I will my Liege.

[Exit Williams]

King Henry. Here, Fluellen, wear you this favor for me, and stick it in your cap; when Alanson and myself were down together, I plucked this glove from his helmet. If any man challenge this, he is a friend to Alanson, and an enemy to our person; if you encounter any such, apprehend him, and you do me love.

Fluellen. Your Grace doo's me as great honors as can be desired in the heart's of his subjects; I would fain see the man, that ha's but two legs, that shall find himself agriefed at this glove; that is all; but I would fain see it once, and please God of his grace that I might see.

King Henry. Know you Gower?

Fluellen. He is my dear friend, and please you.

King Henry. Pray you go seek him, and bring him to my tent.

Fluellen. I will fetch him.

[Exit Fluellen]

King Henry. My Lord of Warwick, and my brother Gloucester,
Follow Fluellen closely at the heels.
The glove which I have given him for a favor,
May haply purchase him a box a'the ear.
It is the soldier's. I by bargain should
Wear it myself. Follow, good cousin Warwick;
If that the soldier strike him, as I judge
By his blunt bearing, he will keep his word;
Some sudden mischief may arise of it;
For I do know Fluellen valiant,
And touched with choler, hot as gunpowder,
And quickly will return an injury.
Follow, and see there be no harm between them.
Go you with me, Uncle of Exeter.

[Exit All]

[*Before King Henry's Pavilion*]

[*Enter Gower and Williams*]

Williams. I warrant it is to Knight you, Captain.

[*Enter Fluellen*]

Fluellen. God's will, and his pleasure, Captain, I beseech you now, come apace to the King; there is more good toward you peradventure, than is in your knowledge to dream of.

Williams. Sir, know you this glove?

Fluellen. Know the glove? I know the glove is a glove.

Williams. I know this, and thus I challenge it.

[*Strikes him*]

Fluellen. 'Sblood, an arrant traitor as any's in the Universal world, or in France, or in England.

Gower. How now Sir? you villain.

Williams. Do you think I'll be forsworn?

Fluellen. Stand away, Captain Gower, I will give treason his payment into plows, I warrant you

Williams. I am no traitor.

Fluellen. That's a lie in your throat. I charge you in his Majesty's name apprehend him, he's a friend of the Duke Alanson's.

[*Enter Warwick and Gloucester*]

Warwick. How now, how now, what's the matter?

Fluellen. My Lord of Warwick, here is, praised be God for it, a most contagious treason come to light, look you, as you shall desire in a summer's day. Here is his Majesty.

[*Enter King and Exeter*]

King Henry. How now, what's the matter?

Fluellen. My Liege, here is a villain, and a traitor, that look your Grace, ha's struck the glove which your Majesty is take out of the helmet of Alanson.

Williams. My Liege, this was my glove, here is the fellow of it; and he that I gave it to in change, promised to wear it in his cap; I

promised to strike him, if he did; I met this man with my glove
in his cap, and I have been as
good as my word.

Fluellen. Your Majesty hear now, saving your Majesty's manhood,
what an arrant rascally, beggarly, lousy knave it is; I hope
your Majesty is pear me testimony and witness, and will
avouchment, that this is the glove of Alanson, that your
Majesty is give me, in your conscience now.

King Henry. Give me your glove soldier;
Look, here is the fellow of it.
'Twas I, indeed, you promised to strike,
And you have given me most bitter terms.

Fluellen. And please your Majesty, let his neck answer for it, if there
is any martial law in the world.

King Henry. How can you make me satisfaction?

Williams. All offenses, my Lord, come from the heart; never came
any from mine, that might offend your Majesty.

King Henry. It was ourself you did abuse.

Williams. Your Majesty came not like yourself; you appeared to me
but as a common man; witness the Night, your garments, your
lowliness; and what your Highness suffered under that shape,
I beseech you take it for your own fault, and not mine; for
had you been as I took you for, I made no offense; therefore I
beseech your Highness pardon me.

King Henry. Here Uncle Exeter, fill this glove with crowns,
And give it to this fellow. Keep it fellow,
And wear it for an honor in your cap,
Till I do challenge it. Give him the crowns;
And Captain, you must needs be friends with him.

Fluellen. By this day and this light, the fellow ha's mettle enough in
his belly; hold, there is twelve-pence for you, and I pray you
to serve God, and keep you out of prawls and prabbles, and
quarrels and dissentions, and I warrant you it is the better for
you.

Williams. I will none of your money

Fluellen. It is with a good will; I can tell you it will serve you to
mend your shoes; come, wherefore should you be so pashfull,
your shoes is not so good; 'tis a good silling I warrant you, or I
will change it.

[*Enter Herald*]

King Henry. Now Herald, are the dead numbered?

Herald. Here is the number of the slaughtered French.

King Henry. What prisoners of good sort are taken, Uncle?

Exeter. Charles Duke of Orleans, nephew to the King,
John Duke of Bourbon, and Lord Bouchiquald;
Of other Lords and Barons, Knights and Squires,
Full fifteen hundred, besides common men.

King Henry. This note does tell me of ten thousand French
That in the field lie slain; of Princes in this number,
And nobles bearing banners, there lie dead
One hundred twenty-six; added to these,
Of Knights, Esquires, and gallant Gentlemen,
Eight thousand and four hundred; of the which,
Five hundred were but yesterday dubbed Knights.
So that in these ten thousand they have lost,
There are but sixteen hundred mercenaries;
The rest are Princes, Barons, Lords, Knights, Squires,
And Gentlemen of blood and quality.
The names of those their nobles that lie dead;
Charles Delabreth, High Constable of France,
Jaques of Chatilion, Admiral of France,
The Master of the Cross-bows, Lord Rambures,
Great Master of France, the brave Sir Guichard Dauphin,
John Duke of Alanson, Anthony Duke of Brabant,
The brother to the Duke of Burgundy,
And Edward Duke of Barr; of lusty Earls,
Grandpre and Roussie, Fauconbridge and Foyes,
Beaumont and Marle, Vandemont and Lestrale.
Here was a Royal fellowship of death.

King Henry. Where is the number of our English dead?
Edward the Duke of York, the Earl of Suffolk,
Sir Richard Ketly, Davy Gam Esquire;
None else of name; and of all other men,
But five and twenty.
O, God, your arm was here;
And not to us, but to your arm alone,
Ascribe we all; when, without stratagem,
But in plain shock, and even play of battle,
Was ever known so great and little loss?
On one part and on the other, take it God,
For it is none but yours.

Exeter. 'Tis wonderful.

King Henry. Come, go we in procession to the village;
And be it death proclaimed through our host,
To boast of this, or take that praise from God,
Which is his only.

Fluellen. Is it not lawful and please your Majesty, to tell how many
is killed?

King Henry. Yes Captain; but with this acknowledgement,
That God fought for us.

Fluellen. Yes, my conscience, he did us great good

King Henry. Do we all holy rights;
Let there be sung Non Nobis, and Te Deum,
The dead with charity enclosed in clay;
And then to Calais, and to England then,
Where never from France arrived more happy men.

[*Exit All*]

Act Five

Chorus. Vouchsafe to those that have not read the story,
　That I may prompt them; and of such as have,
　I humbly pray them to admit the excuse
　Of time, of numbers, and due course of things,
　Which cannot in their huge and proper life,
　Be here presented. Now we bear the King
　Toward Calais; grant him there; there seen,
　Heave him away upon your winged thoughts,
　Athwart the sea; behold the English beach
　Pales in the flood; with men, wives, and boys,
　Whose shouts and claps out-voice the deep-mouthed sea,
　Which like a mighty whiffler before the King,
　Seems to prepare his way; so let him land,
　And solemnly see him set on to London.
　So swift a pace has thought, that even now
　You may imagine him upon Black-Heath;
　Where, that his Lords desire him, to have borne
　His bruised helmet, and his bended sword
　Before him, through the city; he forbids it,
　Being free from vainness, and self-glorious pride;
　Giving full trophy, signal, and ostentation,
　Quite from himself, to God. But now behold,
　In the quick forge and working-house of thought,
　How London does pour out her citizens,
　The Mayor and all his brethren in best sort,
　Like to the Senators of the antique Rome,
　With the plebeians swarming at their heels,
　Go forth and fetch their conquering Caesar in;
　As by a lower, but by loving likelihood,
　Were now the general of our gracious empress,
　As in good time he may, from Ireland coming,
　Bringing rebellion broached on his sword;
　How many would the peaceful city quit,

367

To welcome him? much more, and much more cause,
Did they this Harry. Now in London place him.
As yet the lamentation of the French
Invites the King of England's stay at home;
The Emperor's coming in behalf of France,
To order peace between them; and omit
All the occurrences, whatever chanced,
Till Harry's back return again to France;
There must we bring him; and myself have played
The interim, by remembering you 'tis past.
Then brook abridgement, and your eyes advance,
After your thoughts, straight back again to France.

[Exit Chorus]

[*France. The English camp*]

[*Enter Fluellen and Gower*]

Gower. Nay, that's right; but why wear you your leek today? St. Davy's day is past.

Fluellen. There is occasions and causes why and wherefore in all things; I will tell you as my friend, Captain Gower; the rascally, scauld, beggarly, lousy, pragging knave Pistol, which you and yourself, and all the world, know to be no petter than a fellow, look you now, of no merits; he is come to me, and prings me pread and salt yesterday, look you, and bid me eat my leek; it was in a place where I could not breed no contention with him; but I will be so bold as to wear it in my cap till I see him once again, and then I will tell him a little piece of my desires.

[*Enter Pistol*]

Gower. Why here he comes, swelling like a turkeycock.

Fluellen. 'Tis no matter for his swellings, nor his turkeycocks. God pless you aunchient Pistol; you scurvy lousy knave, God pless you.

Pistol. Ha, are you bedlam? do you thirst, base Trojan, to have me fold up Parca's fatal web? Hence; I am qualmish at the smell of leek.

Fluellen. I peseech you heartily, scurvy lousy knave, at my desires, and my requests, and my petitions, to eat, look you, this leek; because, look you, you do not love it, nor your affections, and your appetites and your disgestions doo's not agree with it, I would desire you to eat it.

Pistol. Not for Cadwallader and all his goats.

Fluellen. There is one goat for you.

[*Strikes him*]

Will you be so good, scauld Knave, as eat it?

Pistol. Base Trojan, you shall die.

Fluellen. You say very true, scauld knave, when God's will is; I will desire you to live in the meantime, and eat your victuals; come, there is sauce for it. You called me yesterday mountain-squire, but I will make you today a squire of low degree. I pray you fall too, if you can mock a leek, you can eat a leek.

Gower. Enough Captain, you have astonished him.

Fluellen. I say, I will make him eat some part of my leek, or I will peate his pate four days. Bite I pray you, it is good for your green wound, and your ploody coxcomb.

Pistol. Must I bite?

Fluellen. Yes certainly, and out of doubt and out of question too, and ambiguities.

Pistol. By this leek, I will most horribly revenge I eat and eat I swear.

Fluellen. Eat, I pray you, will you have some more sauce to your leek; there is not enough leek to swear by.

Pistol. Quiet your cudgel, you do see I eat.

Fluellen. Much good do you scald knave, heartily. Nay, pray you throw none away, the skin is good for your broken coxcomb; when you take occasions to see leeks hereafter, I pray you mock at 'em, that is all.

Pistol. Good.

Fluellen. Aye, leeks is good; hold you, there is a groat to heal your pate.

Pistol. Me a groat?

Fluellen. Yes, verily, and in truth you shall take it, or I have another leek in my pocket, which you shall eat.

Pistol. I take your groat in earnest of revenge.

Fluellen. If I owe you anything, I will pay you in cudgels, you shall be a woodmonger, and buy nothing of me but cudgels; God be wi' you, and keep you, and heal your pate.

[*Exit Fluellen*]

Pistol. All hell shall stir for this.

Gower. Go, go, you are a counterfeit cowardly knave, will you mock at an ancient tradition began upon an honorable respect, and worn as a memorable trophy of predeceased valor, and dare not avouch in your deeds any of your words. I have seen you gleeking and galling at this gentleman twice or thrice. You thought, because he could not speak English in the native garb, he could not therefore handle an English cudgel; you find it otherwise, and henceforth let a Welsh correction, teach you a good English condition, fare you well.

370

Pistol. Does fortune play the housewife with me now? News have I
that my Doll is dead in the spittle of a malady of France, and
there my rendezvous is quite cut off. Old I do wax, and from
my weary limbs honor is cudgeled. Well, bawd I'll turn, and
something lean to cut-purse of quick hand; to England will
I steal, and there I'll steal; And patches will I get unto these
cudgeled scars. And swore I got them in the Gallia wars.

[*Exit Pistol*]

[France. The Royal Palace]

*[Enter at one side, King Henry, Exeter, Bedford, Warwick,
and others. From the other side enters Queen Isabel, Princess
Katherine, her attendant Alice, the French King, the Duke of
Burgundy, and others]*

King Henry. Peace to this meeting, wherefore we are met;
    Unto our brother France, and to our sister
    Health and fair time of day; joy and good wishes
    To our most fair and Princely cousin Katherine;
    And as a branch and member of this Royalty,
    By whom this great assembly is contrived,
    We do salute you, Duke of Burgundy,
    And Princes French and Peers, health to you all.

King of France. Right joyous are we to behold your face,
    Most worthy brother England, fairly met,
    So are you Princes, English, every one.

Queen Isabel. So happy be the issue, brother Ireland
    Of this good day, and of this gracious meeting,
    As we are now glad to behold your eyes,
    Your eyes which hereto have borne
    In them against the French that met them in their bent,
    The fatal balls of murdering basilisks;
    The venom of such looks we fairly hope
    Have lost their quality, and that this day
    Shall change all griefs and quarrels into love.

King Henry. To cry amen to that, thus we appear.

Queen Isabel. You English Princes all, I do salute you.

Burgundy. My duty to you both, on equal love.
    Great Kings of France and England; that I have labored
    With all my wits, my pains, and strong endeavours,
    To bring your most Imperial Majesties
    Unto this bar, and Royal interview;
    Your Mightiness on both parts best can witness.
    Since then my office has so far prevailed,
    That face to face, and Royal eye to eye,
    You have congreeted; let it not disgrace me,
    If I demand before this Royal view,

What rub, or what impediment there is,
Why that the naked, poor, and mangled peace,
Dear nurse of arts, plenties, and joyful births,
Should not in this best garden of the world,
Our fertile France, put up her lovely visage?
Alas, she has from France too long been chased,
And all her husbandry does lie on heaps,
Corrupting in it own fertility.
Her vine, the merry cheer of the heart,
Unpruned, dies; her hedges even pleached,
Like prisoners wildly over-grown with hair,
Put forth disordered twigs; her fallow leas,
The darnell, hemlock, and rank fumitory,
Does root upon; while that the coulter rusts,
That should deracinate such savagery;
The even mead, that before brought sweetly forth
The freckled cowslip, burnet, and green clover,
Wanting the scythe, withal uncorrected, rank;
Conceives by idleness, and nothing teems,
But hateful docks, rough thistles, keksies, burrs,
Losing both beauty and utility;
And all our vineyards, fallows, meads, and hedges,
Defective in their natures, grow to wildness.

Burgundy. Even so our houses, and ourselves, and children,
Have lost, or do not learn, for want of time,
The sciences that should become our country;
But grow like savages, as soldiers will,
That nothing do, but meditate on blood,
To swearing, and stern looks, defused attire,
And everything that seems unnatural.
Which to reduce into our former favor,
You are assembled; and my speech entreats,
That I may know the let, why gentle peace
Should not expell these inconveniences,
And bless us with her former qualities.

King Henry. If, Duke of Burgundy, you would the peace,
Whose want gives growth to the imperfections
Which you have cited; you must buy that peace
With full accord to all our just demands,
Whose tenures and particular effects
You have enscheduled briefly in your hands.

Burgundy. The King has heard them; to the which, as yet

There is no answer made.

King Henry. Well then; the peace which you before so urged,
Lies in his answer.

King of France. I have but with a cursory eye
Over-glanced the articles; please your Grace
To appoint some of your council presently
To sit with us once more, with better heed
To re-survey them; we will suddenly
Pass our accept and peremptory answer.

King Henry. Brother, we shall go Uncle Exeter,
And brother Clarence, and you brother Gloucester,
Warwick, and Huntington, go with the King,
And take with you free power, to ratify,
Augment, or alter, as your wisdoms best
Shall see advantageable for our dignity,
Anything in or out of our demands,
And we'll consign thereto. Will you, fair sister,
Go with the Princes, or stay here with us?

Queen Isabel. Our gracious brother, I will go with them;
Happily a woman's voice may do some good,
When articles too nicely urged, be stood on.

King Henry. Yet leave our cousin Katherine here with us,
She is our capital demand, comprised
Within the fore-rank of our articles.

Queen Isabel. She has good leave.

[*Exit all except for Henry and Katherine*]

King Henry. Fair Katherine, and most fair,
Will you vouchsafe to teach a soldier terms,
Such as will enter at a Lady's ear,
And plead his love-suit to her gentle heart.

Katherine. Your Majesty shall mock at me, I cannot speak your
England.

King Henry. O, fair Katherine, if you will love me soundly with
your French heart, I will be glad to hear you confess it
brokenly with your English tongue. Do you like me, Kate?

Katherine. Pardonnez-moi, I cannot tell wat is like me.

King Henry. An angel is like you Kate, and you are like an Angel.

Katherine. Que dit-il que je suis semblable a les anges?

Alice. Oui vraiment, sauf votre Grace, ainsi dit-il.

King Henry. I said so, dear Katherine, and I must not blush to affirm it.

Katherine. O, bon Dieu, les langues des hommes sont plein de tromperies.

King Henry. What says she, fair one? That the tongues of men are full of deceits?

Alice. Oui, dat de tongues of de mans is be full of deceits; dat is de Princess.

King Henry. The Princess is the better English-woman. In faith, Kate, my wooing is fit for your understanding, I am glad you can speak no better English, for if you could, you would find me such a plain King, that you would think, I had sold my farm to buy my Crown. I know no ways to mince it in love, but directly to say, I love you; then if you urge me farther, then to say, do you, in faith? I wear out my suit; Give me your answer, please, do, and so clap hands, and a bargain; how say you, Lady?

Katherine. Sauf votre honneur, me understand well.

King Henry. Marry, if you would put me to verses, or to dance for your sake, Kate, why you undid me. For the one I have neither words nor measure; and for the other, I have no strength in measure, yet a reasonable measure in strength. If I could win a Lady at leap-frog, or by vaulting into my saddle, with my armor on my back; under the correction of bragging, be it spoken. I should quickly leap into a wife; Or if I might buffet for my love, or bound my horse for her favors, I could lay on like a butcher, and sit like a jackanapes, never off. But before God Kate, I cannot look greenly, nor gasp out my eloquence, nor I have no cunning in protestation; only downright oaths, which I never use till urged, nor never break for urging. If you can love a fellow of this temper, Kate, whose face is not worth sun-burning? that never looks in his glass, for love of anything he sees there? let your eye be your cook. I speak to you plain soldier; If you can love me for this, take me. If not, to say to you that I shall die, is true; but for your love, by the Lord no; yet I love you too. And while you live, dear Kate, take a fellow of plain and uncoined constancy, for he perforce must do you right, because he has not the gift to woo in other places; for these fellows of infinite tongue, that can rhyme themselves into ladies' favors, they do always reason themselves out again. What? a speaker is but a prater, a rhyme is but a ballad; a good leg will fall, a straight back will stoop, a black beard will turn white, a curled pate will grow bald, a fair face will wither, a full eye will wax hollow; but a good heart, Kate, is the sun and the moon, or rather the sun, and not the moon; for it shines bright, and never changes, but keeps his course truly. If you would have such a one, take me. And take me; take a soldier; take a soldier; take a King Henry. And what say you then to my love? Speak my fair, and fairly, I pray you.

Katherine. Is it possible dat I sould love de ennemy of Fraunce?

King Henry. No, it is not possible you should love the enemy of France, Kate; but in loving me, you should love the friend of France; for I love France so well, that I will not part with a village of it; I will have it all mine; and Kate, when France is mine, and I am yours; then yours is France, and you are mine.

Katherine. I cannot tell wat is dat.

King Henry. No, Kate? I will tell you in French, which I am sure will hang upon my tongue, like a new-married wife about her husband's neck, hardly to be shook off. Je quand sur le possession de Fraunce, and quand vous avec le possession de moi... Let me see, what then? Saint Denis be my speed, Donc votre est Fraunce, et vous etes mienne. It is as easy for me, Kate, to conquer the Kingdom, as to speak so much more French; I shall never move you in French, unless it be to laugh at me.

Katherine. Sauf votre honneur, le François que vous parlez, il est mellieur que l'Anglois lequel je parle.

King Henry. No, faith is it not, Kate; but your speaking of my tongue, and I yours, most truely-falsely, must needs be granted to be much at one. But Kate, do you understand thus much English? Can you love me?

Katherine. I cannot tell.

King Henry. Can any of your neighbors tell, Kate? I'll ask them. Come, I know you love me; and at night, when you come into your closet, you'll question this gentlewoman about me; and I know, Kate, you will to her dispraise those parts in me, that you love with your heart; but good Kate, mock me mercifully, the rather gentle Princess, because I love you cruelly. If ever you be mine, Kate, as I have a saving faith within me tells me you shall, I get you with scambling, and you must therefore needs prove a good soldier-breeder. Shall not you and I, between Saint Denis and Saint George, compound a boy, half-

French-half-English, that shall go to Constantinople, and take the Turk by the beard? Shall we not? What say you, my fair Flower-de-Luce.

Katherine. I do not know dat.

King Henry. No; 'tis hereafter to know, but now to promise; do but now promise Kate, you will endeavour for your French part of such a boy; and for my English moiety, take the word of a King, and a bachelor. How answer you? La plus belle Katherine du monde mon très cher et devin déesse.

Katherine. Your majestee avez fause French enough to deceive de most sage demoiselle dat is en Fraunce.

King Henry. Now fie upon my false French; by my honor in true English, I love you Kate; by which honor, I dare not swear you love me, yet my blood begins to flatter me, that you do; notwithstanding the poor and untempering effect of my visage. Now beshrew my father's ambition, he was thinking of civil wars when he got me, therefore was I created with a stubborn outside, with an aspect of iron, that when I come to woo ladies, I fright them; but in faith Kate, the elder I wax, the better I shall appear. My comfort is, that old age, that ill layer-up of beauty, can do no more spoil upon my face. You have me, if you have me, at the worst; and you shall wear me, if you wear me, better and better; and therefore tell me, most fair Katherine, will you have me? Put off your maiden blushes, avouch the thoughts of your heart with the looks of an Empress, take me by the hand, and say, Harry of England, I am yours; which word you shall no sooner bless my ear withal, but I will tell you aloud, England is yours, Ireland is yours, France is yours, and Henry Plantagenet is yours; who, though I speak it before his face, if he be not fellow with the best King, you shall find the best king of good fellows. Come your answer in broken music; for your voice is music, and your English broken; therefore Queen of all, Katherine, break your mind to me in broken English; will you have me?

Katherine. Dat is as it shall please de Roi, mon père.

King Henry. Nay, it will please him well, Kate; it shall please him, Kate.

Katherine. Den it sall also content me.

King Henry. Upon that I kiss your hand, and I call you my Queen.

Katherine. Laissez mon Seigneur, laissez, laissez, ma foi; je ne veux point que vous abbaissiez votre grandeur, en baisant le main d'une votre Seigneur indigne serviteur. Excusez-moi, je vous supplié mon tres-puissant Seigneur.

King Henry. Then I will kiss your lips, Kate.

Katherine. Les dames et demoiselles pour etre baisée devant leur noces, il n'est pas le coutume de Fraunce.

King Henry. Madame, my interpreter, what says she?

Alice. Dat it is not be de fashon pour le ladies of Fraunce; I cannot tell wat is "baisser" en Anglish.

King Henry. To kiss.

Alice. Your Majesty entendre bettre que moi.

King Henry. It is not a fashion for the maids in Fraunce to kiss before they are married, would she say?

Alice. Oui, vraiment.

King Henry. O, Kate, nice customs curtsy to great Kings. Dear Kate, you and I cannot be confined within the weak list of a country's fashion; we are the makers of manners, Kate; and the liberty that follows our places, stops the mouth of all find-faults, as I will do yours, for upholding the nice fashion of your country, in denying me a kiss; therefore patiently, and yielding. You have witchcraft in your lips, Kate; there is more eloquence in a sugar touch of them, than in the tongues of the French council; and they should sooner persuade Harry of England, than a general petition of Monarchs. Here comes your father.

[*Enter the French Court, and the English Lords*]

Burgundy. God save your Majesty, my Royal cousin, teach you our Princess English?

King Henry. I would have her learn, my fair cousin, how perfectly I love her, and that is good English.

Burgundy. Is she not apt?

King Henry. Our tongue is rough, coz, and my condition is not smooth; so that having neither the voice nor the heart of flattery about me, I cannot so conjure up the spirit of love in her, that he will appear in his true likeness.

Burgundy. Pardon the frankness of my mirth, if I answer you for that. If you would conjure in her, you must make a circle; if conjure up love in her in his true likeness, he must appear naked, and blind. Can you blame her then, being a maid, yet rosed over with the virgin crimson of modesty, if she deny the appearance of a naked blind boy in her naked seeing self? It were, my Lord, a hard condition for a maid to consign to.

King Henry. Yet they do wink and yield, as love is blind and enforces.

Burgundy. They are then excused, my Lord, when they see not what they do.

King Henry. Then good my Lord, teach your cousin to consent winking.

Burgundy. I will wink on her to consent, my Lord, if you will teach her to know my meaning; for maids well summered, and warm kept, are like flies at Bartholomew-tide, blind, though they have their eyes, and then they will endure handling, which before would not abide looking on.

King Henry. This moral ties me over to time, and a hot summer; and so I shall catch the fly, your cousin, in the latter end, and she must be blind to.

Burgundy. As love is my Lord, before it loves.

King Henry. It is so; and you may, some of you, thank love for my blindness, who cannot see many a fair French city for one fair French maid that stands in my way.

King of France. Yes, my Lord, you see them perspectively; the cities turned into a maid; for they are all girdled with maiden walls, that war has entered.

King Henry. Shall Kate be my wife?

King of France. So please you.

King Henry. I am content, so the maiden cities you talk of, may wait on her; so the maid that stood in the way for my wish, shall show me the way to my will.

King of France. We have consented to all terms of reason.

King Henry. Is it so, my Lords of England?

Westmoreland. The King has granted every article;
His daughter first; and in sequel, all,
According to their firm proposed natures.

Exeter. Only he has not yet subscribed this: Where your Majesty demands, that the King of France having any occasion to write for matter of grant, shall name your Highness in this form, and with this addition, in French: "Notre très-cher fils Henry, Roi d'Angleterre Héritier de France"; and thus in Latin;

"Praeclarissimus Filius noster Henricus Rex Angliae et Haeres Franciae."

King of France. Nor this I have not, brother, so denied,
But your request shall make me let it pass.

King Henry. I pray you then, in love and dear alliance,
Let that one article rank with the rest,
And thereupon give me your daughter.

King of France. Take her, fair son, and from her blood raise up
Issue to me, that the contending kingdoms
Of France and England, whose very shores look pale,
With envy of each other's happiness,
May cease their hatred; and this dear conjunction
Plant neighborhood and Christian-like accord
In their sweet bosoms; that never war advance
His bleeding sword between England and fair France.

Lords. Amen.

King Henry. Now welcome Kate; and bear me witness all,
That here I kiss her as my Sovereign Queen.

[*Flourish*]

Queen Isabel. God, the best maker of all marriages,
Combine your hearts in one, your realms in one;
As man and wife being two, are one in love,
So be there between your Kingdoms such a spousal,
That never may ill office, or fell jealousy,
Which troubles oft the bed of blessed marriage,
Thrust in between the paction of these Kingdoms,
To make divorce of their incorporate league;
That English may as French, French Englishmen,
Receive each other. God speak this amen.

All. Amen.

King Henry. Prepare we for our marriage; on which day,
My Lord of Burgundy we'll take your oath
And all the Peers, for surety of our leagues.
Then shall I swear to Kate, and you to me,
And may our oaths well kept and prosperous be.

[*Sennet*]

[*Exit All*]

[*Enter Chorus*]

Chorus. Thus far with rough, and all-unable pen,
  Our bending author has pursued the story,
  In little room confining mighty men,
  Mangling by starts the full course of their glory.
  Small time; but in that small, most greatly lived
  This star of England. Fortune made his sword;
  By which, the world's best garden he achieved;
  And of it left his son Imperial Lord.
  Henry the Sixth, in infant bands crowned King
  Of France and England, did this King succeed;
  Whose State so many had the managing,
  That they lost France, and made his England bleed;
  Which oft our stage has shown; and for their sake,
  In your fair minds let this acceptance take.

The End

a-birding : falconry, hawk hunting
accidence : inflections, word order, accents
accite : cite, summon
accompt : account, story
Achitophel : companion of Absalom in his rebellion
Actaeon : In Greek story, the hunter turned into a stag for having seen Artemis bathing.
Aesculapius : Greek/Roman god of healing and medicine
afeard : afraid
a la cour—la grande affaire : in the heart, the grand affair
alarum : fuss, ado
alligant : elegant
allicholy : melancholy
Amaimon : Egyptian devil
Amurath : Murad I, Ottoman ruler
Anthropophaginian : cannibal
apple-john : summer apple with wrinkled skin
aqua-vitae : brandy, distilled wine
armigero : esquire

baillez : give
Barbason : a demon
bastinado : beating on the soles of the feet
bawcock : fine fellow
beaver : helmet with face protector
beetle : sledgehammer
belike : perhaps
Besonian : rogue, scoundrel
bilbo : sword made in Bilbao
boarded : approached, made advances
bodykins : little body
boitier vert : green wooden box
bona-roba : call girl, high-class prostitute
bootless : useless
bots : botfly larvae, which invade the stomach of horses
boulted : finely woven hard cloth**breed-bate** : instigator of quarrels
broil : brawl, fight
bubukles : red pimples
buck-basket : laundry basket

Bucklersbury : district in London
buck-washing : washing with lye

Cain-coloured : red-haired
caliver : light musket
Cambyses : King Cambyses, according to legend, wounded in the leg and killed the sacred Apis-Bull, went mad, killing his own family, eventually dying from the same leg wound as the one he inflicted on the sacred Bull.
canary : Canary Islands wine
casement : window opening outward
Castalion-King-Urinal : an insult, Castilian king of urine analysis
Cataian : Chinese, native of Cathay
cat-a-mountain : catamount, mountain lion
Caveto : beware (Latin)
cess : luck, military obligation
chamber-lye : urine
chantry : chapel for prayer; endowment for prayer
charge of foot : company of foot soldiers
chariness : wariness, caution
chid : chided
choler : anger, bile
chollors : choler, irritability
clapper-claw : abuse verbally, scratch with fingernails
clerk : cleric
cock-pit : small arena for cock fights
cog : cheat
cogging : swindling, cheating
cogscomb : coxcomb, fop
colt : to trick
complice : associate, accomplice
Congreeing : agreeing
cony-catch : deceive, trick
Coranto : stately dance
cornuto : cuckold
costard : head
costermonger : apple or fruit seller (costard apples)
coulter : harrowing wheel
coz : cousin, friend :
cozenage : scam, swindle
cozening : swindling
crescive : increasing
Cressid, Cressida : Trojan woman who abandons one lover for

another
Cressy Battle : battle at Crécy, France in 1346
crotchets : odd notions, crazy ideas
cry aim : encourage, cheer on
cuckold : husband of a cheating wife
cullion : rascal
currance : occurence
curtal dog : dog with a cropped tail
curtleaxe : broad heavy sword; cutlass
cut and longtail : diversity, whether cut tail or long tail
cypher : nonentity, zero

daubery : disguise
deanery : grouping of several parishes
Dives : rich man (Biblical character)
Doctor Faustus : referring to the recent Christopher Marlowe
    play, an adaptation of the German Faust legend
draff : dregs, cattle fodder
drawer : barkeep; money handler
drumble : sluggish, slow
Duke de Jamany : Duke of Germany

eke : also
eld : old age
ensconce : settle into, conceal
Ephesians : drinking buddies
eringoes : thistle plant
evitate : avoid, shun
exion : action (mispronunciation)
expressure : expression, representation
eyas-musket : young hawk

faining : eagerly
faitor : faker, fraud
fap : befuddled
farthingale : hooped underskirt
fartuous : virtuous
fillip : strike, rap
firk : strike
fobbed, fubbed : put forward, put off
foin : thrust
forbear : wait
forsooth : in truth

foutre : fuck
fracted : broken
frampold : peevish
franklin : freeholder who is not in the nobility
frieze : coarse shaggy wool
fritters : batter cakes
fullam : loaded dice
fumitory : earth smoke; a medicinal herb

gage : mark or symbol of a pledge or surety; challenge
Galen : Greek physician
Gallia : Gaul, France
gallimaufry : hodgepodge, jumble
gammon : smoked ham
gelding : castrated horse
geminy : pair, twins
giantess ... Mount Pelion : Giants tried to storm Olympus by
    putting Mt. Pelion on top of Mt. Ossa
gib : castrated
gibbet : gallows
gibes : taunts, jeers
gimmal : interlocking rings
ging : gang, crew
glover : maker or seller of gloves
gloze : underplay, flatter
gnawn : gnawed
gratis : free
gripe : belly pain
groat : four-pence coin
Guiana : now Guyana, a country in South America settled by the
    Dutch, later seized by the British.
gun-stones : artillery or mortar shells
gyves : shackles

halter : noose
havior : behavior, demeanor
hazard : out of bounds (as in golf)
Hector of Greece : Son of Priam, King of Troy, and hero of the
    Trojan War
Herne the Hunter : Ghost on horseback in Windsor Forest
Hibocrates : Hippocrates
hilding : low wretch
Hiren : courtesan; seductress

honey-seed : homicide (mispronunciation)

Honi soit qui mal y pense : motto of the Order of the Gartere: "evil to him who thinks evil"

horn-mad : raving mad

huswifery : domestic work

Hybla : Siclian town noted for its honey

Hyperion : a Titan, father of Helios, the Sun God

imbrue : stab

impawn : pledge, pawn

insinewed : joined, intertwined

intervallum : interval, recess

intestine : internal matter

iteration : repeating

Jack-a-Lent : small puppet to be pelted during Lent, siimpleton

jackanapes : impudent, mischievous person

jade : nag, worn-out horse; shrewish woman

Jarteer : the Garter Inn

jerkin : tight sleeveless jacket

jointure : agreement that after a man's death a certain amount of property belongs to the wife.

jordan : chamberpot

jutty : jetty

kibes : open chilblain, exposed area inflamed, usually on the heel

kirtle : gown

kite : bounced check, fraud

knog : knock

Lavolta : leaping and turning dance, from Italy

lazar : leper, diseased person

leather-coat : rough-skinned apple

legerity : agility, quickness

leman : mistress, lover

lewdsters : lewd people

lime-kiln : Oven for baking quicklime from limestone

linstock : forked stick used in firing cannon

liquor : lacquer

little page : purse

loach : freshwater fish

luces : pearl buttons or buttons made from seashells

Lucifer : the Devil

lugged : pulled by chain

ma foi, il fait fort chaud : (French) my faith, it grows hot.
malt-worms : drunkards
Mars : Roman god of war
martlemas : fullness
meed : award, gift, earned wage
meeter : more agreeable, more suitable
micher : truant
mickle : great, abundant
milch-kine : dairy cows
milliner : hat maker or designer
Mockwater : jape on doctors' practice of diagnosing diseases by
    examining urine.
montant : upward thrust (fencing)
Moor-ditch : ditch outside London's walls, fetid and foul-smelling
morris-dance : folk dance with bells, representing folk tale
    characters
Mounseur : Monsieur
mummy : wrapped body, mass of pulp
Muse : one of the Greek goddesses of the arts

neat : cow
neif, neaf : fist
noddle : head
nonce : now, the time being
nut-hook : constable

obolus : half-pence
obsque hoc nihil est : nothing but this
'Od's : God's
oeillades : winks, make eyes at
ouches : ornaments
Oui; mette le au mon pocket : Yes, put it in my pocket
ousel : blackbird
onyear, oneyer : fiscal officer

pace : horse's rapid gait lifting both legs on one side at the same
    time
palfrey : saddle horse, usually for a woman rider
panderly : acceding to base emotions
pannier : wicker basket
pantler : pantry boy, baker

parmaceti : spermaceti, a waxy substance from the head of a whale, used for cosmetics, candles
pauca : (Latin) few
pax : small tablet representing the kiss of peace
pendent : hanging
perdurable : permanent
perpend : ponder, consider
Phebus, Phoebus : son of the Sun god
Phrygian Turk : (a jumbled expression: Phrygians and Turks inhabited the same land, but a thousand years apart)
pinnace : a tender; ship's boat for unloading passengers
pipe-wine : long wine cask, used for shipping wine
pismire : ant
pith : strength, mettle
pittie : pit bull
pizzle : penis
posset : hot sweet milk with wine
pottle : a two-quart mug
pouncet box : small perfume box with perforated top
primero : card game
puissance : power
Pulcher : pulchritude; beauty
pumpion : pumpkin
punk : prostitute
punto : (fencing) punto diritto is a direct hit; punto reverso is a backhanded stroke

Qu'ai j'oublie? : (French) What did I forget?
quarter : divide into four pieces; take up residence
quean : impudent woman, prostitute
quiddity : "whatness," essence
quoif, coif : skullcap; cap worn under a helmet
quoit : toss
quondam : former, earlier
quotidian : commonplace, recurring

rate : berate
ratsbane : rat poison
raze : root
red-lattice : Red-lattice signified that a pub was licensed
reins : kidneys
reverse : fencing thrust (*See* punto)
ribands : ribbons

Ringwood : market town
riot : wild behavior
rivage : coast, shore
rout : riot

sack : sherry
salt fish : ocean fish
saltpeter : nitrate used for fertilizer or explosives
'Sblood : God's blood
scall : rapscallion, disreputable person
scambling : awkward, unsteady
scaped : escaped
semper idem : always the same
shent : shamed, chided
ship-tire : traveling clothes
shog : move on, shock
shotten : recently spawned (fish), less tasty
Si fortuna me tormente, sperato me contento : When fortune
    torments me, hope contents me
slops : baggy trousers
sneap : snub
solus : alone, only
sortance : agreement
squire : country gentleman, judge
stews : brothel
stoccadoes : stabs, thrusts
stock : stocking; stoccado
strappado : rope torture by dropping with hands bound
strond : shore
sutler : merchant to the army
swinged : thrashed, beaten

tapster : tavern keeper
tench : a freshwater fish
tertian : tertian fever, occuring every other day, such as malaria
thews : sinews
throng : mob
tire of Venetian : clothing in Venetian style
tire-valiant : gentleman's costume
title-leaf : title page
troth : pledge, oath
trow : think, suppose
Tucket : trumpet flourish

tun : large beer cask, large quantity
two stones : testicles

uncape : uncover, discover
urinals : bottles for urine samples
utis : merriment, din

vail : lower, doff one's hat
varlet : servant, knave
vaward : vanguard, forward position
veneys : (fencing) thrust, bout
vice : grip
vizard : visor, mask, half-mask

ward: defense, defensive move
warrener : gamekeeper, keeper of rabbit warren
welkin : sky, heavens
welladay : alas, a lament
whelm : submerge, overwhelm
whey face : pallid complexion
whipping-cheer : public flogging
whiting : bleaching, washing
whitsters : whiteners, bleachers
Whitsun : Whitsunday, seventh Sunday after Easter
wight : creature
wild mare : leapfrog
wild Prince : reference to Prince Hal, who, after a wayward
    youth, became King Henry V
wittolly : like a cuckold
wont : inclined, eager
wot : became aware of, to know

The continuity of characters throughout these four plays is remarkable. As you can see, the groups form an "upstairs, downstairs" arrangement. Falstaff lives in a world of lower-class and lowlife characters, into which Falstaff has drawn the heir apparent, Prince Hal. Hal, however, undergoes a transformation over the course of these plays, showing bravery in battle, reconciliation with his father the King, and repudiating Falstaff's influence over him. By the third play, the change is complete, and King Henry V earns his acclaim as a national hero. Falstaff, though never seen in the final play, still has a presence through the characters who had known him.

Characters around Falstaff

Sir John Falstaff

Robin

Poins

Bardolph

Nym

Pistol

Peto

Mistress Quickly

Doll Tearsheet

Gadshill

Shallow

Silence

Davy

Mouldy

Shadow

Wart

Feeble

Bullcalf

Fang

Snare

Characters at King Henry IV's court
King Henry IV
Prince Hal (Henry, Prince of Wales, later Henry V)
John of Lancaster
Earl of Westmorland
Sir Walter Blunt

Characters rebelling against King Henry IV
Henry Percy, Earl of Northumberland
Hotspur (Henry Percy the Younger)
Lady Percy (Hotspur's wife)
Thomas Percy, Earl of Worcester
Edmund Mortimer, Earl of March
Owen Glendower
Archibald, Earl of Douglas
Sir Richard Vernon
Richard Scroop, Archbishop of York
Sir Michael
Lady Mortimer
Lord Bardolph

You can see the continuity in the characters in the following charts.

	Henry IV-1	Henry IV-2	Merry Wives	Henry V

Characters in all four plays

	Henry IV-1	Henry IV-2	Merry Wives	Henry V
Sir John Falstaff	▓	▓	▓	▓
Mistress Quickly	▓	▓	▓	▓
Bardolph	▓	▓	▓	▓

Characters in three plays

	Henry IV-1	Henry IV-2	Merry Wives	Henry V
Prince Hal/Henry V	▓	▓		▓
Earl of Westmoreland	▓	▓		▓
Richard Scroop, Archbishop of York	▓	▓		▓
Pistol		▓	▓	▓

Characters in the first two plays

	Henry IV-1	Henry IV-2	Merry Wives	Henry V
King Henry IV	▓	▓		
Poins	▓	▓		
Peto	▓	▓		
Harry Percy (Hotspur)	▓	▓		
Lady Percy, wife of Hotspur	▓	▓		
Prince John of Lancaster	▓	▓		
Sir Walter Blunt	▓	▓		
Henry Percy, Earl of Northumberland	▓	▓		

Characters solely in Henry IV, Part One

Thomas Percy,
    Earl of Worcester

Edmund Mortimer,
    Earl of March

Archibald, Earl of
    Douglas

Owen Glendower

Sir Richard Vernon

Sir Michael

Gadshill

Lady Mortimer

Characters solely in Henry IV, Part Two

Rumor

Earl of Surrey

Lord Bardolph

Thomas, Duke of Clarence

Harcourt

Lord Chief Justice

Lord Mowbray

Lord Hastings

Sir John Colevile

Travers

Morton

Silence

Davy

Mouldy

Shadow

Wart

Feeble

Bullcalf

Fang

Snare

Lady Northumberland

Doll Tearsheet

Characters in Henry IV, Part Two and Merry Wives of Windsor

Shallow

Robin (page to Falstaff)

Characters in Henry IV, Part Two and Henry V

Prince Humphrey,
    Duke of Gloucester

Earl of Warwick

Gower

Character in The Merry Wives of Windsor and Henry V

Nym

Characters solely in The Merry Wives of Windsor

Fenton

Slender

Ford

Page (gentleman)

William Page (boy)

Sir Hugh Evans

Host of the Garter Inn

Simple

Rugby

Mistress Ford

Mistress Page

Anne Page (daughter)

Doctor Caius

Characters solely in Henry V

Duke of Bedford

Duke of Exeter

Duke of York

Earl of Salisbury

Archbishop of Canterbury

Bishop of Ely

Earl of Cambridge

Sir Thomas Grey

Sir Thomas Erpingham

Fluellen

Macmorris

Jamy

Bates

Court

Williams

King of France, Charles VI

Dauphin

Duke of Burgundy

Duke of Orleans

Duke of Bourbon

Constable of France

Governor of Harfleur

Montjoy

French Ambassador

Isabel, Queen of France

Katharine, Princess of France

Alice

www.ingramcontent.com/pod-product-compliance
Lightning Source LLC
LaVergne TN
LVHW011216080426
835509LV00005B/148